FINANCIAL CRISES AND THE POLITICS OF
MACROECONOMIC ADJUSTMENTS

When are policymakers willing to make costly adjustments to their macroeconomic policies to mitigate balance-of-payments problems? Which types of adjustment strategies do they choose? Under what circumstances do they delay reform, and when are such delays likely to result in financial crises? To answer these questions, this book examines how macroeconomic policy adjustments affect individual voters in financially open economies and argues that the anticipation of these distributional effects influences policymakers' decisions about the timing and the type of reform. Empirically, the book combines analyses of cross-national survey data of voters' and firms' policy evaluations with comparative case studies of national policy responses to the Asian financial crisis of 1997–8 and the recent global financial crisis in Eastern Europe. The book shows that variation in policymakers' willingness to implement reform can be traced back to differences in the vulnerability profiles of their countries' electorates.

Stefanie Walter is Full Professor for International Relations and Political Economy in the Department of Political Science at the University of Zurich. Prior to joining the University of Zurich, she held positions as Fritz-Thyssen-Fellow at Harvard University and Junior Professor for International and Comparative Political Economy at the University of Heidelberg. Her research concentrates on the fields of international and comparative political economy, with a particular focus on how distributional conflicts, policy preferences, and institutions affect economic policy outcomes. Her work has been published, inter alia, in *Economics & Politics*, *European Journal of Political Research*, *International Organization*, *International Studies Quarterly*, *Review of International Political Economy*, and *World Development*. She received her PhD in Political Science from ETH Zurich.

Political Economy of Institutions and Decisions

Series Editors

Stephen Ansolabehere, *Harvard University*

Jeffry Frieden, *Harvard University*

Founding Editors

James E. Alt, *Harvard University*

Douglass C. North, *Washington University of St. Louis*

Other Books in the Series

(*continued after Index*)

For Jörn, Nils, and Lukas

Financial Crises and the Politics of Macroeconomic Adjustments

STEFANIE WALTER

University of Zurich

CAMBRIDGE
UNIVERSITY PRESS

CAMBRIDGE
UNIVERSITY PRESS

32 Avenue of the Americas, New York NY 10013-2473, USA

Cambridge University Press is part of the University of Cambridge.

It furthers the University's mission by disseminating knowledge in the pursuit of education, learning and research at the highest international levels of excellence.

www.cambridge.org
Information on this title: www.cambridge.org/9781107529908

First published 2013
First paperback edition 2015

A catalogue record for this publication is available from the British Library

Library of Congress Cataloguing in Publication data
Walter, Stefanie.
Financial crises and the politics of macroeconomic adjustments / Stefanie Walter, University of Zurich.
pages   cm. – (Political economy of institutions and decisions)
Includes bibliographical references and index.
ISBN 978-1-107-02870-8 (hardback)
1. Economic stabilization – Political aspects.
2. Financial crises.   I. Title.
HB3732.W35   2013
339.5–dc23   2013009472

ISBN 978-1-107-02870-8 Hardback
ISBN 978-1-107-52990-8 Paperback

Contents

Figures

Tables

Preface

In 2001, I spent the summer working for a small political foundation in Ecuador. It was an interesting period in Ecuador's history, because just a year earlier, the country had unilaterally adopted the U.S. dollar as the country's official currency. Dollarization occurred amid a major political and economic crisis, characterized by rampant inflation, bank failures, and a coup d'état. Dollarization and its consequences were a frequent conversation topic between my Spanish language teacher and myself. This was perhaps not surprising, because he was outraged about a particular feature of the dollarization decision: The government had replaced the country's national currency, the sucre, with the U.S. dollar at a much depreciated exchange rate. My Spanish teacher had bought a car a few months before this decision, and because he had been unable to secure a loan in sucre, he had taken out a loan denominated in U.S. dollars. Depreciation had massively increased his debt burden, and he explained to me how much he disapproved of his country's exchange-rate policy.

Two years later, when I started working on my dissertation at ETH Zurich in Switzerland on the political economy of currency crises, I was surprised to find out that my Spanish teacher's experience was virtually absent from the political science literature on exchange-rate policymaking. Research on the determinants of exchange-rate policy preferences was full of discussions about competitiveness and purchasing power concerns, as well as the trade-off between exchange-rate stability and monetary policy autonomy, but the financial difficulties experienced by holders of foreign-currency denominated debt fit nowhere in these discussions. This gap in the literature aroused my interest, and I began to look closer into the issue and its consequences for exchange-rate policymaking.

A second gap in the literature increasingly began to puzzle me during my graduate studies. In Switzerland, I lived in a country in which the exchange rate was a daily feature on the front page of most newspapers and in which the ups and downs of the currency constituted a topic of considerable interest for ordinary citizens. Nonetheless, the vast majority of work on exchange-rate policy preferences I was reading talked about the preferences of economic sectors and other special interests and implicitly assumed that the exchange rate was a topic of minor importance for voters. At U.S. conferences, I was repeatedly confronted with the question "Who cares about exchange rates?!" And yet, most of the Swiss I met did care about the value of their currency.

As a result of these puzzling observations, my interest in the exchange-rate policy preferences of ordinary citizens began to deepen. Concentrating first on this narrow topic, I gradually broadened my focus to include voters' preferences regarding the trade-offs exchange-rate policy poses with regard to other economic policies, especially at times of economic crisis. This wider focus sprang in part from the developments that accompanied the writing process of the book. Although currency crises seemed a problem mainly for emerging markets and developing countries when I started working on my dissertation, the global financial and economic crisis, which began in 2007 and gathered full speed in 2008, demonstrated forcefully that this was by no means the case. Instead, policymakers in many developed countries, such as Iceland, Ireland, and Greece, found themselves faced with difficult trade-offs as the crisis swept over their countries. Citizens have been hard hit by this crisis. As a result, their vulnerabilities to different types of policy responses, be it in terms of exchange-rate, monetary, or fiscal policy or in the realm of structural reforms, have gained political significance and have influenced policymakers' crisis management.

Most crises produce their profiteers, and I feel like one of them as the ongoing crisis has provided me with both intellectual food for thought and new empirical data. The main questions I was trying to answer in my book were suddenly at the forefront of the daily news: When are policymakers confronted with economic problems willing to make costly adjustments to their macroeconomic policies? Which types of adjustment strategies do they choose? Under what circumstances do they delay reform, and when are such delays likely to result in currency or other financial crises?

Although an encompassing answer to these questions is probably too much to ask from a single book, this book broadens our understanding of the politics of crisis management by sharpening our understanding of the role of domestic voters. Using a political economy perspective and focusing on domestic politics in democratic countries, it examines how the distribution of voters' vulnerabilities to different types of adjustment strategies influence policymakers' incentives to address macroeconomic imbalances. To this end, it concentrates on balance-of-payments problems in which delayed adjustment followed by a crisis has been a particularly frequent phenomenon. The book identifies the sources of voters' direct and indirect vulnerabilities to changes in macroeconomic policies in economically open economies and shows how these vulnerabilities affect national policy decisions. It argues that policymakers facing an electorate more vulnerable to exchange-rate (or external) adjustment are more likely to adjust monetary, fiscal, and structural policies (i.e., internal adjustment) to address balance-of-payments problems, and vice versa. When sizable parts of the electorate are vulnerable to both external and internal adjustment, policymakers face strong incentives to delay adjustment, especially when electoral incentives discourage timely reform. However, in the long run this strategy frequently ends with a financial crisis.

Empirically, the book examines both the microlevel and the macrolevel to evaluate this argument, concentrating on the two most prominent crisis episodes in recent times: the Asian financial crisis of 1997–8 and the global financial and economic crisis that began in 2007. At the microlevel, quantitative analyses of cross-country survey data from individuals and firms show that both voters and employers evaluate different macroeconomic adjustment strategies in light of their specific vulnerabilities to changes in the exchange and interest rates. At the macrolevel, comparative case studies of four Asian countries affected by the Asian financial crisis of 1997–8 and eight Eastern European countries experiencing balance-of-payments problems in the wake of the global financial and economic crisis that began in 2007 demonstrate that the variation in policymakers' willingness to adjust their macroeconomic policies in response to such problems can be traced back to differences in the vulnerability profiles of the countries' electorates.

The book's main contribution is to show how macroeconomic policy adjustment affects individual voters and how the anticipation of these distributional effects influence policymakers' choice and timing of adjustment strategies. By developing a microfoundation for the effects of adjustment on voters and tracing the consequences of these individual-level distributional effects on national policy decisions, the book emphasizes the distributional conflicts surrounding the domestic politics of adjustment in financially open economies.

Of course, such a book is rarely written in isolation, and I consequently have accumulated a large debt of gratitude over the ten years in which I have worked on this project. The project started with my dissertation research, which examined different aspects of the politics surrounding policymakers' responses to speculative attacks. I was lucky to conduct this research in an intellectually stimulating, demanding, and yet supportive environment, Thomas Bernauer's research group at ETH Zurich. As my main dissertation advisor, Thomas provided guidance and advice, while also encouraging me to present at conferences and to seek input from others. I particularly valued his readiness to read and critically comment on my work whenever I needed feedback. At the Center for International and Comparative Studies (CIS) in Zurich, I also benefited from discussions with Stefanie Bailer, Lars-Erik Cederman, Robin Hertz, Simon Hug, Vally Koubi, Hanspeter Kriesi, Patrick Kuhn, Dirk Leuffen, Thomas Sattler, and Markus Stierli. As a member of my dissertation committee, Katja Michaelowa also gave many helpful comments on my initial ideas for this project.

Big thanks also go to Tom Willett, who served as my second dissertation advisor and has continuously pushed me to take my ideas further, which was at times frustrating, but always productive. Tom not only welcomed me to his research group on international money and finance at Claremont Graduate University, where I spent several months in 2005 and 2006, but he has been a great mentor with his supportive, demanding, and fun character. His comments on early drafts of this book manuscript provided me with many fruitful suggestions.

The actual work on the book began during a post-doc fellowship at the Weatherhead Center for International Affairs (WCFIA) at Harvard University during the 2008–9 academic year, which allowed me to concentrate on my research in a highly welcoming and inspiring research environment. At Harvard, I particularly benefited from discussions with Jeffry Frieden. Not only has Jeff's work on the distributional consequences of economic policies in open economies inspired much of my thinking on the topic, but he also invited me to a number of research seminars in political economy, where I was exposed to many new ideas (as well as intensive lessons in American politics and baseball) and had the opportunity to present my own research. Jeff's sure instinct to put the finger on an argument's weak spot and his interest in both theoretical and real-world developments in economic policymaking, coupled with his encouragement and support, proved extremely inspiring, and the critical discussions we had about my thoughts for the book greatly helped me to carry the project further. My second stay at the WCFIA in spring 2010 marked the beginning of the actual writing process of the book. These two months at Harvard were a highly productive period, and I am enormously grateful to Steve Bloomfield and Michelle Eureka at the WCFIA for making it possible for me to return to this hospitable and intellectually stimulating place. My second visit in Cambridge also marked the beginning of a regular and fruitful exchange with David Singer, who has read and commented on every single chapter in this book. Our frequent discussions in coffee shops or over the phone resulted in many improvements in this manuscript, because David has the ability to get at the depth of an argument, expose potential weaknesses, and propose good and viable alternatives in a highly constructive and gracious manner.

Most of the book was written during my time as a junior professor for international and comparative political economy at the Institute for Political Science at Heidelberg University, Germany, which provided a friendly and supportive atmosphere and a generously funded setting. At Heidelberg, Ruth Beckmann in particular provided me with great support in research and teaching and made many useful suggestions on the manuscript.

Many others have also contributed to the successful completion of this book. At various stages of the project, Bill Bernhard, Bill Clark, Mark Copelovitch, Daniel Finke, John Freeman, Mark Hallerberg, Eric Helleiner, Simon Hug, Nahomi Ichino, Hanspeter Kriesi, David Leblang, Lucas Leeman, Thomas Oatley, Tom Pepinsky, Peter Rosendorff, Gerald Schneider, Ken Shepsle, David Steinberg, Mike Tomz, Christoph Trebesch, and Joshua Walton gave me detailed and helpful comments on ideas from or parts of the manuscript. Mark Copelovitch, Silja Häusermann, David Leblang, and David Singer additionally gave me much appreciated advice and support on the publication process. My editors at Cambridge University Press, most notably Eric Crahan and Scott Parris, have patiently accompanied the writing process and have been generously providing advice and support. Two anonymous reviewers carefully read the first version of the manuscript and made many useful suggestions, which have made the final product much stronger.

I also received valuable feedback from many participants at conferences and workshops at which I presented parts of the manuscript: the Research Workshop in Political Economy at Harvard University, the International Political Economy Society meeting 2009, the Midwest Political Science Association Meeting 2009, the American Political Science Association Annual Conferences 2009 and 2010, and the Politics in Times of Crisis Workshops in Heidelberg in December 2009 and 2010. Generous funding for this book project and preliminary work was provided by ETH research grant 0–20206–04 and the Fritz-Thyssen-Foundation, which funded both my stay at Harvard's WCFIA in the 2008–9 academic year with a Fritz-Thyssen-Fellowship and my research project "The Politics of Delayed Reform and Crisis: Interests, Elections, and Macroeconomic Adjustment" (Az. 20.10.0.003). Over the years, Laura Allendörfer, Jessica Baker, Renate

Berger, Maria Fiedler, Bastian Herre, Dominik Lober, Joel Schoppig, Stefanie Seibert, Philipp Trein, and Susanne Wolfmaier provided very good research assistance. Writing the chapter on the Asian financial crisis only became possible because numerous interviewees agreed to patiently answer my questions. Jungsik Kim, Ek Nitithaprapas, Ning Sitthiyot, Calvin Lin, and Wen-Cheng Chiu deserve great thanks for guiding me through Seoul, Bangkok, and Taichung. Because much of this book has been written in coffee shops, many thanks are also in order to the 1369 coffee shop in Cambridge, MA; das Kleine Café, Café Sammo, and the Mantei Café Lenaustraße in Mannheim; and the Bergheim 41 Café in Heidelberg for providing tasty latte macchiato, friendly staff, and a high tolerance toward my spending countless hours writing at one of their little tables.

My greatest thanks go to my family. My three wonderful sisters, Kerstin, Amelie, and Christina, maybe provided the earliest impetus for this project by being the first to raise my interest in distributional conflict. My parents, Hans-Michael and Monika Walter, have been my greatest supporters from the start. They instilled in me the desire to learn and understand and have provided a safe haven of unwavering love and support from all the twists and turns of an academic career. In very practical terms, it would have been impossible for me to finish this book without my mother's help in recent months. The many hours she has looked after our little sons Nils and Lukas together with their devotion to their "Oma" gave me the time and peace to work on my book. Nils and Lukas, who sometimes grudgingly, sometimes happily, accepted my absences have supplied me with the great gifts of keeping me firmly rooted in reality and allowing me to completely forget about the book in my free time. Most importantly, my husband Jörn deserves thanks: for his patience with me working on what at times seemed like an endless project, for his willingness to discuss my argument and to contribute the economist's view on it, and above all for being there.

ONE

Introduction

The spectacular crash of Thailand's currency in the summer of 1997 constitutes one of the most memorable events of the Asian financial crisis. The Thai exchange rate had been overvalued for several years, and experts had been warning for some time that without adjustments in economic policies, the currency's peg would become unsustainable. Despite these warnings, the Thai government had been unwilling to implement the required policy changes. Rather than tighten fiscal and monetary policy, implement structural reforms, or introduce more flexibility into the exchange rate regime, they increasingly counteracted the mounting pressure on their currency through interventions on the foreign exchange market. In the process, they sold their entire foreign currency reserves until literally nothing was left. At that point, the authorities were no longer able to avoid adjustment and decided to let the exchange rate float. As a result, the currency crashed and lost half of its value, and the country experienced one of its worst economic crises to date.

From an economic efficiency perspective, this behavior of Thai policymakers is truly perplexing. However, it is far from unique: Policymakers in countries such as Argentina, Mexico, and, more recently, Belarus have also delayed needed macroeconomic adjustment, only to see their currencies crash later on. Typically, policymakers in these countries have delayed devaluations by spending billions of dollars in defense of a given exchange rate against speculative pressure, only to succumb to this pressure and to devalue their currencies later on, usually amid a full-blown currency crisis. This contrasts with the experience of other countries, where policymakers have been able to successfully address emerging balance-of-payments problems at a relatively early stage. For example, Britain's decision to abandon its exchange rate peg in 1992 came relatively quickly after serious speculation had started against the British pound sterling. Even though the central bank lost a lot of money in its one-day attempt to stabilize the currency, the relatively speedy decision to let the currency depreciate led to a quick stabilization and a rapid recovery of the British economy.

Improving our understanding of this puzzling variation in policymakers' resolve to address emerging problems through an adjustment of their economic policies is an important task, because delayed adjustment often ends in a financial and economic crisis. Such crises have caused great disruptions around the globe, affecting developing countries, emerging markets, and advanced economies alike. They usually impose enormous costs, both in economic and political terms. A systemic banking crisis, for example, on average causes the gross domestic product (GDP) to shrink by about 9.3 percent, unemployment to rise by 7 percentage points, and real equity prices to fall by a whopping 55.9 percent (Reinhart and Rogoff 2010: 228–30). Similarly, currency crashes lead to an average output loss of 7.1 percent and significantly higher rates of inflation (Aziz, Caramazza, and Salgado 2000). In addition to these economic costs, macroeconomic crises and the policies implemented to resolve them often carry high political costs. The demonstrations and riots that accompanied the major economic and financial crises in countries as diverse as South Korea (1997–8), Argentina (2001), or Greece (2010–12), which left several people dead, make it evident that citizens are well aware of the pain these crises are causing. This is bad news for incumbents. Not surprisingly, financial crises are associated with higher rates of political turnover (Chwieroth and Walter 2010) and have at times even caused the fall of entire political regimes, as the fall of the Suharto regime in Indonesia demonstrates (Pepinsky 2009).

Much research has shown that the deterioration of certain macroeconomic indicators, such as a negative development of the current account, an increasingly overvalued real exchange rate, or a credit boom, is associated with an increased risk of currency, debt, and banking crises (e.g., Kaminsky, Lizondo, and Reinhart 1998; Berg, Borensztein, and Pattillo 2005; Mendoza and Terrones 2008; Jorda, Schularick, and Taylor 2010). Nonetheless, many episodes that exhibit such an increased risk of crisis pass by without major disruptions in the economy. Oftentimes, such noncrisis episodes are associated with early and decisive policy responses by the government, which reduce the risk of a deterioration turning into a full-blown crisis (Cardarelli, Elekdag, and Kose 2009). Obviously, some policymakers are able to implement corrective policy adjustments early on and to enjoy the benefit of the fact that such a prompt reaction to the initial problems is usually much less costly than the resolution of a crisis (Frankel and Wei 2004). Other policymakers, however, do not act until a full-blown crisis forces them to adjust, even though the deterioration of the economic situation suggests that eventual adjustment will in all likelihood be inevitable. Given the costs associated with such crises, it therefore seems imperative to better understand which circumstances foster early adjustment and which circumstances facilitate delays.

The politics of macroeconomic adjustment is characterized by a second puzzle. Once balance-of-payments problems emerge, policymakers have a number of strategies at their disposal to stabilize the macroeconomic situation. The most important distinction here is between *internal adjustment strategies*, such as fiscal and monetary tightening and structural reforms, and *external adjustment strategies*, which involve an adjustment of the exchange rate, typically a depreciation or devaluation of the currency.[1] Both of these strategies are viable options to address macroeconomic problems, yet one can observe a lot of variation in the adjustment strategies chosen. For example, during the 2007–11 global financial and economic crisis, governments responded quite differently to the problems associated with the crisis. Countries such as Estonia or Latvia addressed the emerging problems by slashing government spending, while keeping the exchange rate firmly pegged to the euro. These measures induced a severe recession in which the Latvian GDP shrank by almost 20 percent and unemployment tripled. Other countries, such as Poland, let their exchange rates depreciate in response to the macroeconomic problems their countries faced, while leaving domestic economic and fiscal policies largely unchanged. Yet others, such as Hungary and Romania, opted for a mixed strategy in which domestic economic tightening was coupled with a moderate adjustment of the exchange rate. Apart from the question of whether necessary policy corrections are delayed or not, this variation raises the question of which type of adjustment strategy policymakers are likely to choose. To gain a better understanding of the politics of macroeconomic adjustment, we consequently also need to understand why some policymakers adjust internally, whereas others opt for external adjustment strategies.

To answer these questions, this book investigates when policymakers are willing to adjust their economic policies in response to macroeconomic problems, which types of adjustment strategies they choose, under what circumstances they delay reform, and when such delays are likely to result in crises. Using a political economy perspective and focusing on domestic politics in democratic countries, it examines how the distribution of voters' vulnerabilities to different types of adjustment strategies and electoral

---

[1] A loss in the currency's value relative to another currency is called a depreciation in flexible exchange rate regimes and a devaluation in fixed exchange rate regimes.

concerns influence policymakers' incentives to address macroeconomic imbalances. The book highlights how the internationalization of financial markets has altered the distributional effects of exchange-rate and monetary policy and has made the resulting vulnerabilities a salient determinant of macroeconomic policy outcomes. It particularly spells out how the liberalization of capital accounts has facilitated the emergence of such vulnerabilities by allowing firms and citizens to borrow abroad. The book shows that the resulting distributional concerns not only inform the type of adjustment strategy chosen by policymakers, but can also create strong incentives for policymakers to implement policies that are detrimental in the long run. Delay is particularly likely when sizeable parts of the electorate are vulnerable to both internal and external adjustment.

1.1 Why Macroeconomic Adjustment Becomes Necessary

Adjusting macroeconomic policies becomes necessary when fundamental balance-of-payments problems emerge. The balance of payments, which records all transactions between a country and the rest of the world, is in balance when inflows of goods, services, and capital approximately equal the outflow of goods, services, and capital.[2] In reality, however, one can often observe an imbalance in the balance of payments. Such imbalances can come in two forms: Surplus countries exhibit current account surpluses and capital account deficits, whereas deficit countries exhibit current account deficits and capital account surpluses. Overall, deficit countries are much more crisis prone than surplus countries and tend to face much stronger pressure to adjust when external financing dries up. A current account deficit typically implies that a country is importing more goods and services than it exports, for example, because foreign goods are cheaper than domestically produced goods. Moreover, domestic savings are smaller than domestic investments in deficit countries. Because exports do not generate enough revenue to finance all the purchases of imported goods and because the funds needed for investments are larger than those domestic citizens can provide in the form of savings, current account deficits are associated with capital inflows into a country.[3] Such inflows usually lead to an

---

[2] The balance of payments consists of the current and the capital account as well as balancing items such as reserve sales.

[3] The current and capital account as well as reserve sales and other balancing items balance each other by definition, so that a current account deficit is usually associated with a capital account surplus (more capital inflows than outflows) and vice versa. The causality between current account deficits and capital account surpluses can run both ways.

increase in foreign debt and foreign ownership of domestic assets, domestic credit expansions, and real exchange rate appreciations, which can fuel a further deterioration of the current account. When these capital inflows dry up – either because of a change in the global investment climate or because international investors become skeptical about the sustainability of the country's economic policies – policymakers need to act, because the current account deficit can no longer be financed with foreign capital. It is this type of balance-of-payments problems that lie at the heart of this book.

There are two ways to address such problems. The first is to use foreign currency reserves to finance the deficit; the second is to implement policies that lead to macroeconomic adjustment and a rebalancing of the current and capital accounts. Financing the deficit – for example, through sterilized foreign reserve sales – is an appropriate policy response to a current account deficit that has emerged in response to a temporary shock, such as a sudden and temporary change in the world market price of an important tradable good, a natural disaster that temporarily disrupts a country's productive capacity, or a temporary dip in international capital flows. In these situations characterized by a fundamentally stable macroeconomic environment, a significant adjustment of macroeconomic policies might do more harm than good by destabilizing economic activity. Consequently, a financing of the deficit is the economically sensible way to proceed. Sterilized intervention means that transactions in the foreign exchange market are conducted in such a way that they have no, or little, consequences for the domestic money supply and therefore do not affect domestic interest rates. Such sales allow the central bank to offset a drop in the demand for domestic currency, which puts downward pressure on the exchange rate, without changing its monetary policy stance. This enables policymakers to alleviate speculative pressure and stabilize the exchange rate, while simultaneously avoiding a serious adjustment of the macroeconomy. Of course, a prerequisite for a successful pursuit of this type of policy response is the sufficient availability of funds. Only countries that hold foreign currency reserves large enough to cover the deficit (or who can borrow such funds on international markets or from institutions such as the International Monetary Fund) can engage in this strategy.

Unfortunately, policymakers usually face a lot of uncertainty about whether the emerging economic problems are just temporary or whether they reflect deeper macroeconomic problems. A considerable debate exists about when current account deficits become unsustainable and under what circumstances they can be sustained for very long periods of time (Freund 2005; Freund and Warnock 2007). What is clear, however, is that sterilized reserve sales can only satisfactorily resolve the problems caused by an economic shock when the economy is fundamentally sound. In contrast, when the underlying problems reflect more fundamental problems, such sales merely delay needed adjustment. This delay oftentimes aggravates existing problems and, hence, not only increases the amount of adjustment that is ultimately required to rebalance the economy, but also intensifies the risk that this adjustment will eventually take place in the context of a severe financial crisis.

This distinction between temporary and fundamental balance-of-payments problems is crucial, because oftentimes current account deficits result from deeper macroeconomic and structural problems, such as an unsustainably high level of consumer demand coupled with a weak industrial and services sector, high budget deficits, high growth rates of money and domestic credit, and/or overvalued exchange rates. In these situations, a more far-reaching policy response is needed. To achieve a rebalancing of the current account, foreign and domestic prices have to be realigned, and this can be achieved in two ways (as well as a combination of both). The first possible adjustment strategy is *external adjustment*, which means that the exchange rate depreciates. The goal of this adjustment strategy is to eliminate the trade deficit by using the exchange rate to make domestic products more competitive internationally and to raise the price of imports. As a result, expenditure is switched away from the consumption of internationally tradable goods and toward the production and export of such goods. A second possible adjustment strategy is *internal adjustment* in which monetary and fiscal policies are tightened and structural reforms are implemented to increase the economy's competitiveness. Here, the goal is to deflate domestic prices through a reduction in overall spending and productivity gains, which once more makes domestic products more competitive internationally and reduces the demand for imports. A tightening of monetary policies slows inflation and, hence, the rise of domestic prices, while also encouraging more savings and less investment. Moreover, higher interest rates can attract foreign capital or at least reduce capital outflows and, hence, reduce speculative pressures. This buys time for more far-reaching fiscal and structural reform measures, whose implementation is more time-intensive because they usually require parliamentary approval.

Both of these macroeconomic adjustment strategies are usually painful. Unfortunately for policymakers, however, avoiding adjustment and financing the deficit instead is not an option when the economy is experiencing fundamental problems. Even though adjustment can be avoided as long as the central bank commands or acquires enough foreign currency reserves to finance the deficit, adjustment will have to occur eventually, either voluntarily by changing economic policies, or involuntarily in form of a crash. The latter often comes in the form of a so-called first-generation-type currency crisis (Krugman 1979).[4] Once a country's macroeconomic fundamentals have deteriorated significantly enough, adjustment becomes inevitable. Surprisingly, policymakers nonetheless frequently try to avoid macroeconomic adjustment. Past research has shown that on average, they wait between six and thirteen months after the beginning of serious balance-of-payments problems (especially a turnaround of capital flows) before genuine macroeconomic adjustment occurs (Frankel and Wei 2004).

1.2 How and When Do Policymakers Adjust? Existing Explanations

When serious balance-of-payments problems emerge, policymakers have to come to a decision on two sets of questions: First, which type of adjustment strategy should they choose to rebalance the economy, and second, when should these measures be implemented? These decisions about the type and timing of macroeconomic adjustment can have severe welfare implications. Both internal and external adjustment strategies tend to be costly in economic and political terms, and sterilized reserve sales carry the risk that they merely delay needed adjustment and let the situation deteriorate into a full-blown financial crisis. Given the high salience of addressing the situation in an appropriate manner, how do policymakers decide on these questions? The existing literature offers several answers.

1.2.1 Choosing between Internal and External Adjustment

Regarding the question of which type of adjustment strategy policymakers are likely to choose, existing research in economics has identified several factors that influence the relative cost of different adjustment strategies in different contexts. In particular, research on optimum currency areas (OCAs)

---

4   Note that not all currency crises occur because of bad macroeconomic fundamentals, and not all speculative attacks on countries' currencies end with exchange-rate adjustments. Rather, exchange rates can come under pressure even when macroeconomic fundamentals are merely of a dubious quality. For example, in so-called second-generation-type currency crises, investors' skepticism regarding the government's determination to adjust to emerging macroeconomic imbalances internally and in a timely manner leads to speculative pressure on the exchange rate because investors anticipate that adjustment will eventually have to take place even though conditions have not (yet) deteriorated beyond policymakers' control (Obstfeld 1994, 1996).

has shown that certain country characteristics such as size, openness, or labor market flexibility influence the ease with which internal and external adjustment can be implemented (Mundell 1961; McKinnon 1963; for reviews, see Masson and Taylor 1993; Frankel 1999; Willett 2003). OCA theory suggests that in terms of aggregate economic efficiency, the costs of external adjustment are lower in larger, less trade-dependent economies, whereas internal adjustment is the less costly adjustment strategy for small open economies. In addition, more recent research has found that as financial globalization has progressed, the types of international capital inflows into an economy and their effects on the country's financial structure are playing an increasingly important role in determining the relative costs of external and internal adjustment (e.g., Frankel and Wei 2004; Eichengreen and Hausmann 2005). However, the effect of an economy's financial structure on the choice of adjustment strategies is not entirely clear. For example, while pervasive liability dollarization increases the costs of external adjustment, it also increases the economy's vulnerability to capital outflows and the likelihood of a drop in the value of the currency.

One of the main conclusions of this research in economics is that policymakers' macroeconomic policy choices are not predetermined solely by economic considerations. For example, looking at how policymakers deal with speculative pressure on countries' currencies, several studies find that the characteristics suggested by OCA analysis and other economic factors do not explain well the observed variation in the outcome of speculative attacks (Eichengreen, Rose, and Wyplosz 2003; Kraay 2003). As a result, political economists have argued that the aggregate economic efficiency effects stressed by traditional OCA analyses and other economic models are often not the only factor influencing exchange-rate and monetary policy choices in open economies (see, e.g., Cohen 2003; Willett 2006). Instead, political economy research suggests that policymakers' responses to speculative pressure depend on political factors as well (Leblang 2003; Sattler and Walter 2009; Walter 2009).

For one, international pressure and international considerations matter. For example, conditionality from the International Monetary Fund (IMF) has been found to increase the incidence of external adjustment (Dreher and Walter 2010). However, this is not always the case, as the recent examples of Latvia, Greece, and Ireland show, where the IMF has explicitly supported policies aimed at internal adjustment and a continuation of the countries' fixed exchange rate regimes.

Second, domestic political considerations are of great importance, which is not surprising if one considers that the decision to implement macroeconomic adjustment can end political careers (see, e.g., Cooper 1971; Frankel 2005; Leblang 2005). The political economy literature on exchange-rate and monetary policymaking in open economies has demonstrated that domestic political factors shape country-specific choices about the relative importance of the two goals of exchange-rate stability and monetary policy autonomy, which are mutually exclusive when capital is fully mobile internationally.[5] With regard to macroeconomic adjustment, this literature has argued that in democracies, the costs of internal adjustment outweigh the costs of external adjustment (Eichengreen 1992, 1996; Simmons 1994). Yet, empirically there are also many cases in which democratic policymakers have chosen internal adjustment over external adjustment – the recent decisions by the Baltic states or Ireland to follow this strategy are such examples.[6] A possible explanation for this contradictory evidence is that existing research has typically assumed that voters have homogenous preferences regarding external and internal adjustment: With regard to internal adjustment, the majority of voters have been assumed to oppose internal adjustment and the increase in unemployment associated with it (Eichengreen 1992; Simmons 1994). Similarly, regarding external adjustment, voters have been assumed to uniformly oppose depreciation because it reduces their purchasing power (Frieden and Stein 2001b; Stein and Streb 2004; Blomberg, Frieden, and Stein 2005).

Empirical research, however, casts some doubt on these assumptions of preference homogeneity. Microlevel evidence suggests that voters' macroeconomic preferences and concerns are in fact quite heterogenous (e.g., Scheve 2004). To arrive at a better understanding of voters' policy preferences

---

[5] This research builds on the insights of the so-called unholy trinity or Mundell-Fleming-model, which implies that, when capital is mobile internationally, fixing the exchange rate means that interest rates cannot be manipulated in pursuit of domestic economic objectives (Mundell 1961; Fleming 1962; for a discussion and the labeling of this model as unholy trinity, see Cohen 1995). Likewise, the ability to gear monetary policy toward domestic objectives comes at the cost of giving up exchange-rate stability. This literature demonstrates that exchange-rate and monetary institutions evolve in the context of this trade-off (see, for example, Bernhard, Broz, and Clark 2003; Clark 2003; Bernhard and Leblang 2006) and that these institutional choices in turn are influenced by political factors, such as the political regime type (Leblang 1999; Broz 2002; Stierli 2006; Hall 2008; Guisinger and Singer 2010; Bearce and Hallerberg 2011), the type of electoral regime (Bernhard and Leblang 1999; Leblang 1999), the timing of elections (Frieden and Stein 2001a; Schamis and Way 2003), the government's partisanship (Garrett 1998; Oatley 1999; Bearce 2003, 2007), and interest group pressure (Frieden 1991b, 1996, 2002; Hefeker 1997; Hall 2005; Helleiner 2005).

[6] For Ireland during the ongoing euro crisis, external adjustment would mean the exit from the European Monetary Union and a reintroduction of the Irish pound at a devalued rate.

regarding external and internal adjustment, it therefore appears necessary to explore in more detail how this variation in policy preferences can be explained. In this context, an important question is how voters evaluate different policy options and which aspects they consider when forming their policy preferences (e.g., Kinder and Kiewit 1979; Mansfield and Mutz 2009; Leblang, Jupille, and Curtis 2011).

Existing research offers many clues as to the sources of such possible variation in voters' policy preferences. Although research on voters' preferences with regard to exchange-rate and other macroeconomic policy preferences has been relatively sparse,[7] the literature on the influence of special interests on exchange-rate and monetary policymaking provides insights into which aspects matter in these policy fields. It shows that different economic sectors favor different types of macroeconomic policies, and this variation in preferences depends on their exposure to international trade and their reliance on domestic economic conditions (e.g., Frieden 1991b; 1996; 2002; Hefeker 1997; Bearce 2003; Hall 2005; Helleiner 2005; Woodruff 2005; Kinderman 2008; Steinberg 2008, 2009; Walter 2008).[8] One implication of this research is that export-oriented industries should favor external over internal adjustment. The empirical evidence does not uniformly support this prediction, however. Quantitative studies have arrived at contradictory conclusions about how the size of the manufacturing or the tradables sector in a country influences exchange-rate policy (e.g., Frieden, Ghezzi, and Stein 2001; Hall 2008; Frieden, Leblang, and Valev 2010; Singer 2010a). For example, highly export-oriented economies, such as South Korea and Hong Kong, have fought unexpectedly hard in the past to avoid external adjustment, a behavior that is at odds with the prediction that export-oriented economies would benefit from a depreciated exchange rate.

A possible explanation for these inconsistent findings is that these studies only look at one half of the story. What they neglect to consider is that financial globalization has vastly transformed governments', firms', and consumers' access to international capital markets. This has had profound effects on their balance sheets, which now often contain not only assets and liabilities denominated in domestic currency but foreign-currency denominated positions as well. As a result, the effects of exchange rate and monetary policy decisions have become more complex. To properly understand the distributional

---

[7]   An exception is the literature on individual preferences about the euro (e.g., Banducci, Karp, and Loedel 2003; Gabel and Hix 2005; Hobolt and Leblond 2009).

[8]   The implementation of economic reforms more generally has been shown to be influenced by the coalitions of opponents and proponents of such reforms (e.g., Gourevitch 1986; Rogowski 1989; Frieden 1991a; Hiscox 2002; Häusermann 2010).

consequences of external and internal adjustment, this complexity needs to be better understood. In addition, existing studies mostly concentrate on interest groups but neglect voters' preferences on exchange- rate and monetary policy decisions. Finally, while much of this literature is very mindful how the long-term trade-off between exchange-rate stability and domestic policy autonomy shapes different actors' policy preferences, it disregards the fact that it is possible to ignore this trade-off in the short run. As we shall see, however, this is an important aspect in the politics of adjustment – and one that leads us to policymakers' second decision problem, the issue of *when* to adjust macroeconomic policies.

1.2.2 The Timing of Macroeconomic Adjustment

The issue of the timing of macroeconomic adjustment is taken up by the literature on the politics of crisis and economic reform, which also sheds light on the dynamics surrounding delayed reforms and macroeconomic stabilizations (for an overview see, for example, Rodrik 1996).

Most importantly, this literature has demonstrated that delays of policy reforms are possible even if reforms are beneficial in the aggregate. One explanation for this finding is the so-called J-curve effect, which frequently characterizes economic reforms such as economic liberalization or macroeconomic adjustment. When a reform is characterized by a J-curve trajectory, it means that it initially makes matters worse before they improve. This is particularly problematic when policymakers operate in an institutional setting that encourages them to discount the future. For example, a lack of economic improvement before the next election presents a difficult challenge for incumbent policymakers dependent on their electorate's vote of approval and creates strong incentives for policymakers to either forgo or delay such reforms (Przeworski 1991).

Macroeconomic policymaking is particularly susceptible to such electoral dynamics. The literature on political business cycles has shown that painful changes in macroeconomic policies are unlikely in the run-up to elections, even if this means that post-election policies will have to be particularly restrictive to correct the preelection developments (e.g., Nordhaus 1975; Rogoff 1990). Evidence for electorally motivated manipulations have been found in a range of macroeconomic policy areas, including exchange-rate policy (Klein and Marion 1997; Frieden and Stein 2001b; Stein and Streb 2004) and monetary policy (e.g., Williams 1990; Clark 2003). In these explanations, delay often results from a tendency of policymakers to avoid the blame for policy decisions that are painful in the short run, even though these decisions are likely to have beneficial consequences in the long run (Weaver 1986; Pierson 1994).[9] However, elections do not always lead to delays in macroeconomic adjustment (Walter 2009), and there have been cases in which substantial adjustment has been implemented just before elections were held. Existing explanations about the effect of elections thus cannot fully account for this variation in the speed of reforms.

A second approach to explaining delay in macroeconomic adjustment emphasizes the role of uncertainty (Fernandez and Rodrik 1991). This approach argues that there is a strong status-quo bias when the winners and losers from a reform cannot be identified in advance. Under these circumstances, there can be strong resistance to reform, even if it is certain that the reform will have positive effects on the country as a whole, and this problem intensifies when it is coupled with distributional conflict (Labán and Sturzenegger 1994). In the case of macroeconomic adjustment, an additional source of uncertainty often impedes the speedy resolution of balance-of-payments problems: the high level of uncertainty about whether adjustment is actually needed or whether the observed problems are the result of a temporary shock that does not require any deeper policy adjustment (Bird and Willett 2008). In fact, the belief among decision makers that the planned policy reforms will in fact deliver long-run social benefits that exceed their costs has been found to be a necessary condition for the implementation of such reforms (Jacobs 2011).

A third set of explanations for delayed reform focuses on the domestic distributional conflict that is frequently associated with such reforms (e.g., Alesina and Drazen 1991; Rodrik 1999; Bird and Willett 2008). In this group of explanations, a fierce distributional conflict is likely to erupt between different societal groups about who is to bear the cost of reform. The resulting "war of attrition" prevents any reform until this conflict is resolved (Alesina and Drazen 1991). In the meantime, economic conditions continue to deteriorate until, finally, the cost of further delay is larger for one of the groups than bearing the cost of reform. Only then can reform be implemented and will be designed such that the conceding group will bear the biggest share of the costs inflicted by reform. The policy preferences of the different groups are static in these models, and delay arises because of conflicting preferences among these groups. However, there is some evidence that policy

---

[9] This is also one of the reasons why IMF programs can speed up macroeconomic adjustment. Not only are these adjustments often part of the conditionality attached to IMF programs but policymakers can also use the IMF as a scapegoat for unpopular policy decisions (Smith and Vreeland 2003; Vreeland 2003; Dreher and Walter 2010).

preferences can evolve over time, from an initial aversion to adjustment to an eventual preference for reform (Walter 2008; Walter and Willett 2012). Such an evolution over time is likely to affect policymakers' incentives to delay needed macroeconomic adjustment. This raises the question when public opinion changes so much that reforms become possible.

In sum, myopic policymaking, high levels of uncertainty, and distributional issues hamper the timely adjustment of macroeconomic policies. The policy measures necessary to combat balance-of-payments problems are typically plagued by all of these features. This suggests that similar dynamics of delay are likely to emerge in the context of the macroeconomic policy adjustments necessary to avoid or combat balance-of-payments crises.

1.2.3 Open Questions

The discussion has shown that there is a lot of literature that speaks to the questions of *how* and *when* policymakers adjust their policies to address balance-of-payments problems. Nonetheless, all of these studies leave unanswered some aspects crucial to the question why necessary adjustments are frequently delayed and which adjustment strategies policymakers eventually choose. Studies focusing on the choice between alternative adjustment strategies usually neglect how profoundly the internationalization of financial markets has altered the distributional effects of exchange-rate and monetary policy. They also underplay the fact that policymakers have a third policy option in the short run, that is the option of engaging in sterilized foreign reserve sales that allows them to avoid – or at least delay– macroeconomic adjustment. Research on delayed reforms, in contrast, spells out why policymakers might face incentives to delay adjustment, but neither specifies under which circumstances these incentives are particularly large in the context of adjustment to balance-of-payments problems nor explains why there is variation in both the effect of elections on the speed of adjustment and the evolution of distributional issues over time. In addition, few studies combine the insights from these two strands of literature, even though the questions of how and when to adjust are closely connected. And finally, although many studies point to the importance of distributional conflict, they are usually characterized by a focus on organized interests, rather than the distributional concerns of voters more generally. This is puzzling because research on economic voting suggests that electoral considerations should strongly influence the decision to implement adjustment.

To answer the questions of *why* some policymakers fail to adjust their policies in a timely manner while others delay this decision, and *which types* of macroeconomic adjustment strategies policymakers choose to address imbalances in their balance of payments, this book builds on and extends the insights from these literatures. It argues that distributional and electoral concerns influence both of these policy choices and places voters in the center of the analysis. For this purpose, it concentrates on the significant distributional direct and indirect consequences of exchange-rate, monetary, and fiscal policy adjustment in a financially globalized economy on individual voters and their effect on policymakers' incentives to pursue certain macroeconomic policies.

1.3 The Argument

This book argues that the distributional consequences of macroeconomic adjustment shape policymakers' incentives to address balance-of-payments problems both with regard to the *type* and the *timing* of adjustment strategies. It proceeds in two steps. First, it examines the sources of voters' vulnerabilities to internal and external adjustment and the effects of these vulnerabilities on their policy preferences regarding macroeconomic adjustment. In a second step, it analyzes how different patterns in the distribution of vulnerabilities across the electorate affect policymakers' incentives on when and how to adjust their economic policies, and under which circumstances delayed adjustment is particularly likely to occur.

1.3.1 Explaining Voters' Vulnerabilities to Internal and External Adjustment

Changes in exchange and interest rates, fiscal policy, and structural reforms can significantly hurt certain groups of citizens, while benefiting others. Some groups will consequently be more vulnerable to the consequences of external adjustment, whereas for others internal adjustment is more painful. To understand how vulnerabilities to external and internal adjustment are distributed across a country's electorate, this book examines the direct and indirect sources of voters' vulnerabilities to different types of macroeconomic adjustment. It argues that the different adjustment strategies directly affect voters' purchasing power and personal balance sheets. Moreover, the effects of these strategies on employers and the economy in general present an additional indirect, although nonetheless important, source of exposure to the consequences of adjustment for voters.

Whereas most previous research on the distributional consequences of exchange-rate and monetary policy decisions has focused on industrial sectors and firms, this book explicitly concentrates on voters. Gaining the support of a majority of voters is one of the principle goals of incumbent policymakers (Downs 1957) so that their anticipated reactions to the government's handling of macroeconomic imbalances matter. Because voters can be assumed to prefer those exchange-rate, monetary, and fiscal policies to which they are least vulnerable and to assess the performance of the incumbent based on how his or her policy choices have affected their economic situation (Fiorina 1981), the distribution of vulnerabilities among voters influences policymakers' choices regarding the type and timing of macroeconomic adjustment strategies.

To identify how these vulnerabilities are distributed among the electorate, this book builds on existing research on the influence of industrial sectors on exchange-rate and monetary policy (e.g., Frieden 1991b, 1996, 2002; Hefeker 1997; Hall 2005; Helleiner 2005; Kinderman 2008; Steinberg 2008, 2009). In contrast to this research, however, it draws attention to the fact that voters are increasingly directly exposed to different macroeconomic policies as well. Moreover, although it applies the classic distinction between the effects of exchange-rate adjustment on purchasing power and international competitiveness (Frieden 1991b; Blomberg et al. 2005), it adds two additional dimensions that become salient determinants of macroeconomic policy preferences in a financially open economy: exposure to foreign-currency debt and vulnerability to interest-rate increases.

Financial globalization has had profound effects on the vulnerability of citizens to the external and internal adjustment of macroeconomic policies. Few policy fields have been as deeply affected by financial globalization as the fields of exchange-rate and monetary policy. Here, the globalization of capital has had two powerful consequences. First, as the liberalization of international capital flows has allowed domestic citizens and firms to engage on foreign financial markets, the distributional consequences of exchange-rate policy have become more complex. Today, many citizens and firms have direct or indirect ties to international markets. People travel throughout the world and consume goods that were produced abroad. Many citizens and firms now borrow capital in foreign currencies, either directly on international capital markets or indirectly through domestic financial intermediaries such as banks, to finance their houses, cars, or other investments with mortgages or loans in foreign currencies. Individuals also invest abroad or send money to their relatives in foreign countries. As a result of this increasing ability to borrow and invest in foreign currencies, exchange-rate movements no longer only affect individuals' purchasing power but often have significant effects on their personal financial situation as well.

Individuals who hold a mortgage in a foreign currency, for example, are very vulnerable to depreciation, because this drives up the amount of money they owe. When large portions of private borrowing are denominated in foreign currency, a depreciation of the currency substantially increases the debt burden in domestic-currency terms, which is particularly damaging when borrowers' income mainly comes from domestic sources and is denominated in domestic currency. However, even individuals who have concentrated on domestic markets can be indirectly vulnerable to exchange-rate adjustments when these adjustments adversely affect their employers or the national economy.

The second important consequence of financial globalization has been that exchange-rate policy has become intricately linked to monetary policy. This follows from the so-called unholy trinity (also known as open economy trilemma), the fact that a fixed exchange rate, monetary policy autonomy, and capital mobility cannot be achieved at the same time.[10] As financial markets are liberalized and capital mobility becomes a defining feature of a country's macroeconomic environment, the unholy trinity reduces to a trade-off between exchange-rate stability and domestic monetary policy autonomy. When capital is completely mobile, policymakers can either influence the exchange rate or the interest rate but cannot retain complete control over both of them at the same time. The following example illustrates this assertion. Imagine that policymakers decide to lower interest rates. The reasons for this decision may be to encourage investments, to spur consumption, and hence to promote growth and job creation. As interest rates are lowered, investors intent on maximizing the return on their investments are likely to reallocate at least some portion of their investments to countries with higher interest rate levels. When their capital leaves the country, demand for the domestic currency decreases, as a result of which the exchange rate depreciates – and consequently no longer remains stable. In contrast, if policymakers want to maintain exchange-rate stability, they need to subject monetary policy to this goal. To offset appreciation or depreciation pressures, interest rates have to be lowered or increased but can no longer be used for domestic objectives such as a boost in consumption and growth. The unholy trinity thus implies that in financially open countries, decisions concerning the level of the exchange rate necessarily always have implications for monetary policy, and vice versa. For example, if the authorities want to strengthen their currency, an appreciation can be achieved if they

---

[10] For discussions of the unholy trinity and its policy implications, see Cohen (1995) and Obstfeld (1998).

increase interest rates. This can have painful consequences for voters, however, especially when they hold loans or mortgages whose repayment is tied to domestic interest rates. They are also indirectly exposed as high interest rates discourage new investments and slow down economic activity, which in turn leads to job losses and decreases in income and wealth – developments that have negative consequences for most voters.

As a result of these developments, financial liberalization has deeply affected the distributional consequences associated with both external and internal adjustments of macroeconomic policies. This book therefore suggests an approach for identifying macroeconomic policy preferences, which takes into account the interrelationship between exchange-rate and monetary policy in a financially integrated world, and the effects of these policies on balance sheets.[11] Voters' overall vulnerabilities to different adjustment strategies depend both on how exchange-rate, monetary, and fiscal policy changes as well as structural reforms affect their purchasing power and personal balance sheets and how they influence the business operations of their employers as well as the economy in general. Voters' specific configurations, or profiles, of direct and indirect vulnerabilities then influence their overall policy preference regarding external and internal adjustment. Voters who overall are less vulnerable to depreciation than monetary and fiscal tightening will prefer external adjustment to internal adjustment, and vice versa. Voters who have little to fear from either form of adjustment are likely to be indifferent. In contrast, voters who are very vulnerable to both external and internal adjustment will oppose any type of adjustment.

1.3.2 Explaining Government Choices on Type and Timing of Macroeconomic Adjustment

How do these distributional effects of adjustment influence policymakers' decisions about how and when to respond to balance-of-payments problems? Why do some governments decide to adjust internally, whereas others opt for external adjustment? And why are some policymakers able to adjust their policies in response to deteriorating economic conditions in a timely manner, whereas other policymakers delay adjustment as long as possible, a policy path that typically ends with an economic and financial crisis?

This book emphasizes that distributional issues strongly influence the politics of macroeconomic adjustment. Building on the characterization of the distributional effects associated with different strategies of macroeconomic

---

[11] See also Walter (2008).

adjustment developed in the first part of the book, the second part argues that a government's choice of adjustment strategy depends on voters' specific vulnerability profiles. When a majority of voters are more negatively exposed to losses in the currency's value than internal adjustment, policymakers are more likely to implement policies that tighten domestic economic conditions. In contrast, when a majority of constituents are more vulnerable to exchange-rate changes than monetary and/or fiscal contraction as well as structural change, internal adjustment becomes more likely.

When citizens are highly vulnerable to both external and internal adjustment, this choice becomes more difficult. In this case, any type of adjustment has painful consequences for the country's citizens. Particularly in democratic countries in which governments hope to be reelected, implementing reforms can then come at a high political cost to the incumbent. This creates strong incentives not to adjust at all. This in itself is unproblematic as long as the balance-of-payments problems result from transitory economic shocks that will eventually rectify themselves without any major intervention. However, adjustment cannot be avoided in the long run when the economy experiences fundamental problems. Under these circumstances, adjustment eventually will have to occur, either voluntarily by changing economic policies or involuntarily in the form of a crash. However, there is one important qualification to this mechanism: The trade-off between exchange-rate stability and domestic policy autonomy in financially open countries holds in the medium to long run but not necessarily in the short run. In the short run, policymakers have the option of selling foreign currency reserves to offset any downward pressure on their currencies – without any significant adjustments to the interest rate and fiscal policy. Thus, as long as a country commands enough funds, either in form of its foreign currency reserves or in terms of international financial support, adjustment can be avoided. As soon as these funds are no longer available, however, adjustment will have to occur. When the time bought by this financing of the deficit is not used to implement economic reforms, however, delay usually results in a further deterioration of the imbalances. As a result, delayed adjustment usually has to be much more extensive than adjustment that is implemented early on.

Faced with the emergence of balance-of-payments problems, policymakers are hence confronted with the following dilemma. If adjustment is undertaken in a fundamentally stable economy, it is unnecessary but nonetheless painful and politically costly. If, however, the shock is in fact a sign of fundamental economic problems, adjustment ultimately cannot be avoided. In this case, relatively small adjustments will often be sufficient when

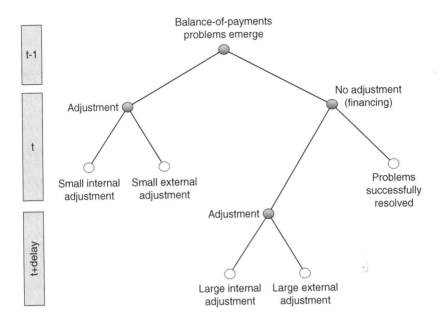

Figure 1.1. Government decision tree.

the problems are addressed early on. In contrast, the adjustment policies required to stabilize the economy will usually be much larger if adjustment has been delayed in the past, because the delay allows fundamentals to deteriorate further. The amount of external and internal adjustment necessary to address the economy's fundamental problems thus increases the longer it has been put off in the past.

When confronted with a deteriorating balance of payments, policymakers thus need to identify whether this deterioration reflects a temporary deviation from the equilibrium path or more serious fundamental problems. This is a difficult task and often creates a situation of uncertainty in which policymakers have to decide how to respond to the country's economic problems. Figure 1.1 depicts the decision problem governments face. Provided that enough funds are available to finance the current account deficit at least temporarily, policymakers have to make two decisions: First, should they adjust or not adjust, and second, if they decide to adjust, should they adjust externally or internally? If policymakers decide to adjust immediately, they need to decide on the type of adjustment strategy – that is, internal or external adjustment. If they decide not to adjust and to finance the deficit instead, this can either be sufficient to quench the pressure on their currency (the least costly outcome), or not, in which case a more extensive adjustment at a later point will become necessary (the most costly option).

Assuming that policymakers want to be reelected, they will base these decisions on a comparison of how the different options will affect their expected election chances. These chances, in turn, depend on the distributional effects of the different adjustment strategies. Policymakers' responses to economic shocks will therefore vary by the type of vulnerability dominant among their countries' voters. If a majority of voters are likely to benefit more from an adjustment of economic policies than from not adjusting, then an early adjustment is likely. For example, in highly export-oriented countries in which little foreign borrowing has occurred, depreciations are often not particularly painful for many voters, because their personal balance sheets are not vulnerable to this type of adjustment, whereas the depreciation is likely beneficial for export performance and growth from which voters indirectly benefit. In these countries, governments are hence expected to quickly adjust externally. If, on the other hand, voters are vulnerable to both types of adjustment, the government faces much larger incentives to follow a wait-and-see strategy. In this case, policymakers' preferred outcome is the one in which they do not adjust and instead sell foreign reserves, and in which this is sufficient to quench the transitory problems of the economy. The problem with choosing this option is that the decision to forego early adjustment carries the risk that more wide-ranging adjustment might be necessary in the future. Given that the electorate is vulnerable to both types of adjustment, such large adjustments will be very painful and cost the incumbent a lot of votes. When voters are vulnerable to both types of adjustment, the incentive to delay is therefore particularly high when policymakers believe that there is a high probability that the economic shock is only transitory, so that adjustment can be avoided altogether.

The distributional effects of adjustment consequently affect both the timing and the type of adjustment strategy chosen. Delay is particularly likely when many voters are vulnerable to both external and internal adjustment and when the government can reasonably hope that the problems are only of a transitory nature. In terms of adjustment strategy, policymakers will choose the strategy, which is likely to minimize the pain imposed on voters. Whether this is internal or external adjustment (or a combination of both) depends on voters' particular distribution of direct and indirect vulnerabilities to changes in macroeconomic policies.

Elections can magnify the incentives to delay adjustment, because they shorten the time horizon of policymakers. When the vulnerability profile of a country's electorate creates a setting in which not adjusting is the preferred policy outcome – not an uncommon scenario – upcoming elections make delaying adjustment particularly attractive to policymakers. This is because even though they know that delay may result in more drastic adjustment measures later on, policymakers can discount this possibility when they are reasonably confident that they can delay adjustment at least until election day. If the uncertainty about the nature of the problem is sufficiently large among voters, they are likely to reward the incumbent at the polls for not inflicting any major pain on them. Consequently, the lower the risk that adjustment becomes unavoidable before voters go to the polls, the stronger the incentive for policymakers to delay adjustment until after the election, even though this strategy carries the risk of even larger and more costly adjustment in the future. This implies that the incentive to delay adjustment will be highest when elections are close, whereas policymakers have more incentives to act like welfare maximizers when the next elections are far away. However, when incumbents believe that they will not be able to put off adjustment until after the next election, they have an incentive to adjust as soon as possible in an attempt to limit the extent of adjustment necessary. In this case, elections can speed up the adjustment process.

In sum, the argument implies that distributional concerns coupled with electoral incentives condition the incentives for policymakers to delay timely macroeconomic adjustment and affect their choice of adjustment strategies. When balance-of-payments problems emerge, voters more vulnerable to exchange-rate (or external) adjustment will favor adjustment of monetary, fiscal, and structural policies (i.e., internal adjustment), and vice versa. When actors are vulnerable to both internal and external adjustment, however, policymakers face large incentives to maintain current policies. Although this is impossible in the long run, policymakers can achieve this goal in the short run by financing the deficit through sterilized sales of foreign currency reserves. The distributional effects of adjustment can therefore create incentives for policymakers to delay reform, especially when citizens are vulnerable to all types of adjustment strategies, when policymakers expect short-term electoral advantages from such delay, and when policymakers have (or can acquire) enough funds to pursue this strategy. However, this strategy is risky: When the current account deficit reflects fundamental macroeconomic problems, financing the deficit allows the misalignment to accumulate and raises the eventual the costs of adjustment. Major financial crises are particularly likely when voters are highly vulnerable to both exchange-rate changes and internal adjustment policies and when political incentives have prevented timely reforms in the past.

1.4 The Plan of the Book

To explain the variation in the speed and the types of adjustment strategies to balance-of-payments problems, the book is organized in two parts.

The first part of the book analyzes the distributional consequences of different adjustment strategies. Chapter 2 discusses the direct and indirect effects of external and internal adjustment strategies on individual voters. Taking into account the effects of financial globalization on personal and corporate finances and on the interrelationship between exchange-rate, monetary, and fiscal policy in a financially integrated world, the chapter argues that voters' vulnerabilities to different adjustment strategies depend on how external and internal adjustment affects their personal economic situation, that of their employers, and the economy as a whole. Importantly, different adjustment policies have very diverse effects on voters. Even though adjustment can sometimes have an overall positive effect, a majority of voters tend to be hurt by macroeconomic adjustment, and for some voters their economic livelihood is on the line when certain adjustment policies are implemented. These vulnerabilities translate into policy preferences about whether and how the government should adjust to macroeconomic imbalances. Voters who are less vulnerable to depreciation than monetary and fiscal tightening will prefer external adjustment to internal adjustment, and vice versa, whereas voters who have little to fear from either form of adjustment are likely to be indifferent. In contrast, voters who are very vulnerable to both external and internal adjustment will oppose any type of adjustment.

Chapters 3 and 4 empirically test this argument about the direct and indirect determinants of voters' vulnerabilities to external and internal adjustment. For this purpose, they use survey data on both the individual level (Chapter 3) and the firm level (Chapter 4) to show that the vulnerability profiles discussed in Chapter 2 do in fact influence assessments of external and internal adjustment strategies, as well as voters' general assessments of their personal and national economic situations. Chapter 3 concentrates on voters' direct vulnerabilities to macroeconomic adjustment. It examines survey data from over 18 thousand voters in 20 European countries, who were surveyed in 2009 about the consequences of the global financial and economic crisis on their personal and their country's overall economic situation. By combining individual-level data with country-level information about national adjustment strategies to the crisis, the chapter analyzes how voters with different vulnerability profiles responded to the different macroeconomic policies implemented by their governments. The results support the argument that voters evaluate different adjustment strategies based on how much pain these strategies are inflicting on them and underline the importance of balance sheet considerations: Voters in countries with a high prevalence of foreign-currency denominated loans were more likely to worry about the repercussions of the crisis when the currency had depreciated. Likewise, voters repaying a mortgage were particularly concerned about the crisis repercussions on their personal situation when monetary policy was tightened and less likely to be concerned when interest rates were lowered.

Turning to the indirect, employer specific, sources of voters' vulnerabilities to macroeconomic adjustment, Chapter 4 investigates how firms assess their governments' monetary and exchange-rate policies and how firm-specific vulnerability profiles shape this assessment. Using survey data from several thousand firms in fifty-three different countries and combining this data with country-level information, the chapter teases out under what circumstances firms feel vulnerable to exchange-rate and monetary policy. The analysis shows that the real and financial vulnerabilities discussed in Chapter 2 do indeed influence corporate policy preferences. Firm-level characteristics such as export orientation and a firm's financial structure are important determinants of firms' vulnerabilities to external and internal adjustment. Balance sheet concerns in particular are influential determinants of firms' vulnerabilities to different adjustment strategies, and that holds for both the currency denomination of liabilities, which matter for firms' exchange-rate policy preferences, and the overall dependence on borrowing, which is an important determinant of their monetary policy preferences. These firm-specific vulnerabilities in turn influence how firms evaluate their country's exchange-rate and monetary polices. The survey also shows that a substantial number of firms report to be vulnerable to both internal and external adjustment, the combination that encourages policymakers to delay adjustment.

Taken together, the chapters in the first part of the book show that different strategies for macroeconomic adjustment can have significant distributional consequences for voters. The second part of the book builds on these insights and analyzes how the vulnerability profile of voters in the aggregate shape policymakers' policy decisions about how and when to respond to balance-of-payments problems. Chapter 5 presents an argument on how voters' distributional concerns affect policymakers' choices of adjustment strategies and under which circumstances they create incentives to delay macroeconomic adjustment. It argues that when a majority of constituents are more vulnerable to exchange-rate changes than a contraction of the domestic economy, internal adjustment becomes more likely, and vice versa. Moreover, it shows that specific vulnerability profiles in the electorate can create incentives for policymakers to avoid timely adjustment, especially when they command sufficient funds or can acquire such funds from external sources to continue to finance the deficit and intervene in international markets. Under these circumstances, policymakers tend to have a strong incentive not to implement painful policy adjustment in the short run. Moreover, elections frequently (although not always) aggravate these incentives not to adjust in time, especially when the median voter exhibits high vulnerabilities to both external and internal adjustment and when policymakers deem it quite probable that they can successfully avoid adjustment at least until after the election. This implies that the incentive to delay adjustment will often be particularly high when elections are close, whereas policymakers have more incentives to focus on the long-run effects of their policies and implement painful adjustment early on when the next elections are far away. Unlike other explanations in the literature, however, the argument also suggests that upcoming elections can sometimes create incentives to adjust sooner rather than later: When macroeconomic conditions deteriorate so strongly that it becomes unlikely that adjustment can be postponed until after election day, policymakers have incentives to implement adjustment quickly, rather than letting the situation get worse and future adjustment even more costly.

Chapters 6 and 7 assess the empirical relevance of these predictions by examining the politics of macroeconomic adjustment in the two most serious global financial crises of recent times: the Asian financial crisis of 1997–8 (Chapter 6) and the global financial and economic crisis that started in 2007 (Chapter 7). Chapter 6 analyzes how the distribution of vulnerabilities and the timing of elections influenced exchange-rate and monetary policy in four countries affected by the Asian financial crisis of 1997–8: Hong Kong, South Korea, Taiwan, and Thailand. The governments of these countries implemented very different macroeconomic policies when balance-of-payments problems and speculative pressures on their currencies emerged, both with regard to the type of adjustment strategies and with regard to the speed with which policymakers chose to implement them. The case studies show that the variation in policymakers' willingness to adjust to emerging pressure on their currencies can be traced back to differences in distributional concerns and the election cycle. In Taiwan, the low vulnerability of most Taiwanese voters to depreciation and their high exposure to interest-rate increases, coupled with an absence of upcoming elections, allowed policymakers to let the currency depreciate early on. As a result, the country emerged as one of the countries least affected by the

Asian financial crisis. In Hong Kong the central importance of exchange-rate stability trumped voters' vulnerabilities to interest-rate increases, allowing policymakers to quickly impose the painful consequences of internal adjustment. In contrast to these two cases in which adjustment was implemented relatively rapidly, in Thailand and Korea large segments of the electorate exhibited high vulnerabilities to both depreciation and monetary tightening. Faced with demands to neither adjust internally nor externally as well as upcoming elections, the authorities in both countries tried to stabilize the currency through the sale of enormous sums of foreign currency reserves. When this strategy ultimately failed, policymakers in both countries chose external over internal adjustment. As a result of the delay, the exchange rates crashed and lost up to half of their value.

Chapter 7 looks at the most recent global financial crisis and concentrates on a set of countries whose policy responses have most puzzled many observers: the new EU member states, and here especially the three Baltic countries and Bulgaria, which successfully confronted their balance-of-payments problems by implementing internal adjustment strategies. The analysis shows that in line with this book's argument, these countries exhibited a vulnerability profile that combined a moderate vulnerability to internal adjustment with a very high vulnerability to external adjustment. In particular, voters and firms in these countries held unusually large amounts of foreign-currency denominated debt, which significantly raised the potential costs of a devaluation of the currency. I argue and show that this vulnerability profile explains why the governments of these countries were able to push through contractionary fiscal and nominal wage policies without serious public opposition. Moreover, the chapter shows that the vulnerability profiles of electorates in these countries differed from voters' overall vulnerabilities in other Eastern European countries, where governments chose externally oriented adjustment strategies (the Czech Republic and Poland) or mixed adjustment strategies (Hungary and Romania). Here, vulnerability to external adjustment was significantly lower and vulnerability to internal adjustment higher than in the Baltic countries and Bulgaria. Overall, the second part of the book thus demonstrates that differences in voters' vulnerabilities can lead to very different policy responses to speculative pressure in countries affected by balance-of-payments crises.

The final chapter concludes by summarizing the book's main findings and discussing their broader implications for researchers and policymakers. The chapter discusses the main insights generated by the book's micro- and macro-level analyses and shows how these insights create an agenda for future research. In doing so, it identifies four main avenues for further research: (1) the origins of crisis-prone vulnerability profiles, (2) the interaction of domestic institutions with the distributional and electoral incentives discussed in this book, (3) the interaction of macroeconomic policy decisions with decisions in other policy areas, and (4) the interplay of the domestic politics of macroeconomic adjustment with international politics. The chapter ends by arguing that a better understanding of the constraints and incentives that distributional and institutional concerns create for policymakers is likely to improve policy prescriptions. The book's findings suggest that a stronger consideration of the political constraints under which domestic policymakers operate is likely to improve the ease with which the recommended policies can be implemented politically. Although the desirability of some of these constraints may be debatable, taking them into account will lead to more feasible policy advice.

TWO

Individual Vulnerability to
Macroeconomic Adjustment

When Jozsef Szepesi, an office clerk from Budapest, Hungary, planned to buy a family home in 2007, he considered several options for financing his new home: One option was a mortgage in Hungarian forint – his country's currency and the currency in which his wage was being paid – at high interest rates, whereas another option was a mortgage in Swiss francs at a much lower interest rate.[1] Given the large difference in interest rates, he followed the advice of his mortgage broker and opted for the Swiss-currency denominated mortgage. Unfortunately, after a few months the global financial and economic crisis hit Hungary in the early fall of 2008, which resulted, among others, in a substantial fall in the value of the Hungarian currency. Because Szepesi's mortgage was denominated in a foreign currency, this resulted in a massive increase of his debt burden in terms of his own currency: His monthly mortgage payments surged from 60,000 to 85,000 forints – at a monthly take-home pay of 175,000 forint. Szepesi was not the only person in Hungary with such an experience. In Hungary, foreign-currency mortgages had become the norm, rather than the exception, in the years preceding the crisis, so that the depreciation of the Hungarian forint created serious financial problems for many Hungarian consumers. In 2009, they faced up to 70 percent higher debt servicing costs than they had originally calculated (The Economist 2009). Many of them organized in the Association of Bank Loan Victims, an advocacy group that actively lobbied parliament to consider the plight of its members and publicized the problems they were facing. Public dissatisfaction with the government grew: A poll in mid-March 2009 showed that 80 percent of Hungarian voters were dissatisfied with the government, and approximately every second voter was of the opinion

---

[1] *The Guardian*, 29 October 2008, Days of New Flats, Cars, and Generous State Benefits over as Currency Collapses.

that parliament should dissolve itself and have early elections.[2] When the discontent exploded in April 2009 as thousands of Hungarians took to the streets to protest against their government and to demand new elections, Hungarian Prime Minister Gyurcsány resigned.

Violent protests have also accompanied the financial crisis in Greece, which has engulfed the country since 2010. The country had experienced a boom phase after euro adoption in 2001. At the same time, a significant decrease in borrowing costs on international financial markets, rising wages, inflation, and a continuously high fiscal deficit contributed to a huge current account deficit and a low competitiveness of Greek exports. In contrast to Hungary, however, the Greek authorities did not opt for external adjustment when the crisis erupted, which in this case would have meant an exit from the eurozone and the reintroduction of the drachma at a much depreciated rate. Instead, in a move supported by the IMF, the EU, and the European Central Bank (ECB), Greek policymakers chose to maintain the euro and to let the economy adjust internally by implementing severe budget cuts and structural reform instead. The consequence was – and continues to be at the time of writing – a sharp fall in wages, a steep increase in unemployment, and a severe recession. Not surprisingly, this pain is not taken lightly by Greece's citizens. Thousands of people have regularly taken to the streets, and protests have repeatedly turned violent, even costing several people's lives. The crisis has also taken its political toll, causing early elections, extreme difficulties in forming a government, and the strengthening of radical right- and left-wing parties.

These examples illustrate that both external adjustment of the economy – that is, a change in the value of the currency – and internal adjustment, – that is, a significant tightening of fiscal and monetary policy as well as structural reforms – can be very contentious and politically costly. The external adjustment of the Hungarian forint and the internal adjustment implemented by the Greek government directly affected, and continue to affect, many of their citizens' lives. Because this was very painful, both approaches came at a high political cost to the respective governments. Considering that adjustment almost always involves an economic downturn, especially when undertaken after imbalances have been allowed to build up, this is not surprising. However, the costs of adjustment are not distributed equally among all citizens. Because exchange-rate, monetary, fiscal, and structural policies have strong distributional implications, some voters will usually be hurt more by certain types of policy adjustments than others, who sometimes

---

[2] http://www.politics.hu/20090330/poll-finds-hungarians-more-pessimistic-than-ever

even benefit from such adjustments (Frieden 1991b). Some groups will be more vulnerable to the consequences of external adjustment, whereas for others internal adjustment is more painful. As a result, different adjustment strategies hit some groups of citizens harder than others. In such situations, political struggles are likely to emerge about how the costs of adjustment are to be distributed.

To understand which type of adjustment strategies policymakers implement and why adjustment is sometimes delayed, it is therefore necessary to gain a good understanding of who will endorse and who will oppose different strategies. An essential concern in this endeavor is to correctly identify the policy preferences of different groups of voters. This chapter consequently examines how the different adjustment strategies at the government's disposal affect the economic well-being of different groups of voters. Based on the assumption that voters assess the performance of the incumbent retrospectively (Fiorina 1981), its purpose is to improve our understanding of how voters evaluate the government's handling of balance-of-payments pressures.[3] This analysis then serves as the basis for the analyses in the second part of this book, which examine how these evaluations create electoral incentives for governments as to when and how to adjust economic policies in response to balance-of-payments imbalances.

This chapter consequently proposes a new, comprehensive approach for identifying preferences on different adjustment strategies, which takes into account the interrelationship between exchange-rate, monetary, and fiscal policies in a financially integrated world (see also Walter 2008). This approach builds on the classic distinction between the effects of exchange-rate adjustment on purchasing power and international competitiveness (Frieden 1991b) but adds two additional dimensions that become salient in a financially open economy: exposure to foreign-currency debt and the vulnerability of balance sheets to interest-rate increases, fiscal tightening, and structural reform. It shows that the effect of different adjustment strategies on individual voters depends on their direct and indirect vulnerabilities to adjustments in the exchange-rate, interest-rate, and fiscal

---

[3] Because this book focuses on adjustment in deficit countries, the discussion concentrates on the effects of exchange-rate depreciation and internal devaluation. The basic logic of the argument can also be used to understand the distributional consequences of adjustment in surplus countries, which mirror those discussed here. For example, although a depreciation tends to have a beneficial effect on voters in the tradables sector, an appreciation often has a negative effect. Similarly, adjustment in surplus countries involves a loosening of monetary policy, which benefits indebted voters.

Table 2.1. *Sources of voters' vulnerabilities to internal and external adjustment*

	External adjustment (depreciation)	Internal adjustment (Monetary/fiscal tightening and/ or structural reforms)
Direct effects	• on personal purchasing power • on personal balance sheets	• on personal balance sheets

Indirect effects	• on employer
	  - competitiveness
	  - balance sheets
	• on general economic conditions
		• on employer
		  - competitiveness
		  - balance sheets
		• on general economic conditions

policies. This vulnerability results from the effects of the different adjustment strategies on voters' purchasing power and personal balance sheets, as well as the effects of these strategies on employers and the economy in general, as summarized in Table 2.1. The chapter argues that voters will advocate those policies that reduce their particular financial vulnerabilities and oppose those to which they are most vulnerable. Whether governments face large coalitions in favor or against certain adjustment strategies depends on the distribution of vulnerabilities across the electorate.

The focus of the analysis is on voters, because the survival of governments in democratic countries ultimately depends on whether or not they can maintain support from a majority of voters. This is not to say that lobbying from firms, which frequently occurs with regard to economic policymaking, is not important, especially because firms and industry associations are likely to be intensely affected by policy responses to speculative pressure on financial markets. Policymakers will seriously consider information provided by firms on the specific effects of adjustment on their businesses, because this provides them with information on how different policies are likely to affect certain groups of voters. Because policymakers must ultimately convince voters, this book thus treats the far-reaching effects of external and internal adjustment strategies on firms as indirect effects on voters' personal well-being. Correctly specifying voters' overall vulnerabilities and the resulting policy preferences consequently also requires understanding how different adjustment strategies affect domestic firms. In the empirical work, I will therefore consider firms' policy preferences as well.

2.1 The Distributional Effects of External Adjustment

Depreciations and devaluations of the national currency strongly affect most individuals living in open economies. These effects emerge both directly and indirectly and originate both from real and financial processes. A loss in the currency's value directly decreases voters' purchasing power. In addition, voters who own foreign-currency denominated assets or owe debt in a foreign currency experience a direct effect on their net wealth – positive in the case of foreign-currency assets, but negative in the (more frequent) case of foreign-currency debt.[4] Indirectly, voters' vulnerabilities depend on how external adjustment affects their employers and the economy more generally, because positive and negative developments in this realm can also have far-reaching consequences for their personal economic situation. To understand the overall effects of external adjustment on individual voters, we thus need to jointly consider these different aspects. In some cases, these effects will reinforce each other, but in other cases they can offset each other. Voters' policy preferences about external adjustment result from the net effect of exchange-rate adjustment on their personal economic situation overall.

2.1.1 Direct Effects of External Adjustment on Voters

The direct effects of external adjustment on voters stem from two sources: the effect of a depreciation or devaluation – terms that I will use interchangeably from now on – on voters' purchasing power and its effect on voters' personal finances.

2.1.1.1 Relative Price Effects: Purchasing Power Concerns

Changes in the exchange rate strongly affect relative prices – at least in the short to medium run – and can therefore increase or decrease voters' purchasing power. Depreciation increases the domestic price of imported goods and, more generally, the prices of all internationally tradable goods relative to nontradable goods. This depresses voters' purchasing power, especially when voters consume large shares of tradable goods, which cannot easily be

---

[4]   Unless they have hedged against currency fluctuations, which is relatively rare among individuals.

substituted with domestically produced goods.[5] The depreciation-induced price increases for imported goods such as automobiles, computers, or consumer electronics therefore make these goods less affordable to voters interested in buying them. This negative consumption effect can also extend to basic goods. For example, in countries with a high dependence on food imports, depreciations can substantially raise food prices, which especially hurts the urban poor.[6]

In addition, depreciation-induced price increases for tradable goods are usually passed through to domestic prices. Even though this pass-through is not perfect and the extent tends to vary by industry, depreciation can therefore lead to increases in inflation.[7] The general increase in prices, in turn, further decreases voters' purchasing power. The higher the pass-through for tradable goods and the higher the proportion of tradable goods in voters' overall consumption basket, the more strongly and negatively a depreciation affects consumers' purchasing power. As consumers, voters are consequently directly and negatively affected by depreciation-based external adjustment. Voters' consumption habits thus directly influence their vulnerability to different external adjustment.

Many studies on the political economy of exchange-rate policy take this negative consumption effect as the starting point for their analyses and assume that voters will always oppose depreciations because they oppose the concomitant loss of purchasing power (e.g., Frieden and Stein 2001b; Stein and Streb 2004; Blomberg et al. 2005). However, depreciations affect voters in more ways than a decrease in purchasing power. First of all, voters' personal finances can be directly affected if they hold any debt or income in foreign currency, as the next section will show. Second, voters are also indirectly affected by depreciations, and these more indirect effects can sometimes offset the negative consumption effect of depreciations. To identify voters' overall vulnerabilities to external adjustment, these additional direct and indirect effects also need to be taken into account.

---

[5]   Baker (2005) shows that individual trade policy preferences are influenced by the price of tradable goods. This suggests that consumption patterns should also influence exchange-rate policy preferences.

[6]   An alternative view suggests that real depreciations increase the purchasing power of consumers of nontradable goods (such as food and housing). To the extent that the poor consume more nontradable goods than tradables, this argument suggests that real depreciations (rather than appreciations) are beneficial for the poor (Agénor 2004).

[7]   For an overview of the literature on this topic, see Goldberg, Koujianou, and Knetter (1997).

2.1.1.2 The Financial Side: Personal Balance Sheet Concerns

The direct effects of exchange-rate changes on voters' personal finances operate through their personal balance sheets. Balance sheets are statements of assets and liabilities. Every firm and institution has balance sheets, but the financial situation of each individual person can be conceptualized in similar terms. For example, an individual's savings are counted as an asset, and the mortgage on her house counts as a liability in her personal balance sheet. Changes in the exchange rate directly affect the value of all personal balance sheet positions that are at least partly denominated in foreign currency. Foreign-currency denominated assets of individuals are, for example, wages that are paid in foreign currency or remittances, which an individual receives from relatives or friends living abroad. Consumer loans, mortgages, and other types of debt in any currency other than the national currency constitute foreign-currency-denominated liabilities.

With the increase in international capital mobility, foreign-currency denominated assets and liabilities have become quite common. In many developing countries, the sum of remittances sent back to the citizens of these countries is now larger than the inflow of foreign direct investments into these countries (Singer 2010a). Moreover, borrowing in foreign currencies is no longer limited to sovereign borrowing by the government or by large corporations; it is now undertaken by the private sector as well, where not only firms but also consumers take out such loans (e.g., Jeanne 2003; Brown, Ongena, and Yesin 2009). In fact, private foreign-currency denominated borrowing now often exceeds public foreign-currency denominated borrowing.

Market participants typically resort to loans in foreign currencies for one of two reasons. First, in many countries, they are simply unable to borrow in their own currency because both domestic and international lenders refuse to issue debt denominated in domestic currency. In this situation, voters looking to borrow money to buy a house or a car have no option but to take out a loan denominated in foreign currency. This phenomenon is particularly common in developing countries, where foreign-currency borrowing often constitutes the only financing available, a phenomenon that has been dubbed "original sin" (Eichengreen and Hausmann 2005). A second reason for taking out foreign-currency denominated debt is that borrowing money from abroad can be financially attractive when foreign interest rates are lower than domestic rates.[8] These interest-rate differentials can be

---

[8] Of course, exploiting this interest-rate differential between foreign and domestic interest rates is only attractive when the (perceived) currency risk is relatively low.

quite substantial: For example, in 2005 Hungarians interested in taking out a mortgage to buy a house were able to choose between loans in a foreign currency such as the Swiss franc or the euro or loans in domestic currency in which interest rates were approximately twice as high as interest rates on foreign-currency loans (OECD 2010: 90). With the increase in capital mobility, exploiting this interest-rate differential has become relatively easy. In many countries, advertisements for foreign-currency loans abound, and such loans can usually be taken out at local bank branches.

It is important to note that the phenomenon of foreign-currency denominated liabilities is not limited to the developing world or emerging economies. Figure 2.1 shows the percentage of loans to nonbank borrowers denominated in foreign currencies in selected European countries for 2007. It demonstrates that foreign-currency borrowing by firms and consumers has become the rule, rather than the exception, in some Eastern European countries such as the Baltic countries. In Latvia, almost 90 percent of all loans to firms and consumers in 2007 were denominated in a foreign currency. Although the emerging markets in Eastern Europe typically have much higher ratios of foreign-currency debt than the advanced economies in Western Europe, Figure 2.1 also shows that even in financially highly developed countries such as Luxembourg, Austria, or the United Kingdom, substantial fractions of private sector loans are denominated in foreign currencies. For instance, in Austria almost one-third of all loans, especially mortgages, held by private households in 2007 were denominated in foreign currency, mostly Swiss francs (Austrian National Bank 2007).[9] Overall, these figures indicate that foreign-currency borrowing has become a regular feature in many countries.

Despite the increasing prevalence of foreign-currency borrowing, political economists have typically not paid much attention to this type of financial vulnerability of voters to depreciation. In a world characterized by high levels of capital mobility, however, this source of vulnerability is at least as important as the relative price effects of depreciation on voters' purchasing power and is likely to significantly influence voters' preferences about exchange-rate policy and external adjustment. This is because any change in the exchange rate immediately affects the value of assets and liabilities denominated in a foreign currency, as the example of Jozsef Szepesi's mortgage at the beginning of this chapter illustrates. Thus, unless foreign-currency liabilities are hedged (that is, simply put, insured against exchange market risk), depreciations immediately increase the debt burden when

---

[9]   This figure is higher than the one recorded in Figure 2.1 because the data used in Figure 2.1 is the stock of foreign-currency loans, rather than the flow in one year.

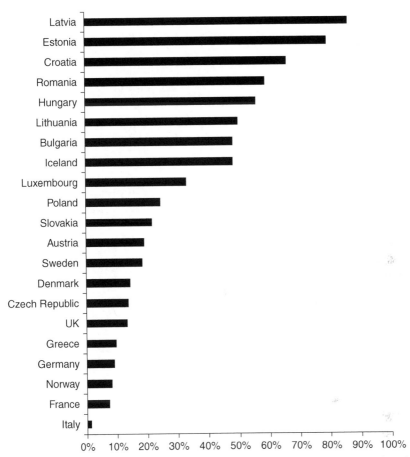

Figure 2.1. Percentage of foreign-currency loans to nonbank clients in 2007, selected European countries.
Source: Brown et al. 2009, : tables 1 and 2; author's calculations.

financial liabilities are denominated in foreign currencies and increase the revenues of foreign-currency denominated assets.[10] However, many holders of foreign-currency debt do not hedge, either because they are unaware of the currency risk or because buying hedges against the currency risk is too costly. For these borrowers, a depreciation of the currency implies an immediate and often substantial increase of their debt burden in domestic currency terms. Servicing the debt, both in terms of interest payments and paying off the principal, suddenly becomes much more expensive. This

[10] In terms of domestic currency.

can seriously disturb balance sheets that were previously well balanced, especially when these are mismatched – that is, when assets, such as wages and other income, are predominantly denominated in domestic currency.

The increasing proliferation of foreign-currency denominated assets and liabilities therefore has turned foreign-currency balance sheet positions and potential balance sheet mismatches into important determinants of voters' exchange-rate policy preferences. Because anyone who holds more foreign-currency denominated liabilities than assets is directly vulnerable to a depreciation of the currency, such prospects can produce a large and vocal constituency against external adjustment. Voters' direct vulnerabilities to external adjustment and their resulting policy preferences thus not only depend on their consumption habits but also on the composition of their assets and liabilities.

2.1.2 Indirect Effects of External Adjustment on Voters

External adjustment has not only direct but also indirect effects on voters. These effects are two-fold and consist of an employment-specific effect and the effect of external adjustment on general economic conditions. The employment-specific effect varies by how adjustment affects a voter's employer, whereas the general economic effect depends on the structure of the economy and on the aggregate macroeconomic effects of external adjustment.

2.1.2.1 Employment-Specific Effects: Competitiveness and Financial Concerns Revisited

The conventional wisdom holds that producers of tradable goods are the main beneficiaries of exchange-rate depreciation because it increases their competitiveness, whereas nontradable producers are hurt by the loss in the currency's value (Frieden 1991b). Exporters gain, because a depreciation of the currency lowers the price of the exported goods abroad and thus boosts exporters' international competitiveness. Firm-level evidence indicates, for example, that firms with greater foreign sales perform significantly better after depreciations than firms that do not sell their products abroad (Forbes 2002b; Echeverry et al. 2003; Pratap, Lobato, and Somuano 2003; Aguiar 2005) – a conclusion that is supported by evidence on the industry level (Nguyen 2007). Depreciation is usually beneficial for import-competing producers as well. As foreign products become more expensive in domestic currency terms, their domestically produced goods become more competitive and attractive as substitutes for imported goods.[11] Thus, in terms of competitiveness, depreciations tend to benefit firms in the tradable sector – whether they export or compete against imported products – and can thus act as an output stimulus for them.[12] This, in turn, benefits both the owners and the workers of firms in the tradable sector.

Recent research has shown, however, that the competitiveness effects of depreciations are less clear than this traditional view suggests. How depreciation affects a firm's competitiveness depends on a variety of factors, including the firm's cost and revenue structure, competitive environment, and the effect of exchange-rate changes on its input and output markets (Muller and Verschoor 2006). Depreciations are not necessarily unambiguously good for export-oriented firms, because the increased competitiveness of their exported products can be dampened by higher prices for imported inputs and intermediate goods. Firm-level studies on the relationship between devaluations and export performance not only indicate that devaluations overall tend to have a positive net effect on exporters but also emphasize that not all export-oriented firms benefit equally. For example, a study on the fate of 1,200 Thai firms in the wake of the Asian financial crisis in 1997–8, during which the Thai currency was substantially devalued, finds that contrary to conventional wisdom, capacity utilization and employment fell in the tradable sector, even though exporting companies were able to weather the crisis slightly better than firms focused on the domestic market (Dollar and Hallward-Driemeier 2000). Another study shows that export-oriented commodity firms in countries that devalue their currencies significantly outperform their competitors in nondevaluing countries in terms of growth and profit rates in the short run but tend to perform worse in the long run, especially when they import a lot of capital goods (Forbes 2002a).[13] Overall, existing research thus indicates that in terms of competitiveness, depreciation tends to be advantageous for employees in the tradables sector, although these gains in competitiveness can at least partially be offset by higher input prices. Voters who work for firms that use a lot of imported inputs are hence more vulnerable to external adjustment than those who work in export-oriented firms with a low reliance on imported inputs.

---

[11] An alternative interpretation leading to the same conclusions is that tradable producers prefer a more depreciated exchange rate because it raises the price of their products relative to the price of nontradable inputs (Frieden and Stein 2001b; Blomberg et al. 2005).

[12] Recent research demonstrates that depreciations and trade protection are frequently treated as substitutes (Férnandez-Albertos 2009; Broz 2010; Copelovitch and Pevehouse forthcoming).

[13] Note that some authors do not even find any positive competitiveness effect of devaluations on export dynamics (e.g., Blaszkiewicz and Paczynski 2003).

Voters working for companies in the nontradable sector tend to be hurt by depreciations, especially when these companies use a lot of imported inputs. Because depreciation increases the domestic price of these imports, the profitability of firms relying on them declines. Depreciations can also hurt financial firms whose competitiveness builds on offering investments with low exchange-rate risk. Because the loss of confidence inspired by a major devaluation makes investments in domestic assets much less attractive to foreigners and raises risk premia, their profitability declines. Down the line, this can have negative consequences for the workers, employees, and owners of these firms and financial institutions.

In addition to these competitiveness effects, voters are also indirectly exposed to the financial effects of external adjustment on the companies and institutions they work for. Analogous to individuals' balance sheets, a depreciation of the national currency strengthens or weakens all those firms whose balance sheets contain positions denominated in foreign currencies. Any firm engaged in cross-border transactions will naturally exhibit such positions: Exporters' revenues abroad result in foreign-currency denominated assets in their balance sheets, and importers often accrue foreign-currency denominated liabilities when they buy products abroad. Moreover, similar to the consumers discussed earlier, firms in financially open economies increasingly borrow money in foreign currency, either because loans in domestic currency are not available or because the interest rates on these loans are much higher than those on foreign-currency loans. The extent of this foreign borrowing can be substantial but differs across countries. For example, in the year 2000, Peruvian and Argentinean firms held on average more foreign-currency debt than domestic currency debt, whereas the average share of foreign debt relative to total debt was much lower in Colombia (5.5%) and Brazil (11.8%) (Galindo, Panizza, and Schiantarelli 2003). The extent of foreign-currency borrowing also varies by sector. Typically, exporters and foreign-owned firms tend to borrow more in foreign currency than firms in the nontradables sector (Bleakley and Cowan 2008; Brown et al. 2009).

When a firm's balance sheet is characterized by substantial currency mismatch, a depreciation of the exchange rate poses a great threat to its net worth and ultimately its survival. This is because its debt burden increases significantly when the domestic currency depreciates, which can trigger a decrease in investment, output, and profitability for firms with high levels of unhedged foreign-currency debt (e.g., Aghion, Bacchetta, and Banerjee,

2004; Cook 2004).[14] Empirical studies show that large depreciations indeed substantially increase the risk of bankruptcy and decrease investment and the profitability of firms with a high international debt exposure (e.g., Claessens, Djankov, and Xu 2000; Aguiar 2005; Chue and Cook 2008).

These risks associated with exchange-rate fluctuations can be lowered through hedging, which means that companies counterbalance the currency risk created by their foreign-currency debt. Hedging can be achieved in two ways. The first option is to purchase financial derivatives such as forwards, futures, and options that offset the negative effects of exchange-rate fluctuations. Although financial hedges are usually very effective, they can be quite expensive and are not always available, especially in countries in which capital markets are not fully developed. A second option is to naturally hedge against currency risk, which means that the foreign-currency liabilities are offset with foreign-currency assets. Exporters are often naturally hedged when they receive payments for their exported goods in foreign currency. Firms with higher levels of foreign-currency debt therefore do not necessarily fare worse after a depreciation when their revenues increase because of this change in the currency's value (Bleakley and Cowan 2008). Despite its attraction, natural hedging is not possible for all firms. For domestically oriented firms, for example, natural hedging is usually not an option. It is therefore not surprising that despite these potential advantages of hedging, the empirical evidence suggests that most firms do not fully hedge their exchange-rate risk, and many do not hedge at all (Dollar and Hallward-Driemeier 2000; Fosler and Winger 2004).

This means that depreciations often do pose substantial threats to firms who have borrowed in foreign currency, especially in emerging markets and developing countries where financial markets are not yet fully developed.[15] Voters, who work for such firms, are indirectly vulnerable to external adjustment as well, because the problems experienced by their employers can put their jobs and incomes in jeopardy.

2.1.2.2 General Economic Effects of External Adjustment

The second indirect effect of external adjustment on voters is its effect on the country's general economic conditions. Depending on the country's economic structure, depreciations can trigger economic expansions

---

[14] For a good review of the theoretical and empirical literature on the effect of international debt on firms more generally and its mixed findings, see Chue and Cook (2008)

[15] In line with this finding, Hall (2005) and Woodruff (2005) show that severe currency mismatches in balance sheets make depreciation less likely. Shambaugh (2004) argues that reliance on different types of capital generate distinct capital-specific exchange-rate regime preferences.

and contractions in the overall economy. This depends mostly on how the country-specific real and financial effects of a downward adjustment of the exchange rate discussed earlier add up in the aggregate. The traditional textbook view has been that depreciations often have expansionary effects on output and employment, because a depreciated exchange-rate increases foreign demand for domestic products and therefore boosts exports, which then spill over into the general economy. The positive effects on employment and output associated with such an expansion are clearly positive for voters as well.

Unfortunately, it is by now well established that devaluations of the currency can also have significant contractionary effects, because it can negatively affect both aggregate supply and aggregate demand (Caves, Frankel, and Jones 2002). Domestic aggregate supply can fall when the positive effects of devaluation for tradable-goods producers are offset by rising costs for imported inputs and for borrowed capital, as investors are more reluctant to lend to companies in an adverse economic environment. One particularly relevant aspect in this context is the effect of a depreciation on the country's financial sector. When a country's financial institutions exhibit large currency mismatches, substantial depreciations can cause liquidity or even solvency problems among these institutions (Chang and Velasco 2001). This can result in credit crunches, bank runs, and full-blown financial crises, which impose vast costs on the economy. However, even banks whose balance sheets do not exhibit a currency mismatch can be harmed substantially by depreciation if their borrowers exhibit a mismatched portfolio. Because a depreciation raises the risk of default amongst these borrowers, depreciations create a considerable indirect risk for their creditors as well (Mishkin 1996). It is therefore not surprising that currency and banking crises, which tend to be very costly and painful to resolve, often coincide (Kaminsky and Reinhart 1999).

Because depreciations reduce consumers' purchasing power and can increase their debt burden, depreciations also have a contractionary effect on aggregate demand, as both of these effects typically lead consumers (and firms) to cut back their spending because of the negative effects on purchasing power and balance sheets discussed earlier. These individual effects sum up to depress aggregate demand in the economy, which can cause or prolong an economic downturn.

Thus, individuals can face substantial indirect risks if the overall effect of external adjustment on the economy is contractionary. When a banking crises emerges in the wake of the devaluation, voters not only face the risk of losing their deposits with failing banks and difficulties in securing financing but also suffer from the general economic downturn associated with financial crises. In addition, as taxpayers, they typically have to pay for the resolution of these crises. In the same vein, when the devaluation has expansionary effects on the aggregate economy, voters indirectly benefit from the external adjustment that leads to a boost in output and employment. Devaluations can thus have substantial indirect effects on voters, both positive and negative. How exactly external adjustment will affect the general economy depends on the specific structural, economic, and financial environment in which it takes place.

2.1.3 The Net Effect of External Adjustment on Voters

In sum, downward exchange-rate adjustments can affect voters in very different ways that can partially offset each other. Individuals are directly affected by devaluations in terms of their purchasing power and their personal balance sheets. Voters who consume a lot of tradable products and hold substantial amounts of unhedged foreign-currency debt are most negatively affected, whereas voters who derive large portions of their income from foreign-currency denominated assets can directly benefit from a devaluation. Indirectly, voters are affected by the consequences of the devaluation on their employers and the general economy. Voters working in export-oriented industries and voters in countries where the depreciation has an expansionary effect on the economy as a whole tend to benefit from a depreciation. In contrast, voters working in nontradable industries or for firms that either import a lot of their inputs or exhibit large positions of unhedged foreign-currency denominated liabilities in their balance sheets (or both) are more vulnerable to losses in the currency's value, as are voters who live in economies where the overall effect of a depreciation is contractionary.

The overall vulnerability of each voter to a depreciation thus depends on the net effect of these direct and indirect effects. It consequently arises from a joint consideration of voters' consumption patterns and financial situations, the type of firm in which they are employed, as well as the general aggregate effect of a depreciation on the economy.[16] These different effects can either offset or reinforce each other. For example, imagine a voter who consumes a

---

[16] Note that the direct effects on purchasing power and balance sheets surface very quickly and are clearly linked to the loss in the currency's value, whereas the more indirect (income) effects associated with overall economic performance are likely to be lagged and less obviously linked to exchange-rate adjustments (Willett 1998, 2007). Evidently, the bigger the changes in the exchange rate, the larger and more noticeable their effects are likely to be.

lot of imported products, whose balance sheets contain no foreign-currency denominated positions, and who works for an export-oriented firm, when the government adjusts externally and lets the currency depreciate. If the depreciation has contractionary effects on the economy, our voter faces a negative direct consumption effect and indirectly suffers from the depreciation, but the devaluation has no direct effect on her financial situation and the boost to her employer's competitiveness might even lead to a positive income effect. This example also demonstrates that individuals, who are relatively sheltered from the direct effects of a devaluation, can nonetheless face substantial indirect risks if the overall effect of a devaluation on their employer or the economy is contractionary, and vice versa.

Voters' preferences regarding external adjustment and the level of the exchange rate more generally arise as a consideration of their overall vulnerabilities to these effects. The more negative the direct and indirect consequences of a depreciation, the more opposed voters will be to external adjustment. In addition, because these effects increase with the amount of depreciation, vulnerable voters will always prefer less devaluation to more devaluation. In contrast, when depreciations overall have a more positive effect, voters will strongly favor this adjustment strategy over alternative policy paths.

2.2 The Distributional Effects of Internal Adjustment

Internal adjustment strategies similarly affect voters in direct and indirect ways. The goal of internal adjustment is to deflate domestic prices to such a level that the domestically produced products regain competitiveness on international markets. The resulting change in relative prices leads to a rebalancing of the current account and, more generally, the economy. Such price deflation can be achieved by tightening monetary conditions, especially through an increase in interest rates; fiscal contraction, achieved by significant cuts of public expenditure and/or tax increases; and structural reform, for example labor market deregulation. Usually, policymakers will pursue a combination of these contractionary internal adjustment policies. As with external adjustment, voters can exhibit both direct and indirect vulnerabilities to these policies. For example, highly indebted voters are directly and negatively affected by rising interest rates, whereas all voters are indirectly hurt when budget cuts and monetary tightening push the country into recession. The overall effect of internal adjustment on individual voters is thus once more a combination of these different direct and indirect effects, which can reinforce and, in more rare circumstances, also offset each other. Voters' assessments of internal adjustment directly follows from the net impact of internal adjustment on their personal economic situation.

2.2.1 Direct Effects of Internal Adjustment on Voters

Internal adjustment means that the economy is rebalanced through a contraction of the economy induced by monetary tightening, contractionary fiscal policy, and/or structural reform. All three can have significant direct effects on voters' personal economic situations.

2.2.1.1 Monetary Tightening: Personal Balance Sheet Concerns

Internal adjustment strategies that tighten domestic monetary conditions directly affect voters' savings and debts. Consequently, monetary tightening affects any balance sheet position that is tied to the domestic interest rate. Voters holding more assets than liabilities benefit from a monetary tightening, but net borrowers are hurt. Voters with net savings in domestic currency benefit because the yield on savings increases when interest rates go up. Voters with net savings and other interest-bearing assets in domestic currency receive higher interest payments on their investments, especially when these investments have variable interest rates. They therefore experience a direct positive effect of internal adjustment on their investments. In contrast, net borrowers are hurt by interest-rate increases, because they raise their debt burden. Monetary tightening is thus immediately painful to a wide variety of voters: homeowners who have to repay their mortgages, consumers who have to repay credit card debt or consumer loans, and any other indebted voter. This direct effect of interest-rate increases is particularly severe when a loan has variable interest rates that are closely tied to short-term interest rates and when debtors have not hedged against interest-rate movements. Because such hedges are rare, a majority of debtors are therefore likely to be quite vulnerable to interest-rate increases.

Monetary tightening is most painful for those borrowers who either are highly leveraged or already have difficulties servicing their debts. In such instances, even a small increase in interest rates can cause major difficulties for borrowers. The problems of subprime mortgage holders in the U.S. housing market crisis of 2007–8 provide a vivid example of this phenomenon. Many of the mortgages these individuals took out to buy (or refinance) their houses had very low, introductory interest rates for the first few years. Even though the Federal Reserve had begun to raise interest rates in 2004, mortgage holders who had taken out their mortgages around this time were initially unaffected by the tightening of monetary policy. After this initial period, however, their mortgages turned into adjustable-rate mortgages, which tracked the interest-rate level set by the monetary authorities. As interest rates continued to rise, these homeowners suddenly were obliged to pay much higher monthly house payments after their initial "honeymoon" period with low fixed interest-rate payments ended. In some cases, the monthly installments increased by more than 40 percent. In one example, the monthly house payment increased from $2,000 to $2,789 within a few months.[17] This, obviously, caused many homeowners enormous problems. Many were not able to pay these higher interest rates and ultimately either had to sell their homes or face foreclosure. As a result, foreclosure rates in the United States began to increase, and housing prices began to decline in late 2006 and worsened further in 2007 and 2008, ultimately initiating the global financial crisis that is still ongoing at the time of writing.

This example shows that voters can exhibit substantial direct vulnerabilities to monetary tightening. Because interest-rate adjustments have opposite effects on savings and debts, the net direct effect of interest-rate adjustments on voters depends on their net position. Net savers directly benefit from higher interest rates, but net borrowers are directly hurt. Higher interest rates also hurt those voters interested in buying a new home, car, or other consumer goods because high interest rates make financing these purchases more expensive. As with devaluations, these effects become stronger the bigger the changes in the interest rate become.

2.2.1.2 Contractionary Fiscal Policy: Direct Effects on Voters

Internal adjustment strategies that include spending cuts in the government's budget and tax increases also usually have direct effects on voters. Any individual whose income is decreased by these fiscal policy measures is directly and negatively affected. For example, a reduction in unemployment benefits directly hurts the unemployed, whereas increases in the income tax hurts all individuals with regular earnings. In contrast to the direct effects of external and internal adjustment via monetary tightening, however, it is more difficult to identify general groups of voters who will be hurt or helped by contractionary fiscal policies because the specific effects of these policies depend on the specific policy measures chosen. Not only can fiscal contraction and a rebalancing of the budget deficit be achieved by budget

---

[17] *New York Times*, 14 October 2007, The American Dream Foreclosed.

cuts and tax increases (or both), which tend to affect different groups of voters, but the specific effects also depend on which taxes are increased and which budget items are cut. An increase in the property tax will, for example, hurt a different group of people than an increase in the value-added tax. Similarly, budget cuts can be achieved by measures as diverse as social welfare reductions, the closing of public libraries and swimming pools, reduced subsidies to certain industries, or an increase in the retirement age. Again, the groups affected will vary widely.[18]

Which groups of voters are directly vulnerable to internal adjustment of fiscal policy consequently depends on the specific policies that are implemented. This is not to say that these vulnerabilities are small. For example, the fiscal policy measures implemented by the Estonian government as a part of its internal adjustment strategy in response to the 2008–9 economic crisis included, among others, tax increases in the value-added tax by 2 percentage points, an increase in contributions to unemployment insurance, and higher excise taxes on alcohol, cigarettes, and fuel (Sikk 2011). The government also implemented significant cuts in government spending: For example, pensions were frozen, the operational expenditures in the public sector were cut by 20 percent, and employees in the public sectors were dismissed. These measures imposed high and immediate costs on Estonian voters.

In sum, even though identifying which voters are directly hurt by fiscal contraction depends on the specific fiscal consolidation measures proposed, it is clear that this form of internal adjustment can directly and negatively affect many voters to a significant degree. While the intensity of these direct effects vary, they are painful across the board.

2.2.1.3 Structural Reform: Direct Effects on Voters

As with contractionary fiscal policies, it is difficult to identify the direct effects of structural reform without knowledge about the details of the implemented reforms. However, other than with fiscal contraction, these direct effects can be both positive and negative for voters. For example, as consumers, they often benefit from deregulation and other measures that introduce more competitiveness and, hence, lower prices. At the same time, structural reforms on the labor market, which lead to lower wages or less

---

[18] The possibility to distribute the costs of fiscal adjustment in a variety of ways makes strong political conflict about who is to bear the main burden of adjustment almost unavoidable and significantly complicates the speedy implementation of such reform (Alesina and Drazen 1991).

job security, directly affect workers negatively. Moreover, structural reforms have significant distributional effects, pitting one group of voters against others. For example, the plans of the Greek government to liberalize the highly regulated taxi business by giving taxi licenses at a low fee to professionals interested in entering the market generated furious protests and strikes by Greek taxi drivers. Because taxi licenses in the old system had been a high-priced possession – costing up to 100,000 euros a license – the governments' plans to deregulate this market directly threatened taxi drivers' investments. At the same time, the reform was expected to decrease taxi fares and to improve service at the benefits of taxi users. Thus, the direct effects of this reform were unevenly distributed among Greek voters.

Overall, the direct effects of structural reform thus depend on the specific measures implemented by the government and on the specific position voters find themselves in relation to these reforms. It is clear that structural reforms can have very negative direct effects on certain voters, but in contrast to fiscal contraction, other voters can be positively affected by the same reform.

2.2.2 Indirect Effects of Internal Adjustment on Voters

Like external adjustment, internal adjustment also affects voters indirectly through an employment-specific effect, which depends on how adjustment affects a voter's employer, and its effect on general economic conditions.

2.2.2.1 The Employment-Specific Effect of Internal Adjustment

Voters are indirectly affected by internal adjustment when it has negative consequences for their employers. Monetary tightening influences firms' propensity to invest, their balance sheets, and their business opportunities. First, monetary tightening reduces firms' willingness to invest in new machines, inventories, buildings, and their work force. This is because interest-rate increases make it more expensive to borrow the funds needed to undertake such investments and therefore lower the future return that a firm can expect to obtain from the investment. As a consequence, firms tend to invest less when monetary policy is tightened. Second, corporate balance sheets are affected because interest-rate increases enlarge a firm's debt burden when these debts are tied to the domestic interest rate, although they also increase the return on interest-bearing assets. The higher debt burden, in turn, reduces firms' profitability. These negative effects on firms' balance sheets are likely to be particularly pronounced for firms that hold high levels of debt relative to their equity. For such highly leveraged firms, an increase in interest rates can lead to serious financial problems, including bankruptcy. Finally, as I will discuss in the next section, monetary tightening depresses aggregate demand and slows down overall economic activity. This reduces firms' business opportunities to sell their products and services. As firms face mounting difficulties, their employees' incomes and jobs become increasingly insecure, posing substantial risks for these individuals.

Research in political economy makes quite specific predictions about the economic sectors that are most vulnerable to the adverse consequences of monetary tightening (e.g., Frieden 1991b; Henning 1994; Hefeker 1997; Bearce 2003). According to this research, the nontradables and import-competing sectors tend to be particularly exposed to interest-rate increases because they have a strong orientation toward the domestic economy. They typically borrow and invest in domestic currency and derive their income from domestic business transactions. Not surprisingly, firms in these sectors are likely to be much harder hit by monetary tightening than their more internationally oriented counterparts in the export-oriented sector or the banking and financial services sector, as well as international investors (Bearce 2003: 378). As a consequence, workers employed in the more domestically oriented sector are likely to have a higher indirect vulnerability to monetary tightening than voters employed by more internationally oriented firms.

A tightening of fiscal policy and structural reforms can equally affect firms negatively. Akin to the direct effects of contractionary fiscal policy and structural reform on voters, however, it is not possible to make general predictions as to which industries or sectors will be affected by tax increases, budget cuts, or deregulatory measures because the effect depends on the specific measures implemented by the government. Nonetheless, the costs of these measures for individual firms can be substantial, for instance, when subsidies are cut, taxes are increased, or special protectionist arrangements are abolished. In addition, as with monetary tightening, a contractionary fiscal policy weakens aggregate demand and hence reduces firms' business opportunities, which will predominantly hurt those firms concentrated on the domestic market. Structural reforms, on the other hand, can also have positive effects for employers, especially when they allow them to operate more efficiently – although these positive effects often take some time to materialize.

Overall, voters employed in the private sector, by firms whose subsidies are cut or who are otherwise adversely affected by the contraction of fiscal policy and structural reforms, have a high indirect, employment-specific vulnerability to internal adjustment.

2.2.2.2 General Economic Effects of Internal Adjustment

Finally, internal adjustment of fiscal, monetary, and structural policies indirectly hurts all voters because it typically weakens the national economy, as the effects of internal monetary and fiscal adjustment on individuals and firms discussed earlier sum up to depress aggregate demand and supply. This slows down economic activity and usually causes the economy to enter a phase of recession. The widespread job losses and negative income effects of this slowdown are painful for every voter who depends on the state of the domestic economy, especially the majority of voters whose main source of income is their own labor. Labor is less mobile internationally than capital and therefore much more affected by a domestic economic downturn. There is much research showing that labor is hurt by tight monetary policies, especially in the short run (e.g., Alesina, Roubini, and Cohen 1997). This effect is particularly pronounced when labor markets are characterized by a high level of labor market inflexibility because internal adjustment then often leads to increases in unemployment rather than lower wages or a (temporary) reduction in working hours.

Moreover, the negative general economic effects of contractionary policies can have specific negative consequences for individual voters. For example, a homeowner who has long repaid his mortgage and hence is not exposed to interest-rate increases is likely to see the value of her house decline when economic conditions worsen. As monetary tightening makes it increasingly difficult for other homeowners to either service their mortgages or to afford buying new houses, house prices are likely to fall. One of the starkest examples of such a dynamic is the effect of the subprime mortgage crisis on the U.S. housing market. Instigated by the problems of subprime mortgage holders in servicing their debts, house prices in the United States collapsed and lost, on average, about 30 percent of their value between the housing market peak in 2006 and January 2010.[19] American homeowners who always serviced their mortgages with no difficulties have consequently been indirectly hit badly by the sharp drop in demand on the housing market.

2.2.3 The Net Effect of Internal Adjustment on Voters

Overall, internal adjustment strategies have a number of direct and indirect effects on voters that can either offset or – more frequently – reinforce each

---

[19] *Washington Post*, 27 January 2010, Housing Recovery Could take a Decade, Economists Warn.

other. Fiscal retrenchment is always painful but mostly hurts those voters whose taxes are increased, whose benefits are cut, and who work for firms directly affected by the fiscal consolidation measures implemented by the government. Structural reforms tend to hurt some groups while benefiting others, but typically the costs are more pronounced in the short run, whereas the benefits are more likely to accrue in the long term. Monetary tightening is also painful, particularly for indebted voters and voters working for firms that are vulnerable to interest-rate increases. A tightening of monetary policy can also directly benefit those voters who hold more interest-bearing assets than debts, but this group typically comprises only a minority of voters. In addition, even voters who are not directly affected by the adjustments in monetary and fiscal policies can be indirectly vulnerable to their negative consequences because of the adverse consequences on their employers and on general economic conditions. Most voters are indirectly vulnerable to rising interest rates, contractionary fiscal policies, and, to a lesser extent, structural reform.

As a consequence, internal adjustment strategies tend to be painful for a majority of voters, even though the extent of this vulnerability varies with voters' direct and indirect exposure and, particularly in the case of fiscal policy adjustment and structural reforms, the specific measures implemented by the government. The more negative the direct and indirect consequences of these strategies are likely to be for each voter, the more opposed the voter will be to internal adjustment. Moreover, because the negative effects grow with the extent of interest-rate increases and fiscal adjustment, vulnerable voters will always prefer less adjustment to more adjustment. Not surprisingly, political economy research has argued that internal adjustment is particularly difficult – or even impossible – to achieve in democratic countries, because the median voter will be negatively affected by this adjustment strategy (Simmons 1994; Eichengreen 1992, 1996; Bearce and Hallerberg 2011).

2.3 The Vulnerability Profile and Voters' Preferences on External and Internal Adjustment

It should be clear by now that the different adjustment strategies at governments' disposal to resolve balance-of-payments problems have strong distributional implications. Their costs are not distributed equally among voters, and different adjustment strategies will hurt certain groups of citizens more than others. Despite this heterogeneity, it is possible to derive predictions about how these vulnerabilities shape voters' policy preferences with regard to external and internal adjustment. What is crucial in this respect is a voter's overall (or net) vulnerability to internal and external adjustment. As this chapter has shown, this overall effect depends on voters' specific direct and indirect vulnerabilities to the different types of macroeconomic adjustment. Whether voters will ultimately prefer external or internal adjustment depends on the relative size of the overall costs each type of adjustment will impose on them. Assuming that voters always prefer those policies to which they are least vulnerable, the type and extent of voters' vulnerabilities to different adjustment strategies will influence their preferences about how the government should adjust to balance-of-payments imbalances.

Voters' specific vulnerability profiles can be conceptualized in terms of a 2x2 matrix in which the horizontal axis denotes how vulnerable voters overall are to external adjustment, while the vertical axis denotes this vulnerability to internal adjustment, as depicted in Figure 2.2. Distinguishing between low and high levels of vulnerability, each voter can be placed in one of four quadrants, each of which denotes a specific vulnerability profile and is associated with a specific policy preference about macroeconomic adjustment.

The upper left-hand corner (quadrant I) represents voters for whom internal adjustment implies high direct and indirect costs, but who are hardly affected by a depreciation. As an example, picture a voter who receives part of his income in a foreign currency, who works in an export-oriented, but highly leveraged firm, who receives many state benefits, whose workplace is highly protected by labor regulation, and who has just taken out an adjustable-rate mortgage in domestic currency. Voters in this quadrant will accordingly prefer external adjustment to adjustment policies that lead to higher interest rates, a fiscal contraction of the domestic economy, or major structural reforms.

Similarly, the lower right-hand corner (quadrant III) represents the case in which voters are highly vulnerable to external adjustment, but much less so to internal adjustment. An example for this kind of voter is an individual who consumes many imported goods and has borrowed extensively in a foreign currency but holds many interest-bearing assets in domestic currency. For this voter, an increase in the domestic interest rate is much less threatening than a depreciation of the currency. Consequently, individuals exhibiting such a vulnerability profile will prefer adjustment in the form of monetary tightening and/or fiscal retrenchment rather than a depreciation of the exchange rate.

Only few voters are likely to be vulnerable to only one type of adjustment, but not the other. Rather, the much more common case is that

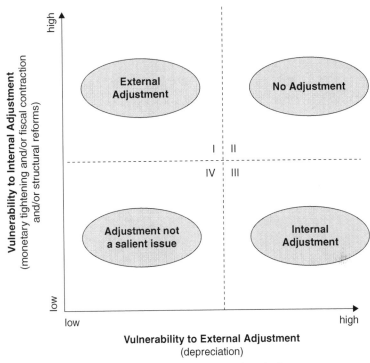

Figure 2.2. Overall vulnerability and preferred adjustment strategy.

voters are vulnerable to both external and internal adjustment, albeit to different degrees. For example, in many cases balance sheets contain both domestic-currency denominated and foreign-currency denominated positions, so they are affected by both changes in the exchange rate and the interest rate. In these more mixed cases, voters' preferences arise as a consideration of their net vulnerabilities to the different policy alternatives. Voters with mixed balance sheets, for example, weigh their vulnerability to depreciation relative to their vulnerability to interest-rate increases. The higher a voter's weighted overall vulnerability to depreciation, the more exchange-rate adjustment threatens the voter's economic outlook. Similarly, debtors with a higher overall balance sheet vulnerability to interest-rate increases will usually be harmed more by a significant tightening of monetary policy than a depreciation.[20]

The picture becomes particularly complicated when voters are equally vulnerable to both types of adjustment. In this case we can distinguish

---

[20] Of course this always also depends on the relative sizes of the changes in interest and exchange rates.

between voters who exhibit equally small vulnerabilities to both adjustment strategies (the lower left-hand quadrant IV) and voters who would be severely hurt by any type of adjustment (the upper right-hand quadrant II). For the former type of voters, the choice of adjustment strategy is not going to be a salient issue. Because neither type of adjustment imposes large costs on them, they can live with both internal and external adjustment. In contrast, for the high-vulnerability voters in quadrant II, any adjustment can quickly turn into a matter of economic survival. To illustrate this, imagine a voter who has to repay his mortgage in a foreign currency but who has also taken out other loans in domestic currency, so that both a depreciation and an increase in interest rates can push him into bankruptcy. Similarly, a voter who works for a firm that holds very high levels of unhedged foreign-currency debt and imports most of its inputs, but whose success also depends on sizeable government subsidies, is at a high risk of losing her job both as a result of a depreciation and a budget cut that reduces or abolishes the firm's subsidies. These voters are consequently strongly opposed to any type of adjustment. As we will see in the second part of this book, such a vulnerability profile can create strong incentives for policy-makers to postpone needed adjustments when adjustment can be avoided in the short run.

2.4 Conclusion

The goal of this chapter was to further our understanding of who will endorse and who will oppose different strategies available to policymakers faced with balance-of-payments imbalances. For this purpose, it showed that both external and internal adjustment policies vary in their effects on different groups of voters and that these distributional effects will be harsher for some voters than for others. Voters can be vulnerable to adjustment in both direct and indirect ways. Some of the factors, which make voters more or less vulnerable to depreciation, monetary tightening, contractionary fiscal policy, and structural reform are well known, but others, especially the importance of voters' and their employers' balance sheets, have so far received very limited attention in previous research. In financially open economies, these balance sheets are likely to contain foreign-currency denominated positions, which immediately increase the salience of decisions surrounding the level of the exchange rate. To demonstrate empirically that balance sheet concerns indeed play an important part in determining policy preferences about internal and external adjustment, the next two chapters analyze survey data and show that these financial concerns significantly influence voters' evaluations of and firms' policy preferences about exchange-rate and monetary policies.

In addition to identifying the sources of voters' direct and indirect vulnerabilities to different types of macroeconomic adjustment, this chapter has argued that their specific net vulnerability profile is an important determinant of their policy preference about whether and how the government should adjust to macroeconomic imbalances. Voters who are less vulnerable to depreciation than monetary and fiscal tightening will prefer external adjustment to internal adjustment, and vice versa. Voters who have little to fear from either form of adjustment are likely to be indifferent. In contrast, voters who are very vulnerable to both external and internal adjustment will oppose any type of adjustment. Chapter 5 will show that the relative size of these different groups can have important policy consequences, because policymakers have strong incentives to delay adjustment when the group of voters vulnerable to any type of adjustment is large.

THREE

Direct Vulnerabilities to Adjustment

European Voters in the 2008–2009
Global Financial Crisis

The previous chapter argued that macroeconomic adjustment to balance-of-payments problems can affect voters considerably because they can exhibit substantial direct and indirect vulnerabilities to adjustments in their country's macroeconomic and structural policies. These vulnerabilities depend on how these policies affect voters' personal situations, their employers, and their general economic conditions. Importantly, different adjustment policies have very diverse effects on voters. Even though adjustment can sometimes have an overall positive effect, a majority of voters tend to be hurt by macroeconomic adjustment, and for some voters, their economic livelihood is on the line when certain adjustment policies are implemented. These vulnerabilities translate into policy preferences about whether and how the government should adjust to macroeconomic imbalances. Voters who are less vulnerable to depreciation than monetary and fiscal tightening will prefer external adjustment to internal adjustment and vice versa, whereas voters who have little to fear from either form of adjustment are likely to be indifferent. In contrast, voters who are very vulnerable to both external and internal adjustment will oppose any type of adjustment.

The second part of this book will argue and show that these distributional consequences ultimately affect policymakers' decisions about both the choice of adjustment strategies and the speed with which they are implemented. This argument builds on the crucial assumption that voters' vulnerabilities do in fact translate into policy preferences and influence voters' propensities to reelect the incumbent. Before turning to an analysis of how these distributional considerations affect the politics of adjustment and delay, this chapter and the next examine more closely whether this assumption holds empirically. For this purpose, they use survey data on both the individual level (Chapter 3) and the firm level (Chapter 4) to show that the specific vulnerability profiles discussed in the previous chapter do in fact influence assessments of external and internal adjustment strategies, as well as voters' general assessments of their personal and national economic situation. Because survey data containing information both on voters' direct and indirect vulnerabilities as well as on their policy preferences, government evaluations, and ultimately vote intentions in the context of one single dataset is scarce, I use a composite approach to evaluate the distributional argument advanced in the two theoretical chapters of this book.[1] The first survey, analyzed in this chapter, looks at voters' direct vulnerabilities to macroeconomic adjustment. It uses the responses of over eighteen thousand voters in twenty European countries to examine how these vulnerabilities affect voters' evaluations of their personal and their country's economic situation and how this effect is conditioned by changes in exchange and interest rates. The second survey, analyzed in Chapter 4, focuses on voters' indirect, employer-specific vulnerabilities to macroeconomic adjustment. For this purpose, it uses a survey of several thousand firms in more than sixty countries to assess how firms' real and financial vulnerabilities shape their exchange-rate and monetary policy preferences. Taken together, the results gleaned from these two analyses offer insights into how different vulnerabilities shape individual policy preferences about external and internal adjustment and how they ultimately influence electoral politics.

The first component of voters' overall vulnerabilities to different types of adjustment is their direct, personal exposure to these policies in terms of their purchasing power and their balance sheets. Whereas the purchasing power argument has received some scholarly attention in the past (Blomberg et al. 2005), previous research has overlooked the importance of personal balance sheets in determining voters' direct vulnerabilities to different adjustment strategies. The analysis presented here therefore explicitly concentrates on the exposure of voters' personal finances to changes in exchange and interest rates and domestic economic conditions more generally.[2] It builds on a survey of individual voters in over twenty European countries, which was conducted during the first peak of the 2008–10 global

---

[1] Survey questions on the conduct of exchange-rate and monetary policy are particularly rare. Similarly, the information needed to gauge respondents' direct and indirect vulnerabilities is almost never solicited in surveys.

[2] Because the effects of fiscal policy adjustments depend on the specific policies implemented by a national government and on specific characteristics of individuals not elicited by the Eurobarometer survey used in this study, I do not evaluate the effects of fiscal policy adjustments in this chapter.

economic and financial crisis. The survey asked respondents to assess to what extent the crisis had affected their personal and their country's overall economic situation. Much research on the phenomenon of "economic voting" has shown that such evaluations critically influence voters' decisions on whether to reelect the incumbent government or not (e.g., Key 1966; Fiorina 1981; Anderson 2000; Duch and Stevenson 2008; for overviews of the literature, see Lewis-Beck and Stegmaier 2000; Lewis-Beck and Stegmaier 2007). By combining the individual-level data with country-level information about national adjustment strategies to the crisis, this survey allows me to tease out how voters with different vulnerability profiles evaluated the different macroeconomic policies implemented by their governments in response to the crisis.

The results underline that variation in balance sheet exposure leads to differences in voters' evaluations of macroeconomic policy outcomes. Voters in countries with a high prevalence of foreign-currency denominated loans were much more likely to worry about the repercussions of the crisis when the currency had depreciated. Likewise, voters repaying a mortgage were somewhat more concerned about the crisis repercussions when monetary policy was tightened and domestic economic conditions more generally deteriorated sharply and were less likely concerned when interest rates were lowered or the economy continued to grow. These findings strongly support the argument that voters evaluate different adjustment strategies with an eye toward how much pain these strategies are inflicting on them. Because these evaluations are likely to influence voters' electoral decisions, policymakers need to take these vulnerabilities into account. The critical distributional consequences that adjustment can have for voters are therefore likely to play an important role in the politics of adjustment.

The empirical analyses presented in this chapter make two important contributions to the literature on the politics of macroeconomic adjustment. First, whereas previous studies have focused exclusively on the firm or country level, the analyses in this chapter examine the direct implications of exchange-rate and monetary policy for individual voters, the ultimate sovereign in democratic politics. The results show that these direct effects strongly influence voters' assessments of the government's management of the economy. Second, the analyses emphasize that in financially open countries, the composition of personal balance sheets is an important determinant of voters' vulnerabilities and, as a consequence, their individual assessments of macroeconomic policy outcomes.

3.1 Voter Evaluations of Economic Policy Outcomes during the 2008–2010 Global Financial and Economic Crisis: Research Design

Voters' evaluations of the economy are a matter of great importance for incumbent policymakers. Voters base their decision on whether or not to reelect the incumbent government at least partly on these evaluations, as extensive research on the phenomenon of economic voting has shown (for overviews, see Lewis-Beck and Stegmaier 2000, 2007). When voters observe that their personal or their country's national economic situation is deteriorating, they are more likely to punish the incumbent, whereas improvements in the economy tend to increase the incumbent's vote share. This effect can be observed in most democratic countries (Duch and Stevenson 2008), including both Western European (Anderson 2000) and Eastern European countries (Fidrmuc 2000), and tends to be particularly pronounced during economic downturns and among voters most vulnerable to such downturns (Singer 2010b; Singer and Gélineau 2012). Understanding how different groups of voters evaluate different macroeconomic adjustment strategies in terms of their personal and their country's general economic situation therefore improves our understanding of how the distributional consequences of macroeconomic adjustment shape policymakers incentives in terms of their crisis management and politically constrain their options to reform the economy.

3.1.1 Research Strategy

To examine the question of how voters' vulnerabilities to internal and external adjustment influence their assessments of the economy, I use survey data from European individuals in early 2009, when the global economic and financial crisis of 2007–10 was in full swing. Because both the vulnerability profiles of European voters as well as the policy responses of European governments varied widely, I am able to examine how voters' vulnerabilities shaped their assessments of their governments' crisis management.

For this purpose, I use individual-level survey data from the Eurobarometer project. The Eurobarometer is a series of cross-national public opinion surveys conducted on behalf of the European Commission that covers issues relating to the European Union, broadly conceived. The specific data used come from Eurobarometer 71.1, which was fielded between January and February 2009, when the first phase of the global economic and financial crisis of 2007–10 was in full swing (European Commission 2009b). This survey was specifically designed to elicit the effects of the crisis on the views and perceptions of Europeans. Among others, it asked respondents to assess the extent to which they believed that the crisis was having repercussions on their personal and their country's overall economic situation. Because the economic voting literature tells us that a more pessimistic view of these repercussions implies a lower probability of reelecting the incumbent government in the next election, these evaluations can have far-reaching political consequences. To investigate how voters' vulnerabilities shaped their evaluations of the outcome of their governments' policy responses to the global economic and financial crisis, I combine individual-level information on voters' direct vulnerabilities to internal and external adjustment, in particular information on their balance sheet vulnerabilities, with macro-level information on the specific adjustment strategies chosen by the different countries.

This research strategy is promising because all respondents surveyed were asked identical questions but answered these questions against the backdrop of very different macroeconomic policy responses of European governments.[3] The global economic and financial crisis of 2008–10 hardly left any country unscathed. Nonetheless, a lot of variation exists both with respect to the severity of the crisis and with respect to governments' policy responses to the crisis. Most Western European countries initially responded with an easing of monetary policy and expansive fiscal policy to jump-start the economy in the Keynesian tradition. Other countries experienced balance-of-payments problems and severe speculative pressure on their currencies and bond markets and consequently adjusted their policies to accommodate this pressure. Here, the approaches have varied widely.[4] Some countries, such as Poland, have predominantly adjusted externally, letting their currencies depreciate. Other countries, such as Estonia or Latvia, have defended their exchange rates, responding to the pressure through reserve sales and massive internal adjustment while keeping the exchange rate stable. Yet others, like Hungary, have responded with a mix of external and internal adjustment, letting the exchange rate depreciate to some extent while simultaneously increasing interest rates and pursuing fiscal consolidation and structural reform, although less aggressively

---

[3] The following countries are included in the analysis: Austria, Belgium*, Bulgaria, Czech Republic, Denmark, Estonia, Finland*, France, Germany, United Kingdom, Greece, Hungary, Ireland*, Italy, Latvia, Lithuania, Luxembourg, Netherlands*, Poland, Portugal*, Romania, Slovakia, Slovenia*, Spain* and Sweden. Countries with an asterisk are only included in the internal adjustment analyses because of missing information on private foreign-currency debt in these countries.

[4] For a more detailed discussion of crisis responses in Eastern Europe, see Chapter 7.

than countries pursuing purely internal adjustment strategies. Different governments thus chose very different strategies to address the macroeconomic problems caused by the crisis.

Given this variation in policy responses, the 2009 Eurobarometer survey is uniquely suited for teasing out how specific vulnerability profiles shape voters' evaluations of the consequences of their governments' crisis management on their personal and the national economic situation.[5] The analyses also exploit the fact that not all the countries covered by this survey experienced severe balance-of-payments problems, which increases the variation in macroeconomic policies.[6] Because the argument advanced in the last chapter also implicitly predicts how voters in surplus countries might benefit or be hurt from currency appreciations and a lowering of interest rates, using the full spectrum of countries and a higher variation in policy outcomes allows me to better estimate the conditional effect of voter vulnerabilities and macroeconomic policies on individual evaluations of the economy.

3.1.2 The Dependent Variable: Economic Repercussions of the Crisis

Given the importance of voters' subjective evaluations of their personal economic situation and the state of the national economy for their voting decisions, I use these evaluations as dependent variables in the following analyses.[7] The 2009 Eurobarometer 71.1 survey asked respondents to assess the extent to which the crisis had affected their personal and their country's overall economic situation. In two questions, respondents were asked to rate to what extent they considered that the then current economic and financial crisis was having repercussions on their personal situation and their country's economy.[8] The possible answers were (1) "no repercussions at all," (2) "not really any repercussions," (3) "fairly important repercussions," and (4) "very important repercussions." Even though the word *repercussion* leaves respondents some room for interpretation,

---

[5] The European experience is also interesting because those European countries that are members of the EMU face a limitation in their possible adjustment strategies because they share a common currency and monetary policy.

[6] Germany or Finland, for example, exhibited significant current account surpluses in 2009.

[7] Ideally, one would also include information on respondents' voting preferences. Regrettably, however, although elicited in the survey, this information has been embargoed by the European Commission and is therefore not publicly available. At this point it is unclear, when (and whether) the embargo will be lifted; therefore, unfortunately, I am not able to investigate the effect of voters' vulnerabilities on their vote choice.

[8] Questions QD1_3 (national economy) and QD1_4 (personal situation).

it appears plausible to assume that in the context of an economic crisis, higher values in this variable denote a more pessimistic evaluation of the impact of the crisis on voters' personal and the country's national economic situation.

3.1.3 Independent Variables: Voter Vulnerabilities and Macroeconomic Adjustment Strategies

To gauge voters' vulnerabilities to external and internal adjustment, I focus on the exposure of their personal balance sheets to changes in the exchange and interest rates. Because the effect of these vulnerabilities on voters' assessments of crisis repercussions depends on the policy responses implemented by the government, these vulnerabilities are then interacted with measures of the extent of external and internal adjustment pursued in each country.

3.1.3.1 Direct Vulnerability to External Adjustment

As discussed in the previous chapter, voters' personal balance sheets are vulnerable to a depreciation of the currency when they contain substantial unhedged and unmatched liabilities denominated in foreign currencies. Because the Eurobarometer survey does not elicit this information from respondents directly, respondents' personal balance sheet vulnerabilities to external adjustment are measured on the country level as the percentage of foreign-currency denominated loans to nonbank borrowers – that is, consumers and nonfinancial firms – in 2007 (see Figure 2.1 in Chapter 2 and Brown, Peter, and Wehrmüller 2009: tables 1 and 2). This variable covers countries like Italy, where foreign-currency denominated loans are very rare (only 1.4% of all loans), as well as countries like Latvia, where most loans (86.1%) are denominated in foreign currencies, such as euros or Swiss francs. Even though this is a fairly crude measure and concentrates only on liabilities but neglects foreign-currency denominated assets, the large variation in this measure implies that it still approximates the average exposure of a country's voters to foreign-currency debt. It can be interpreted as the likelihood that an individual owes foreign-currency denominated debt. The higher this exposure, the higher the probability that voters in this country are vulnerable to external adjustment – that is, a depreciation of their country's currency.

The discussion in Chapter 2 about the distributional effects of adjustment suggests that voters in countries with a high incidence of foreign-currency debt should be more pessimistic about the repercussions of the crisis when the currency has depreciated in the course of the crisis, because the loss in the currency's value increases their debt burden. At the same time, they should be more optimistic when the exchange rate has appreciated, because an appreciation reduces their debt burden in domestic currency terms. The effect of foreign-currency debt on voters' evaluations of the economy is thus conditional on the direction of external adjustment.

To capture this conditional effect empirically, it is necessary to measure the extent of external adjustment that occurred in response to the crisis in each country. To capture this country-level variation, I use data from the IMF's *International Financial Statistics*. External adjustment is operationalized as the year-on-year change in a country's nominal exchange rate between January 2008 and January 2009. For all countries having a separate national currency, the exchange rate to the euro is used for these calculations, whereas the exchange rate between the euro and the Swiss franc is used for members of the European Monetary Union (EMU). Even though there was of course no change in the exchange rate among EMU member states, the significant depreciation of the euro vis-à-vis the Swiss franc should have negatively affected those Europeans holding Swiss franc denominated debt.[9] The external adjustment variable is coded thus that higher values represent a depreciation of the currency, whereas lower values denote an appreciation of the exchange rate. It varies from a 14 percent depreciation in Poland to a 12 percent appreciation in Slovakia.

To model the effect of voters' direct balance sheet exposure to external adjustment conditional on the country's exchange-rate development, I include an interaction term between voters' average foreign-currency debts and the country's exchange-rate behavior in the past year. If the theoretical expectation is correct, the interaction term should be positive and statistically significant, indicating that respondents are particularly pessimistic about the country's crisis trajectory when they are exposed to high levels of foreign-currency debt and live in a country in which the exchange rate depreciates.

---

[9] It should be noted that the appreciation of the Swiss franc against the Euro did not reflect macroeconomic fundamentals but rather the so-called safe haven-effect mirroring investors' desires to invest in safe Swiss assets in light of the turbulence caused by the global financial crisis. Nonetheless, the CHF appreciation hurt European voters holding Swiss franc denominated debt and should therefore influence their assessment of crisis repercussions. Results are robust to using the euro exchange rate with the U.S. dollar, which equally appreciated vis-à-vis the euro. The results are also robust to restricting the sample to non-EMU countries.

3.1.3.2 Direct Vulnerability to Internal Adjustment

Voters' direct vulnerability to internal adjustment is measured with information on whether they are paying a mortgage on their apartment or house.[10] Mortgage holders should be vulnerable to internal adjustment for two reasons. First, because they are repaying a large sum of money, they should on average be more sensitive to interest rate increases than voters not repaying a mortgage. Second, because they need to service their mortgage payments, they depend on their income and, hence, are particularly vulnerable to economic downturns. Obviously, repaying money on a mortgage is only one way in which voters can be vulnerable to internal adjustment, and this vulnerability will vary among mortgage holders because many mortgages have fixed interest rates that are not affected by short-term changes in monetary policy. In addition, mortgages can differ in their length to maturity and, in some countries, are likely to be denominated in foreign currency and linked to foreign interest rates. Nonetheless, on average, mortgage holders should be more vulnerable to internal adjustment than other groups of voters. The operationalization therefore still seems a reasonable proxy for voters' vulnerability to internal adjustment. If anything, this operationalization is likely to underestimate the effects of vulnerability to internal adjustment on voters' assessments of the severity of crisis repercussions, because it neglects many other sources of vulnerability.

Because the debt burden of mortgage holders usually rises when interest rates are increased, this group of voters is more vulnerable to a tightening than a loosening of monetary policy. As a result, these individuals should be particularly concerned about rising interest rates and benefit from decreasing rates. Moreover, indebted individuals tend to be more dependent on domestic economic conditions because they need to earn enough money to repay their mortgage. They should therefore be particularly concerned about a downturn in economy activity. The effect of voters' direct vulnerability to internal adjustment on their evaluations of the government's crisis management is hence conditional on the monetary policy decisions implemented by the authorities in response to mounting financial difficulties and the general developments of the domestic economy.[11]

---

[10] Question Q46–8. The question asked respondents whether they had a house or an apartment they were currently paying for.

[11] Mortgage holders should also be concerned about fiscal tightening. However, because fiscal policy adjustments need time and therefore were mostly not yet implemented by

To measure the extent of internal adjustment, I consequently focus on two aspects of internal adjustment: monetary tightening and developments in the aggregate domestic economy. Monetary tightening is measured as the difference between the nominal interest rate in January 2008 and the nominal interest rate in January 2009, calculated as percentage change relative to the 2008 value.[12] These changes vary between a decrease in interest rates of 72 percent, representing the UK's slashing of interest rates from 5.5 to 1.5 percent and a 64-percent increase in Romania, where interest rates were increased from 8.0 percent in January 2008 to 13.1 percent in January 2009. These numbers show that monetary policy followed a rather unusual pattern in the early months of the crisis: When the crisis created severe problems for global financial markets, most countries loosened, rather than tightened, monetary policy in an attempt to support struggling banks and other financial institutions and to boost economic activity.[13] Nonetheless, the extent of these monetary policy adjustments varied considerably across the countries covered by the Eurobarometer survey. The effects of the crisis on domestic economic conditions are measured as the change in per capita GDP between the first quarter of 2009 and the first quarter of 2008, relative to the 2008 level.[14] This variable shows that on average, economies contracted by 7.8 percent over this period, reflecting the seriousness of the crisis.

To account for the conditional effect between voters' direct vulnerability to internal adjustment and the monetary policy strategy pursued by their country's authorities or the development of domestic economic conditions, I include two interaction terms between the individual-level mortgage-dummy and (1) the country-level measure of interest rate and (2) the GDP change in the past year. For monetary policy tightening, the theoretical expectation is that the interaction term should be positive, indicating that interest-rate increases intensify mortgage holders'

---

the time the survey was fielded in January 2009 and because the survey moreover lacks information about respondents' direct vulnerabilities to specific tax increases and cuts in benefits, fiscal policy tightening is not included in the following analyses.

[12] The data are taken from the IMF's International Financial Statistics. I use money market rates (line 60b), or the discount rate (line 60) when the former is not available. Results are robust, especially for the assessment of voters' personal situations, to using absolute changes in nominal interest rates between January 2008 and 2009 and to using nominal interest-rate levels for January 2009.

[13] Seventeen countries (including all eurozone countries that pursue a common monetary policy) lowered interest rates, and only three countries increased interest rates.

[14] Data are from Eurostat, except for Bulgaria, Ireland, Romania, and Turkey, where data from the IMF's International Financial Statistics are used.

pessimism about the economic situation.[15] In contrast, the interaction term between repaying a mortgage and change in per capita GDP should be negative, indicating that mortgage holders worry more about a fall in domestic growth rates.

3.1.4 Control Variables and Method

Because other personal characteristics of voters are also likely to influence their assessments of their personal and the national economic situation, controls for voters' level of education, their status of employment, gender, and age are included.[16] In the analyses on the effects of external adjustment, I additionally control for the change in per capita GDP between the first quarter of 2009 and the first quarter of 2008 as an indicator for internal adjustment. In the analyses on the effects of internal adjustment, the variable measuring exchange-rate change is included as a control. Finally, a dummy variable indicates whether the respondent lives in a EMU member state or not. All descriptive statistics are listed in the appendix.

Because the analysis combines individual- and country-level data, I employ multilevel regression techniques (Steenbergen and Jones 2002). These models account for the fact that respondents from the same country share a common context, although they vary with regard to their individual characteristics. I use a single equation, random-intercept model to jointly estimate the effects of both individual- and country-level variables.[17] Because the dependent variable is an ordinal measure, I perform ordered logit analyses using the STATA command *gllamm*. Because the number of countries covered by the Eurobarometer survey is limited, I run separate analyses for the effects of external and internal adjustment, respectively, on

---

[15] If respondents are more concerned about the indirect effects of the crisis on the economy, as signaled by a slashing of interest rates, it is possible that mortgage holders, who are likely to be more aware of monetary policy decisions, become more concerned as interest rates are further lowered. This in turn would imply a negative coefficient on the interaction term.

[16] Education levels: dummy variables based on variable D8 for low education (less than 15 years or no full-time education, answer categories 1 and 5) and medium education (between 16 and 19 years of education or still studying, answer category 2 and 4). The base category represents individuals with 20+ years of education. Status of employment: dummy variables based on question D15-AR for self-employed (answer category 1), employed (answer category 2) and unemployed (answer category 3). The residual category represents those not working and includes students and retirees. Gender: dummy variable for female respondents based on question D10. Age: age in years, based on question D11.

[17] Results are generally robust to using random slopes models.

respondents' assessments of the severity of the repercussions of the global financial and economic crisis.[18]

3.2 How Exchange Rate Changes Affect Voters Vulnerable to External Adjustment

How does vulnerability to external adjustment affect voters' evaluations of how the economic crisis of 2008–09 had influenced their personal situation and the national economy by January 2009? Chapter 2 argued that for voters who owe money in foreign currencies and have not hedged against potential movements of the exchange rate, a depreciation substantially increases their debt burden and thus can have very negative effects on their prosperity. They should therefore be particularly likely to voice concern about the repercussions of the crisis. In the same vein, an appreciation lowers the debt burden on foreign-currency denominated debt, leading to an improvement of the personal finances of individuals holding such debt and therefore less concern about the economic crisis.

Table 3.1 presents the results of multilevel ordered logit analyses addressing this question.[19] The first column shows the determinants of voters' evaluations of the effects of the crisis on their personal situation, and the latter column focuses on their evaluations of the national economy. These results support the argument that foreign-currency borrowing is an important determinant of voters' vulnerability to external adjustment. They suggest that voters' balance-sheet vulnerabilities strongly influence their concern about the consequences of the crisis for their personal situation as well as the national economy. The share of foreign-currency denominated debt in a country's total private debt significantly affects respondents' assessments of the nature of the repercussions of the economic crisis, especially when the exchange rate has depreciated in recent months. As expected, the direction of this effect depends on the recent behavior of the exchange rate: When the exchange rate has depreciated in the past year, respondents living in countries with a higher incidence of foreign-currency debt are significantly more pessimistic about the repercussions of the economic crisis than in countries where the exchange rate has appreciated.

---

[18] Results are generally robust to using full models in which both vulnerabilities to different types of adjustment and country-level adjustment indicators are included.

[19] The effects are similar when voters were asked to assess the future repercussions of the crisis for their personal situation and the national economy over the next five years.

Table 3.1. *Vulnerabilities to external adjustment and voters'*
assessment of crisis repercussions

	Crisis repercussions on personal situation (1)	Crisis repercussions on national economy (2)
% of private debt in foreign currency	1.930*** (0.48)	1.183** (0.44)
Exchange-rate depreciation, January 2008–09	−14.376*** (2.44)	−12.056*** (2.51)
Foreign-currency debt x Depreciation	37.996*** (8.37)	24.620*** (6.89)
Change in per capita GDP	−0.445 (1.32)	−4.788*** (1.36)
Low level of education	0.221*** (0.05)	−0.138** (0.05)
Medium level of education	0.148*** (0.04)	−0.114** (0.04)
Self-employed	0.314*** (0.06)	0.173** (0.06)
Employed	0.251*** (0.03)	0.019 (0.04)
Unemployed	1.061*** (0.06)	0.261*** (0.06)
Female	0.094** (0.03)	−0.026 (0.03)
Age	−0.002+ (0.00)	0.003** (0.00)
EMU member	−0.377 (0.30)	−0.440+ (0.25)
Number of individuals (countries)	17,624 (18)	17,732 (18)
Baysian Information Criterion (BIC)	39,973.8	29,898.9
Country-level variance	0.347	0.196
Reduction in country-level variance	55.98%	52.75%
Intraclass correlation	0.092	0.056

Notes: Multilevel ordered logit regression analysis (random-intercept models). The dependent variable is respondents' assessments of the repercussions the crisis is having on their personal situation (model 1) or the national economy (model 2), ranking from (1) no repercussions to (4) very important repercussions. Values in parentheses are standard errors. Cutoff points are not reported. The proportional reduction in country-level variance is estimated relative to a model, which only contains the individual-level variables. Countries included in the analysis are Austria, Bulgaria, Czech Republic, Denmark, Estonia, France, Germany, United Kingdom, Greece, Hungary, Italy, Latvia, Lithuania, Luxembourg, Poland, Romania, Slovakia, and Sweden.
+p ≤ .1; *p ≤ .05; **p ≤ .01; ***p ≤ .001

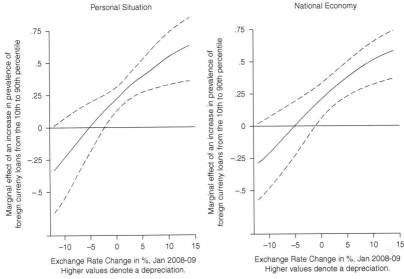

Figure 3.1. Marginal effect of private foreign-currency debt on the probability that respondents report severe repercussions of the crises.

Notes: Graphs are based on the regression models presented in Table 3.1.
Dotted line denotes 95% confidence interval.

Figure 3.1 illustrates this conditional effect of the national exposure of private debt to foreign-currency liabilities graphically.[20] The graphs present the marginal effect of foreign-currency debt at different levels of exchange-rate appreciation and depreciation on respondents' assessments of the severity of crisis repercussions on their personal situation and the national economy. Substantively, they show the difference in the predicted probability that an "average" respondent reports severe repercussions of the economic crisis between respondents living in countries with a high prevalence of foreign-currency denominated debt and those living in countries with a low pervasiveness of foreign-currency denominated debt.[21] The figures demonstrate that the effect of foreign-currency debt on

[20] All graphs in this chapters were created using STATA code provided by Brambor, Clark, and Golder (2006).
[21] High levels are defined as the 90th percentile of the foreign-currency-debt variable (79.2% of all private loans in foreign currency, as in Estonia), low levels as the 10th percentile (7.4% of all private loans in foreign currency, as in France). The average respondent is a 48-year old employed woman with an intermediate level of education, who lives in a country outside the eurozone country in which the economy has contracted by 7.8% over the past year.

respondents' concern about the repercussions of the crisis increases as the exchange rate depreciates. When the exchange rate depreciates, such debt significantly increases voters' concerns about the repercussions of the crisis. Interestingly, this elevated concern about the repercussions of the crisis begins when exchange rates are still relatively stable. In contrast, in countries in which the currency appreciated over the past year, respondents with a higher probability of holding foreign-currency debt are less concerned about the repercussions of the economic crisis than those living in countries characterized by low levels of foreign-currency debt, although this effect is not statistically significant. This finding is in line with the argument that an appreciation reduces the debt burden on foreign-currency liabilities in domestic currency terms.

The results also show that voters do not only take these vulnerabilities into account when assessing the effects of the crisis on their personal situation but also when asked about the national economy. Higher average levels of foreign-currency denominated private debt increase respondents' pessimism about the repercussions of the crisis when the exchange rate has depreciated both with regard to their personal situation and to the national economy, whereas it increases their optimism on both counts when the currency has appreciated. In substantial terms, the incidence of foreign-currency debt increases respondents' concern about their personal situation slightly more than their concern about the national economy. For example, the probability that respondents living in an environment with a high exposure to foreign-currency debt report negative personal consequences of the crisis is 55 percentage points higher than that of respondents living in a low-exposure environment. When asked about the repercussions of the crisis on the national economy, this difference still amounts to 50 percentage points.

Overall, these findings present strong support for the argument that voters' vulnerability to external adjustment depends to a significant degree on the composition of their personal and other private sector balance sheets. When balance sheets contain substantial positions denominated in foreign currency, depreciations of the currency have significant negative effects on voters' financial viabilities. Not surprisingly, they evaluate both their personal situation and that of the national economy accordingly. Moreover, the analysis of the determinants of voters' views on the national economy suggests that voters are also aware of their indirect vulnerability to external adjustment. By taking into account the vulnerability of other actors to external adjustment, they use this information to assess the effects of macroeconomic shocks and policies on the country's overall economic performance.

3.3 How Internal Adjustment Affects Voters' Evaluations of the Severity of Crisis Repercussions

Do voters' vulnerabilities to internal adjustment equally affect their assessments of crisis repercussions on their personal situations and the national economy? The previous chapter argued that internal adjustment strategies are likely to be painful for most voters, even though the extent of this vulnerability varies with voters' direct and indirect exposures to a tightening of monetary and fiscal policies, the specific structural reforms implemented, and a downturn in domestic economic activity more generally. The results of the ordered logit analyses presented in Table 3.2 suggest that these painful consequences of internal adjustment do indeed affect how voters evaluate the consequences of the economic crisis. This effect is observable both with regard to the monetary policies implemented in response to the crisis and with regard to policy outcomes in terms of domestic economic conditions. As expected, the magnitude of this effect differs both between respondents who are currently repaying a mortgage and those who are not and between respondents' evaluations of their personal situations and their evaluation of the national economy.

Turning first to the effects of monetary policy decisions, models 3 and 4 in Table 3.2 analyze the effect of interest-rate changes on respondents' assessments of crisis repercussions. The results show that respondents assess the repercussions of the crisis based on both their direct and indirect vulnerabilities to monetary tightening. Respondents are much more optimistic about the repercussions of the crisis if interest rates were lowered and much more pessimistic when interest rates were increased.

Figure 3.3 displays this effect graphically. It shows that interest-rate changes have a particularly strong effect on voters' assessments of their personal situation. For example, in a context like the eurozone, in which interest rates were slashed by two-thirds relative to the previous year in an effort to combat the consequences of the global financial crisis, respondents were on average not very worried about the repercussions of the crisis on their personal situation: Model 3 estimates the likelihood that an average respondent will report severe personal repercussions of the crisis to be only 12.1 percent (13.2% for respondents repaying a mortgage). In contrast, with a predicted probability of 63.7 percent (68.8% for mortgage

Table 3.2. *Vulnerabilities to internal adjustment and voters' assessments of crisis repercussions*

	Monetary tightening		Economic downturn	
	Personal situation (3)	National economy (4)	Personal situation (5)	National economy (6)
Mortgage holder	0.151* (0.06)	0.089 (0.07)	−0.001 (0.05)	−0.113* (0.05)
Interest-rate increase	2.695*** (0.64)	1.243** (0.44)		
Mortgage holder x Interest-rate increase	0.145 (0.11)	0.029 (0.12)		
Change in p.c. GDP, Q1/08–Q1/09			1.634 (2.44)	−2.654 (1.86)
Mortgage holder x GDP change			−0.950+ (0.49)	−2.276*** (0.55)
Exchange-rate depreciation	−11.098*** (3.07)	−8.096** (2.57)	−2.511 (2.50)	−4.371* (2.07)
Low level of education	0.249*** (0.04)	−0.150*** (0.04)	0.250*** (0.04)	−0.143*** (0.04)
Medium level of education	0.136*** (0.03)	−0.131*** (0.03)	0.142*** (0.03)	−0.120*** (0.03)
Self-employed	0.348*** (0.05)	0.165** (0.05)	0.355*** (0.05)	0.170** (0.05)
Employed	0.225*** (0.03)	0.020 (0.03)	0.218*** (0.03)	0.022 (0.03)
Unemployed	1.066*** (0.05)	0.278*** (0.06)	1.058*** (0.05)	0.282*** (0.05)
Female	0.090*** (0.02)	−0.003 (0.03)	0.095*** (0.02)	0.004 (0.03)
Age	−0.002* (0.00)	0.004**** (0.00)	−0.001+ (0.00)	0.004*** (0.00)
EMU member	−0.202 (0.38)	−0.419 (0.32)	−0.572 (0.43)	−0.482 (0.32)
Number of individuals (countries)	24,194 (25)	24,360 (26)	24,647 (25)	24,819 (26)
BIC	54,982.3	40,803.9	56,055.7	41,576.6
Country-level variance	0.447	0.306	0.783	0.306

	Monetary tightening		Economic downturn	
	Personal situation (3)	National economy (4)	Personal situation (5)	National economy (6)
Reduction country-level variance	35.48%	61.83%	2.42%	26.58%
Intraclass correlation	0.120	0.192	0.085	0.091

Notes: Multilevel ordered logit regression analysis. The dependent variable is respondents' assessments of the repercussions the crisis is having on their personal situation (models 3 and 5) or the national economy (models 4 and 6), ranking from (1) no repercussions to (4) very important repercussions. Values in parentheses are robust standard errors. Cutoff points are not reported. The proportional reduction in country-level variance is estimated relative to a model, which only contains the individual-level variables.
⁺p ≤ .1; ˙p ≤ .05; ˙˙p ≤ .01; ˙˙˙p ≤ .001

holders), the likelihood that respondents will experience severe repercussions of the crisis on their personal situation is much higher in a context like Hungary, where interest rates were increased by about one-third. These findings suggest that individuals are quite aware that falling interest rates decrease their personal debt burden whereas rising interest rates increase it, in addition to adverse indirect effects of monetary tightening. Moreover, among respondents whose direct vulnerability to interest-rate adjustment is particularly high because they are currently repaying a mortgage on a house or apartment, concern about the personal repercussions of the crisis becomes somewhat more pressing as interest rates increase.[22]

Monetary policy adjustments equally affect voters' evaluations of crisis repercussions on the national economy and hence economic developments to which they are indirectly vulnerable. The right-hand panel in Figure 3.2 shows that higher interest rates raise concern about the national economy. In contrast to the findings for respondents' evaluations of their personal situation, however, concern about the consequences is relatively high even in contexts where interest rates were significantly reduced.[23] This is

---

[22] The difference in predicted probabilities between mortgage holders and those not repaying a mortgage is statistically significant across most values of interest-rate changes.

[23] The predicted probability that an average respondent will report severe personal repercussions of the crisis is 47.5% (49.1% for respondents repaying a mortgage).

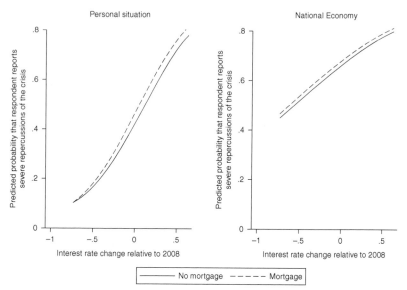

Figure 3.2. Effect of relative interest change on repercussions on the predicted probability that respondents report severe repercussions of the crises.

Notes: Graphs are based on regression models 3 and 4 presented in Table 3.2.

not surprising if one considers the specific circumstances in January 2009: To prevent a freeze-up of credit markets and significant bank failures in the wake of the global financial crisis, the monetary authorities in many countries had resorted to an unprecedented slashing of interest rates. For example, British banks and financial institutions faced enormous difficulties during the crisis, which included a bank run and the closure of several financial institutions. To support the struggling financial sector, the authorities lowered interest rates by 4 percentage points, which amounted to a year-on-year decrease in interest rates of almost three quarters relative to the January 2008 level. In such a setting, the disturbing signals sent by these policy decisions about the health of the financial sector are likely to counteract the stimulative effects of loose monetary policy. The findings presented here imply that while voters appreciated that lower interest rates ease their personal debt burden, they also recognized that the drastic cuts in interest rates witnessed in late 2008 and early 2009 were instituted in response to the severe problems in the financial sector caused by the crisis. Consequently, interest-rate reductions led respondents to assess the repercussions of the crisis on the national economy more pessimistically. As before, this effect is slightly more pronounced among mortgage holders.

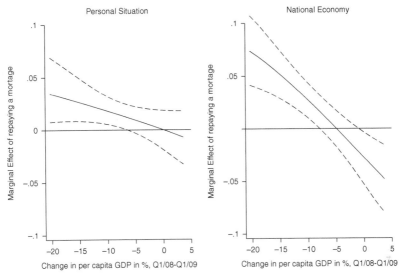

Figure 3.3. Marginal effect of repaying a mortgage on the predicted probability that respondents report severe repercussions of the crises.
Notes: Graphs are based on regression models 5 and 6 presented in Table 3.2.
Dotted line denotes 95% confidence interval.

This might reflect a higher level of information, because individuals who are repaying a mortgage have stronger incentives to follow both monetary policy and their bank's business more carefully than voters not concerned about repaying such debt.

Turning to policy outcomes, models 5 and 6 in Table 3.2 show that compared with nonmortgage holders, mortgage holders, who are particularly vulnerable to worsening conditions in the domestic economy, indeed respond with higher concern the more the economy shrinks in the wake of the crisis.[24] Figure 3.3 displays the marginal effect of holding a mortgage on respondents' evaluations of how severely the crisis had affected them personally and the national economy – that is, the difference in predicted probabilities of reporting severe repercussions between mortgage holders and nonmortgage holders. It shows that when the economy is contracting

---

[24] Somewhat counterintuitively, concern about the personal situation in general tends to decrease, rather than increase, in response to a contraction of the domestic economy. The coefficient displays the expected negative sign, however, when, in addition to exchange-rate changes, foreign-currency loans and the interaction with exchange-rate changes is controlled for.

substantially, mortgage holders show significantly more concern than individuals not repaying a mortgage, both with regard to their personal and the national situation. They are less concerned than individuals not repaying a mortgage when the economy either contracted only slightly, stagnated, or grew a little bit; however, this difference is only statistically significant with regard to their evaluations of the crisis repercussions on the national economy. Mortgage repayment has a stronger marginal effect on individuals' assessments of the situation in the national economy than on their personal situation, possibly because economic downturns tend to affect individuals with a certain time lag. Taken together, the analyses on the effect of changes in aggregate economic activity suggest that voters are well aware of their indirect vulnerability to a shrinking economy. In addition, those individuals with a particularly high vulnerability recognize this elevated vulnerability by reporting more severe consequences of the crisis both for them personally and for the national economy.

Echoing the findings on the effects of external adjustment, the findings about the effects of both monetary tightening and developments in the wider economy suggest that voters' vulnerability to internal adjustment depends significantly on the composition of their personal balance sheets. Voters who are repaying a mortgage see a reduction in interest rates as directly benefiting their personal situation, whereas their concern increases when interest rates soar. They also show a higher level of concern about their personal situation than respondents not repaying a mortgage when the economy is contracting. In addition, the analyses show that respondents are able to differentiate between the effects specific policy decisions and economic developments are having on their personal situation – and as such, their direct vulnerability to adjustment and the effects of these decisions and developments on the economy as a whole – representing their indirect vulnerability to adjustment. In countries in which monetary policy was loosened in response to the spreading crisis, mortgage holders in particular saw this as a positive development for their personal situation, although they responded to this policy with much more concern when asked about the national economy.

3.4 Conclusion

This book argues that both the choice of adjustment strategies to macroeconomic problems as well as delayed adjustment are influenced by how these policies affect the electorate. This argument builds on the assumption that both internal and external adjustment have significant distributional consequences, which drive voters' policy evaluations and their willingness to reelect the incumbent. This chapter has empirically tested this claim. Using survey data from European individuals living through the peak of the global economic and financial crisis in late 2008 and early 2009, it has shown that voters are aware of the distributional consequences of macroeconomic policy adjustment and that they evaluate the consequences of government policy based on their specific vulnerability profiles.

Three main conclusions follow from the analyses presented in this chapter. First, when asked about the repercussions the global economic and financial crisis had on their personal situation and the national economy, respondents answered in line with their personal vulnerabilities to adjustment: In countries that had undergone external adjustment, individuals vulnerable to a depreciation of the exchange rate were significantly more worried about the repercussions of the crisis than those less exposed to such adjustment. Similarly, in countries that had tightened monetary policy – a policy measure typical for internal adjustment – those respondents with a high vulnerability to rising interest rates showed more concern about the implications of the crisis on their personal situation than those respondents whose personal balance sheets were less vulnerable to internal adjustment. Likewise, vulnerable individuals were also more likely to view a slowdown of the national economy as problematic. Voters' specific vulnerabilities in combination with their government's policy response to this crisis thus significantly influenced their evaluations of the consequences of the crisis on their personal situation and the national economy.

Second, the analysis of the determinants of voters' views on the national economy suggests that voters are also aware of the vulnerability of other actors to external and internal adjustment and, hence, their indirect vulnerability to different adjustment strategies. Voters are sensitive to these more general vulnerabilities in the economy and express more concern when external or internal adjustment inflicts losses on the national economy in general. This finding is particularly noteworthy as the results probably underestimate the true effect of voter vulnerabilities on their assessments of their personal and national economic situation, because the choice of adjustment strategy is likely to be influenced by the electorate's vulnerability profile, as Chapter 5 will argue. Because policymakers are likely to implement those adjustment strategies to which their voters are least vulnerable, voters in countries with high levels of vulnerability to a certain type of adjustment are less likely to witness such an adjustment in their country. In this context it is also notable that the analyses that investigated the effects of specific policies (exchange-rate or interest-rate adjustments) were able to explain a much higher percentage of the country-level variation in economic assessments than the analyses that looked at policy outcomes (GDP growth).

Finally, the findings demonstrate clearly that balance sheet concerns constitute an important source of these vulnerabilities. Voters who are more likely to have borrowed in foreign currency are particularly concerned about and hurt by external adjustment, whereas those who are indebted in domestic currency are harmed by and worried about a tightening of monetary policy.

Overall, the findings presented in this chapter strongly support the book's argument that macroeconomic adjustment has significant distributional consequences, which depend on voters' specific vulnerabilities to exchange-rate depreciation on the one hand and internal adjustment on the other. The chapter mainly focused on voters' direct vulnerabilities and on their vulnerabilities to developments in the aggregate economy. However, as discussed in Chapter 2, voters' are also indirectly vulnerable to the effects of different forms of macroeconomic adjustments on their employers. The next chapter therefore explores how firms' vulnerabilities to internal and external adjustment affect their evaluations of their country's monetary and exchange-rate policies. Together, this chapter and the next provide a sound microfoundation for the argument that an electorate's direct and indirect vulnerabilities to macroeconomic adjustment importantly influence the politics of macroeconomic adjustment and delay.

Table 3.3. *Appendix: Descriptive statistics*

Variable	Observations	Mean	Standard deviation	Minimum	Maximum
Crisis repercussions on personal situation	24,660	2.988	0.782	2	4
Crisis repercussions on national economy	24,407	3.490	0.595	2	4
% of private debt in foreign currency	17,916	0.303	0.250	0.014	0.861
Mortgage holder	24,660	0.259	0.438	0	1
Exchange-rate depreciation	23,753	0.065	0.066	−0.119	0.140
Interest-rate increase	24,660	−0.411	0.344	−0.727	0.642
Low level of education	24,660	0.190	0.392	0	1
Medium level of education	24,660	0.430	0.495	0	1
Self-employed	24,660	0.074	0.261	0	1
Employed	24,660	0.426	0.495	0	1
Unemployed	24,660	0.074	0.261	0	1
Female	24,660	0.537	0.499	0	1
Age	24,660	48.259	17.907	15	98
EMU member	24,660	0.513	0.500	0	1

FOUR

Indirect Vulnerabilities to Adjustment

The Determinants of Firms' Monetary and Exchange-Rate Policy Preferences

The last chapter showed that voters' vulnerabilities to internal and external adjustment influence how they evaluate the consequences of economic crises on their personal situations and the national economy. However, macroeconomic adjustment strategies also affect voters indirectly through their effect on employers. Because these employment-specific effects of adjustment influence voters' income and their future job prospects, they should equally influence their evaluation of different adjustment policies. Moreover, in the aggregate, the firm-specific effects of adjustment combine to significantly influence how adjustment affects the country's general economic conditions. Because this constitutes a second indirect channel through which voters are affected by internal and external adjustment, insights into how different adjustment strategies affect the corporate sector help us to understand the full picture of the distributional effects of adjustment. To illuminate this indirect source of voter vulnerability, this chapter therefore investigates how firms assess national monetary and exchange-rate policies and how firm-specific vulnerability profiles shape this assessment.

Focusing on firms and their specific policy evaluations improves our understanding about the politics of macroeconomic adjustment in two additional respects. First, relatively few studies examine the determinants of corporate exchange-rate and monetary policy preferences, although these are likely to play an important role in the political struggles surrounding adjustment. This lack of research is particularly pronounced with regard to exchange-rate policy preferences. The few studies that exist either focus only on the relative price effects of adjustment and disregard the composition of firms' balance sheets (Broz, Frieden, and Weymouth 2008; Férnandez-Albertos 2009; Duckenfield and Aspinwall 2010), or concentrate only on one particular aspect of balance sheets, such as hedging (Cleeland

Knight 2010). In contrast, the firm-level analysis conducted in this chapter is the first one to demonstrate on the microlevel that both firms' export orientation and balance sheet concerns have a direct effect on their policy preferences regarding macroeconomic adjustment. Moreover, it is the first study to jointly analyze firms' exchange-rate and monetary policy preferences. This allows me to assess whether the specific vulnerability profiles discussed in Chapter 2 translate into the predicted exchange-rate and monetary policy preferences.

Second, economic policies, such as exchange-rate or monetary policy, are often complex and difficult to understand (McNamara 1998), so that voters often do not think about the effects of these policies ex ante. Nonetheless, voters care about the outcome of these policies and act and vote on the basis of their effects on their personal, employers', and the general economic situation ex post. It is therefore important for policymakers to know about the distribution of these effects before they adjust macroeconomic policies. Governments that face the question of how to respond to balance-of-payments imbalances therefore need to evaluate a large number of questions: Which groups of voters are directly and indirectly affected by different types of macroeconomic policy responses? Are these effects positive or negative, strong or weak, and how large – and hence electorally influential – are the different groups of voters? How likely is it that the emerging problems signal a fundamental economic disequilibrium or only represent transitory economic problems? And finally, how likely is it that adjustment can be postponed until after the next election? Answering these questions requires an enormous amount of information.

Because firms are particularly important for the functioning of the economy and responsible for providing (or maintaining) jobs for voters, voters' indirect vulnerabilities to different adjustment strategies significantly depend on the effects of macroeconomic adjustment on firms, so that firms can provide the authorities with information on these questions. Firms typically have a much better understanding of these policies and their economic consequences than voters.[1] For example, business representatives can give the government their estimates about how many jobs might be lost if interest rates were significantly increased and representatives of the financial sector can give the government information about the extent and

---

[1] Needless to say, governments also collect information from their statistical offices, the central bank, and other public entities, as well as additional sources, such as business associations, private banks, trade unions, homeowner associations, and consumer groups, which can provide the government with important additional information about the direct and especially the indirect vulnerabilities of voters.

pervasiveness of foreign-currency liabilities among small enterprises and individuals. Much research in political economy has argued that firms hold very distinct policy preferences with regard to exchange-rate policy (Frieden 1991b, 1996, 2002; Frieden and Stein 2001a; Shambaugh 2004; Blomberg et al. 2005; Hall 2005; Helleiner 2005; Broz et al. 2008; Duckenfield and Aspinwall 2010) and monetary policy (Hefeker 1997; Bearce 2003). It is therefore not surprising that firms are much more active in lobbying the government on macroeconomic policies than voters, a fact that many case studies illustrate (see, for example, Kinderman 2008; Walter 2008; Steinberg 2009; Cleeland Knight 2010). Firms can therefore send informative signals to policymakers about how their policy choices are likely to affect their voters, even though these signals are likely to be noisy and biased because interest groups naturally have their own reasons for sharing this information with the government and have incentives to distort this information in their favor.[2] Nonetheless, this implies that firms' vulnerabilities to and their evaluations of government policy matter to policymakers. Understanding the origins of these vulnerabilities therefore advances our understanding of the politics of adjustment.

To undertake this analysis of firm assessments of exchange-rate and monetary policy, I use data from the World Bank's *World Business Environment Survey* (WBES), a large international survey of several thousand firms in sixty different countries that was conducted in the aftermath of the Asian Financial Crisis and provides uncharacteristically detailed information about firms' balance sheets and business activities, as well as their assessment of a number of economic policy issues, including exchange-rate and monetary policy (Batra, Kaufmann, and Stone 2004). Combined with macro-level country information, this firm-level survey data allows me to tease out under what circumstances firms feel vulnerable to exchange-rate and monetary policy.

The analysis of this data shows that the real and financial vulnerabilities discussed in Chapter 2 do indeed influence firms' policy preferences in the expected ways. Firm-level characteristics such as export orientation and a firm's financial structure are important determinants of firms' vulnerabilities to external and internal adjustment. Balance sheet concerns in

---

[2] Note that in many political economy models firms hold policy preferences that diverge from the median voter's policy preference (e.g., Grossman and Helpman 2001). In these models, policymakers arbitrage the firms' preferred policies against the electorates' wishes because firms provide them with certain benefits, such as campaign contributions, which they can use to improve their reelection chances. In contrast, I assume that firms' preferences at least partly overlap with the preferences of their employees, that is, voters.

particular are influential determinants of firms' vulnerabilities to different types of macroeconomic adjustment, and that holds for both the currency denomination of liabilities, which matter for firms' exchange-rate policy preferences, and the overall dependence on borrowing, which is an important determinant of their monetary policy preferences. These firm-specific vulnerabilities in turn influence how firms evaluate their countries' exchange-rate and monetary policies. The survey also shows that a substantial number of firms report to be vulnerable to both internal and external adjustment, which poses considerable problems for the monetary authorities: Whether they let the exchange rate depreciate, or tighten monetary policy to strengthen the currency, these firms will be hurt.

4.1 How Firms Assess Their Vulnerabilities to Exchange-Rate and Monetary Policy

External and internal macroeconomic adjustment can have considerable ramifications for individual firms. Not only do different adjustment strategies affect all firms through their general effects on the national business climate, firms are also affected in firm-specific ways, which vary depending, inter alia, their export orientation and the composition of their balance sheets. This suggests that firms' evaluations of macroeconomic policies on firms should vary both across countries and across firms.

4.1.1 The Data

To test this proposition, I use cross-national firm-level survey data collected by the World Bank's WBES. For this survey, conducted between the end of 1998 and the middle of 2000, the World Bank surveyed 10,032 firms in 80 countries about their perceptions of their business environment, such as the regulatory environment, national governance and corruption, infrastructure, financial barriers, and services to businesses.[3] The dataset contains a wealth of information on firm characteristics, such as firm size, the sector of production, and some information on the firm's financial situation. The survey also asked questions about domestic economic policy and the extent to which certain macroeconomic parameters – such as the exchange and the interest rate – posed obstacles to the firm's operations.

---

[3] In each country at least 100 firms were surveyed. Most interviews were conducted in personal meetings with managerial staff. In Africa, most surveys were conducted by mail. Because of missing data, the number of firms used in this analysis is lower.

I use this information to gauge firms' perceived vulnerabilities to different types of macroeconomic adjustment. Because the vulnerabilities to fiscal policy adjustments and structural change are highly context dependent and are hard to generalize for any subgroup of firms and because the WBES questionnaire lacks good questions on these topics, the analysis concentrates on firm-specific vulnerabilities to exchange-rate and interest-rate adjustments.

Given that the WBES surveyed firms in different countries using a uniform methodology and an identical questionnaire, the answers can be compared both across countries and across firms. This is particularly interesting as the dataset covers a diverse set of both countries and firms. There was significant variation in countries' exchange-rate and monetary policies in the years preceding the survey, which therefore includes information on firms operating in very different macroeconomic environments and under different economic policies. In addition, different types of firms are covered by the survey, which should lead to variation in their vulnerability to different macroeconomic policies. This combination allows me to investigate how different vulnerability profiles and macroeconomic policies affect firms' policy evaluations and the operation of their businesses. The discussion in Chapter 2 would suggest, for example, that exporters perceive an appreciated exchange rate as a problem but should be much less concerned by a depreciated currency. The structure of the dataset allows me to investigate whether such conjectures correctly represent firms' self-reported vulnerabilities to their country's macroeconomic policies and to examine the importance of balance sheets for shaping exchange-rate and monetary policy preferences.

To exploit this variation in macroeconomic contexts, country-specific information on the economy and relevant economic policy instruments and institutions, such as the interest rate or the type of exchange-rate regime, was added to the survey data. The country-level data was taken from Dreher and Walter (2010), which is mostly based on the *International Financial Statistics* published by the IMF. Because firms in most of the countries included in the WBES were surveyed in the year 1999, the country-level data represents the country's macroeconomic environment in 1998, which by the time of the survey was common knowledge for these firms. The timing of the survey constitutes both a challenge and an opportunity. The year 1998 was marked by the Asian financial crisis, which had started in 1997 and continued to affect many countries across the globe in 1998 and early 1999. The year 1998 therefore exhibits unusually large variation in terms of both exchange-rate changes and interest rates in this year. This is advantageous, because it allows me to investigate how external and internal adjustment in different combinations and to different degrees affect firms' perceptions of vulnerability. However, it also poses a problem: Many particularly vulnerable firms did not survive the Asian financial crisis, one of the most severe financial crises of the twentieth century. Because the WBES survey was conducted immediately after this crisis, the firms included in the survey therefore only represent firms that were strong enough to survive the crisis. The result is likely to be a downward bias in my findings: The surviving firms are likely to report less problems with the prevailing exchange-rate and monetary policies than those firms that went bankrupt as a result of these policies would probably have reported. When interpreting the findings of the survey, one should therefore keep this biased selection in mind.

4.1.2 Measuring Firm-Specific Vulnerabilities to Exchange-Rate and Monetary Policy

To measure firms' vulnerabilities to exchange-rate and monetary policy, I use their judgment of how problematic the exchange rate and high interest rates are for the operation and growth of their business.[4] These evaluations are used as proxies for firms' vulnerabilities to exchange-rate adjustment and monetary tightening (for similar approaches, see Broz et al. 2008; Férnandez-Albertos 2009).

To measure exchange-rate-related problems, the WBES presented firm representatives with a list of ten policy fields, which included the exchange rate in addition to issues such as inflation, infrastructure, or corruption.[5] Respondents were asked to evaluate to which extent these items were problematic for the operation and growth of the firm's business on a four-point scale. The possible answers were (1) no obstacle, (2) minor obstacle, (3) moderate obstacle, and (4) major obstacle. Of course, the wording of the question, which only inquires to which extent the exchange rate poses a problem, leaves open to interpretation which specific aspect of exchange-rate

---

[4] Ideally, to identify how vulnerable firms are to exchange-rate and monetary policies, one would like to have their evaluations of specific aspects of their country's current policies. For example, to measure how firms react to external adjustment, one would like to have information about their assessment of both the current level and the recent changes in the exchange rate. Unfortunately, the WBES survey does not provide such detailed information.

[5] WBES question 38f. Respondents were asked not to classify more than three items as major obstacle.

policy, such as exchange-rate variability or the level, firms find problematic. Nonetheless it does provide some indication of the firm's vulnerability to exchange-rate adjustments.

In contrast to the question on exchange-rate policy, the survey question about firms' assessments of monetary policy is more specific. In a second battery of questions, eleven different types of financing constraints, such as collateral requirements, bank bureaucracy, lack of money to lend, or corruption of bank officials, were listed. Another item in this list was high interest rates.[6] Analogous to the exchange-rate question, respondents then were asked to rate the extent to which these financing issues were problematic to the operation and growth of their business on the same four-point scale ranging from (1) no obstacle to (4) major obstacle.

These two ordinal measures of firms' opinions about the exchange and interest rate allow me to proxy firms' own evaluations of their vulnerability to external and internal adjustment. Chapter 2 discussed that these vulnerabilities can be classified into four different types of overall vulnerability to external and internal adjustment, which should determine firms' support for or opposition to certain types of adjustment strategies (see Figure 2.2, Chapter 2): low vulnerability to any type of adjustment, high vulnerability to external but not internal adjustment, high vulnerability to internal but not external adjustment, and the unfortunate fourth category with high levels of vulnerability to both types of macroeconomic adjustment. I therefore construct a third variable, which combines the measures of firms' vulnerabilities to the exchange rate and the interest rate presented earlier and represents these four categories. The new variable is a nominal variable with four potential outcomes: (1) The firm is concerned about neither the exchange rate nor the interest rate, (2) the firm views only the exchange rate, but not the interest rate, as a major obstacle to its operation, (3) the firm views only the interest rate, but not the exchange rate, as a major obstacle and (4), the firm views both the exchange and the interest rate as major obstacles to the operation and growth of its business.

4.1.3 Firm-Level and Country-Level Variation in Vulnerabilities

Figure 4.1 shows the distribution of these three measures of firms' self-perceived vulnerabilities to (1) exchange-rate and (2) monetary policy, as well as their (3) overall vulnerability. The first panel indicates that

---

[6] WBES question 29c. In this set of questions respondents were not asked to limit the number of items classified as major obstacle.

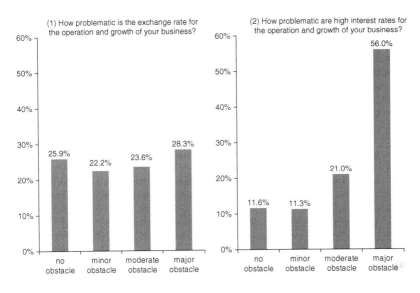

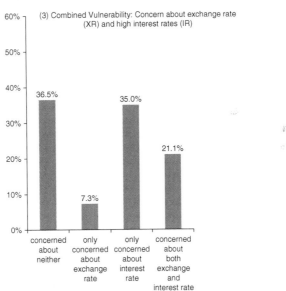

Figure 4.1. Distribution of firms' perceived vulnerabilities to external and internal adjustment in the WBES sample.

firms' concern about the exchange rate is quite equally distributed. About 28 percent of firms see the exchange rate as a major obstacle to their business. In contrast, a majority of firms are concerned about high interest rates. This finding supports the conventional wisdom that a tightening of monetary policy is contractionary and therefore hurts everyone with business interests in the domestic economy.[7] Finally, the last panel shows the combined measure of firms' overall vulnerability to external and internal adjustment. It demonstrates that a substantial fraction of firms perceive their vulnerability to both the exchange rate and high interest rates to be moderate at most. However, there is also a sizeable group of firms vulnerable to both exchange-rate and monetary policy: About one in five firms report both policies to be major obstacles to their business operations. According to the logic developed in Chapter 2, these firms are likely to oppose any type of macroeconomic adjustment and are therefore likely to complicate the government's attempts to adjust macroeconomic policy. The rest of the firms divide into a small group of firms vulnerable to external, but not internal, adjustment and a large group vulnerable to internal adjustment, but not to exchange-rate policy.

Firms' average self-perceived vulnerabilities vary a lot across countries. This is not surprising considering that, as discussed earlier, there was also a lot of variation in countries' exchange-rate and monetary policies in 1998, the year preceding the WBES survey. Figures 4.2 and 4.3 show that firms' self-reported vulnerabilities to exchange rates and interest rates on the country level are associated with how policymakers have managed macroeconomic policies in the past months. Figure 4.2 shows that the percentage of firms seeing the exchange rate as an obstacle to the growth of their business tends to be higher in countries in which the exchange rate depreciated sharply in 1998, even though there is a lot of variation.[8] Surprisingly, in countries with extraordinarily high levels of depreciation, such as Zimbabwe, Malawi, or Russia, firms are less concerned about the exchange rate than in countries with depreciation rates that are lower, although still substantial (e.g., in Ecuador, Thailand, or the Philippines). A closer look at the data reveals, however, that this is a result of rising concern about other policy issues, in particular inflation, policy instability and uncertainty, and financing constraints, which are significantly higher in these countries when compared to countries exhibiting lower rates of exchange-rate depreciation.[9]

---

[7] Note, however, that the number of items that respondents could list as major problems in the battery containing exchange rate was limited, whereas there was no limitation in the list containing high interest rates, so that the difference between these two items might also be an idiosyncratic result of the survey design.

[8] This finding is robust to using the average depreciation rates in the preceding two years, the year-on-year change in the nominal effective exchange rate, and the year-on-year change in the real effective exchange rate.

[9] Recall that respondents were asked to name only three items in the major obstacle category.

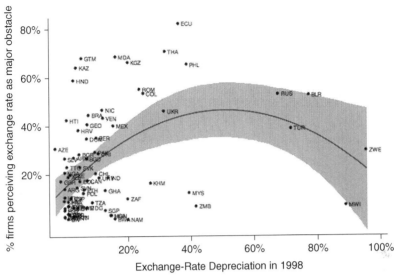

Figure 4.2. Exchange-rate depreciation and firms' vulnerabilities to the exchange rate.

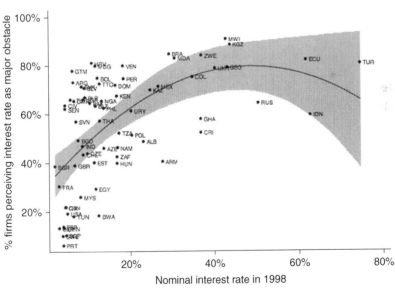

Figure 4.3. Level of interest rates and firms' vulnerabilities to high interest rates.

Similarly, Figure 4.3 shows that higher nominal interest rates in 1998 are associated with a higher percentage of firms expressing a high vulnerability to tight monetary policy. This association remains positive when real interest rates are used. Monetary tightening – that is, interest rate increases – is also associated with higher proportions of firms expressing concern about high interest rates (not shown).

Overall, the data show that the extent to which firms perceive themselves to be vulnerable to external and internal adjustment varies substantially both between countries and between firms. To better understand this variation, the next sections examine how firm characteristics interact with macroeconomic policymaking to shape firms' perceptions of vulnerabilities to adjustments in exchange-rate and monetary policy.

4.2 The Determinants of Firms' Vulnerabilities to External Adjustment

External adjustment affects firms through its effects on relative prices and on balance sheet positions denominated in foreign currencies. As discussed in Chapter 2, depreciation makes exports more competitive internationally and thus tends to benefit export-oriented firms, whereas more domestically oriented firms are often hurt by rising prices for their imported inputs and therefore tend to exhibit a higher vulnerability to depreciation. External adjustment also disturbs firms' balance sheets when they contain mismatched positions denominated in foreign currencies. When firms have borrowed in foreign currencies, but most of their assets are denominated in domestic currency, a depreciation of the exchange rate considerably increases their debt burden. Such firms are therefore particularly vulnerable to external adjustment. Overall, domestically oriented firms and firms holding foreign-currency debt should be most concerned when the exchange rate depreciates, whereas export-oriented producers should worry more about an appreciated exchange rate.

Do these expectations match firms' self-reported vulnerabilities to the exchange rate? To examine this question, this section investigates how firm characteristics, such as firms' export orientation and exposure to foreign-currency debt, influence the probability that they will see the exchange rate as a major obstacle to their business in different macroeconomic environments.

Before we begin, it should be noted that the analyses in this chapter are likely to underestimate the effects of firm characteristics on their vulnerabilities to external and internal adjustment, because the context in which firms evaluate their government's policies is not completely independent from their vulnerability profile. While the argument about the distributional effects of internal and external adjustment makes clear predictions about which firm characteristics should drive firms' vulnerabilities to internal and external adjustment, the remaining chapters in this book will demonstrate that these vulnerabilities also influence governments' policy decisions: When sizeable parts of the electorate are very vulnerable to a certain adjustment strategy, it becomes less likely that this policy will be implemented. Moreover, when the electorate is vulnerable to both types of possible macroeconomic adjustment, the likelihood increases that, in the short run, no adjustment occurs at all because policymakers use their foreign-currency reserves to buffer the speculative pressure on their economy. Firms with very high vulnerabilities to macroeconomic adjustment are hence more likely to be located in countries where no or only small policy adjustments have taken place, especially because highly vulnerable firms located in countries that have undergone significant adjustment in the recent past are more likely to have gone bankrupt and, hence, have no chance of being included in this survey. Moreover, when the WBES survey asks firms to evaluate the extent to which the country's macroeconomic policies are representing obstacles to their business operations, firms are likely to base their answer on recent policies, rather than a possible future adjustment in these policies. Vulnerable firms in countries where no or only limited adjustment of macroeconomic policy has taken place so far can therefore be expected to be less concerned about these policies in their current form. As a result, the estimated effects of firm characteristics on their vulnerabilities to external and internal adjustment are likely to be downwardly biased.

4.2.1 Operationalization

A firm's export orientation is measured as the percentage of its sales that is generated from exports.[10] To deal with the challenge of many missing answers on this variable, I use firms' answers on a second question, which asked whether they were an exporter, without specifying the percentage of sales generated from exports in more detail. If firms answered no and did not give any information on the amount exported, the firm's export share was recoded as zero percent. If firms identified themselves as exporters but did not give any further information, I recoded the variable with the median export share (28%) given by exporters who had additionally given information about their export share.[11] Because exporters' competitiveness is enhanced by exchange-rate depreciation, but decreased by an appreciating

---

[10] WBES question X.
[11] Results are robust to substituting this value with a lower value such as 10%.

exchange rate, the expectation is that a higher export share will be related positively to concern about the exchange rate in countries with appreciated rates and negatively in a context of depreciating exchange rates.

Firms' exposure to foreign-currency denominated debt is measured as the share (percentage) of a firm's financing over the previous year coming from foreign banks.[12] This measure is only an incomplete approximation of the full extent of a firm's exposure to foreign-currency debt. Although financing from foreign banks is likely to be denominated mostly in foreign currency, the survey gives no information about the denomination of the loans. Moreover, domestic banks often lend in foreign currencies as well, but this aspect is not covered by the survey. The measure is therefore likely to underestimate the true vulnerability of firms' balance sheets to a depreciation of the exchange rate, especially in countries with pervasive liability dollarization. Nonetheless, because the WBES survey does not provide any more detailed information on the denomination of firms' liabilities or the extent of a firm's hedging activities, this measure serves as an acceptable proxy for firms' exposure to foreign-currency denominated debt. Firms with a high proportion of funding from foreign banks are assumed to hold more foreign-currency denominated liabilities in their balance sheets. The exchange rate should therefore play a particularly important role for them, and they should be particularly concerned about the exchange rate when the currency is depreciating.

Chapter 2 argued that the real and financial vulnerabilities to external adjustment can also reinforce or offset each other. For example, exporters who hold foreign-currency denominated debt are naturally hedged against depreciation, because their revenues are denominated in foreign currency as well. Foreign-currency denominated liabilities should therefore have a more muted effect on their overall vulnerability to depreciation. To capture this conditional effect, I create an interaction term between firms' export orientation and the share of their financing from foreign banks. This term captures the combined effects of being an exporter and of holding foreign debt: Depreciation benefits exporters, but less so when they hold foreign-currency denominated debt. Similarly, an appreciating exchange rate benefits firms that have borrowed in foreign currency, but less so when a large share of their revenues is derived from exports.

The effects of firms' export orientation and foreign-currency debts are conditional on the level of the exchange rate. Luckily, as illustrated in Figure 4.2a, there is a lot of cross-country variation in exchange-rate changes

---

[12] WBES question 27.

in the sample, ranging from a 3-percent appreciation over the course of 1998 in Azerbaijan to a whopping 244-percent depreciation in Indonesia, caused by the Asian financial crisis. I use the annual exchange-rate change over the previous years (1997–8) to operationalize the adjustment of the exchange rate.[13] As in the previous chapter, negative values denote a currency appreciation, whereas positive values denote a depreciating exchange rate over the past year. The average exchange-rate adjustment in the sample is a 16.5-percent depreciation, which is not surprising if one considers that 1998 was a year plagued by several currency crises. To gauge the effect of more depreciated and more appreciated rates on corporate vulnerability to the exchange rate, I interact the variables measuring firms' export orientation and foreign-debt exposures with the country-specific exchange-rate change over the previous year. To probe this conditional relationship further, I estimate a second regression model, which includes a triple interaction term between firms' export orientation, foreign-debt exposures, and the recent behavior of the exchange rate.

Finally, I include several control variables at the firm and the country level. On the firm level, information on firm size and the firm's ownership status (public, private foreign-owned, and private domestically owned firms) is included, because they are likely to affect both firms' export orientation and debt situations as well as their exposure to macroeconomic policy developments.[14] On the country level I control for the specific circumstances encountered by firms in different countries. Looking at the institutional context, I control for the country's de jure exchange-rate regime, because Broz et al. (2008) and Férnandez-Albertos (2009) have shown that firms' assessments of their exchange-rate vulnerability in the WBES dataset is influenced by the exchange-rate regime. It is measured with two dummy variables for fixed and intermediate exchange-rate regimes, which are based on Ghosh, Gulde and Wolf's (2003) de jure exchange-rate classification.[15] To control for different levels of development, real per capita GDP (logged) is included in the analysis.[16] The descriptive statistics for all variables are

---

[13] The results are robust to using a longer time period as well, such as the two-year average of exchange-rate changes in 1997 and 1998. They are also robust to excluding Indonesia, which recorded an unusually large rate of depreciation in 1998.

[14] WBES questions II (firm size) and VIII and IX (ownership status).

[15] The results are robust to using Reinhart and Rogoff's (2004) de facto classification of exchange-rate regimes.

[16] The results are robust to a variety of additional control variables, such as whether or not a currency crisis occurred in the country in the preceding three years or the level of trade openness.

listed in Appendix A. Appendix B lists the countries and number of firms included in the analyses.

4.2.2 Method

The goal of the analysis is to assess whether the factors associated with firm-specific vulnerability to external adjustment – firms' international orientation and their foreign-currency exposure – influence the probability that they perceive the exchange rate as a major obstacle to their business. To exploit the fact that firms from the same country share a common context, which varies across countries, I once more employ multilevel (hierarchical) regression analysis. Because the dependent variable – perceived vulnerability to the exchange rate – is measured on an ordinal scale, I estimate a random intercept ordered logit model, with firms nested in countries.

4.2.3 Results

This book argues that external adjustment can have considerable distributional effects that benefit some firms, but hurt others. Domestically oriented firms and firms holding foreign-currency debt are expected to be vulnerable to exchange-rate depreciation, whereas export-oriented producers should be more concerned about an appreciated exchange rate. Do these expectations correspond to the concerns voiced by the firms surveyed in the World Business Environment Survey?

To answer this question, Table 4.1 presents the results of multilevel regression analyses of firms' self-reported vulnerabilities to the exchange rate. Model 1 accounts for the variation in the effects of firms' export orientation and foreign-currency borrowing in different exchange-rate policy contexts by including interaction terms between these firm characteristics and the year-on-year change in the exchange-rate level.[17] Model 2 extends this model by adding a triple interaction term between export orientation, foreign financing, and exchange-rate changes.

The regression analyses support the expectations about the distributional consequences of macroeconomic adjustment. The results show that in comparison with domestically oriented firms, export-oriented firms tend to be very concerned about the exchange rate when it has appreciated in the

---

[17] Note that the introduction of the interaction terms means that the individual coefficients on export orientation, foreign financing, and exchange-rate change now only represent the effect of these factor when the other two factors are zero.

Table 4.1. *Determinants of self-reported vulnerability to the exchange rate*

	Model 1	Model 2
% of output exported	0.411***	0.409***
	(0.11)	(0.11)
% of financing from foreign banks	0.843**	0.812*
	(0.28)	(0.33)
Exchange rate depreciation	0.886*	0.884*
	(0.35)	(0.35)
% exports x % foreign financing	−1.329*	−1.278*
	(0.52)	(0.59)
% exported x depreciation	−0.822**	−0.809**
	(0.30)	(0.31)
% foreign financing x depreciation	0.480	0.717
	(0.59)	(1.43)
% foreign fin. x % exports x depreciation		−0.303
		(1.64)
Foreign-owned firm	0.106	0.105
	(0.07)	(0.07)
Publicly owned firm	−0.228**	−0.228**
	(0.08)	(0.08)
Large firm	−0.152*	−0.152*
	(0.08)	(0.08)
Medium-sized firm	−0.062	−0.062
	(0.06)	(0.06)
Fixed exchange-rate regime	−1.281***	−1.281***
	(0.38)	(0.38)
Intermediate exchange-rate regime	−0.161	−0.161
	(0.25)	(0.25)
Real GDP per capita	−0.000***	−0.000***
	(0.00)	(0.00)
Number of firms (countries)	6591 (61)	6591 (61)
BIC	16336.7	16345.5
Country-level variance	0.756	0.756
Reduction in country-level variance	45.13%	45.15%
Intraclass correlation	0.187	0.187

Notes: Random-intercept multilevel ordered logit regression models. Dependent variable is the extent to which the exchange rate poses an obstacle to the operation and growth of a firm's business, ranking from (1) no obstacle to (4) major obstacle. Values in parentheses are standard errors. Cutoff points are not reported. The proportional reduction in country-level variance is estimated relative to a model that only contains the individual-level variables.

†p ≤ .1; *p ≤ .05; **p ≤ .01; ***p ≤ .001

past year or only mildly depreciated, but they are less concerned about the currency in a context of strongly depreciating exchange rates. This effect is moderated when exporters hold foreign-currency denominated debt: Because an appreciation reduces firms' debt burdens on foreign-currency denominated liabilities, exporters who hold such debt are much less concerned about appreciated exchange rates than exporters who have not borrowed money from foreign banks. On the other hand, a depreciation is less advantageous for these firms as well.

In addition, firms that have borrowed money from foreign banks are more likely to be concerned about the exchange rate than firms whose financing mainly comes from domestic sources. This concern increases when the exchange rate depreciates and among less export-oriented firms. Moreover, the triple interaction term in model 2 suggests that this effect of foreign financing is mitigated for exporting firms, although not at a statistically significant level. Especially when one considers that the focus on a firm's financing from foreign banks as a measure for foreign-currency denominated liabilities probably underestimates the true extent of a firm's exposure to foreign-currency debt, these results once more suggest that balance sheet concerns play an important role in determining firms' vulnerabilities to external adjustment.

In addition to these main results, the control variables suggest that firms owned by foreigners are somewhat (although not statistically significantly) more sensitive to the exchange rate than firms that are privately and domestically owned, whereas publicly owned firms exhibit significantly less concern about the currency. This finding is not surprising as foreign firms are likely to interact more with the international economy than domestic firms, whereas public firms are likely to have a privileged relationship with the government that shelters them from economic duress. Moreover, large- and medium-sized firms tend to be less concerned about the exchange rate than small firms, possibly because they have more opportunities to hedge against exchange-rate risk. On the country level, the results suggest that, overall, firms tend to worry most about the exchange rate in intermediate exchange-rate regimes and least in fixed exchange-rate regimes (for detailed discussions of the effect of the exchange-rate regime type on firms' exchange rate vulnerabilities, see Broz et al. 2008; Férnandez-Albertos 2009). Moreover, firms in advanced economies tend to be somewhat more concerned about the exchange rate overall.

Overall, the analysis confirms that firm characteristics are important determinants of their vulnerability to external adjustment. In line with previous research, the results show that export-oriented firms are vulnerable to appreciated exchange rates but much less vulnerable to depreciated rates

(Frieden 1991b; Broz et al. 2008). Moreover, the results support this book's argument that international capital mobility has increased the importance of balance sheet considerations for exchange-rate policy preferences. Firms that hold foreign debt tend to be more concerned about the exchange rate, and this concern is particularly large when the exchange rate depreciates. The findings thus support the conjecture that external adjustment has strong distributional effects. The next section investigates whether this holds true for internal adjustment as well.

4.3 The Determinants of Firms' Vulnerabilities to Internal Adjustment

Turning to firms' vulnerability to internal adjustment, I focus on the effect of monetary policy adjustment, measured as interest rate increases. Monetary tightening increases firms' debt burdens on liabilities linked to the domestic interest rate, lowers their propensity to undertake new investments, and reduces their business opportunities by slowing down aggregate demand. As a consequence, more highly leveraged firms, firms interested in making new investments, and domestically oriented firms should be particularly concerned about high interest rates. The following section investigates whether these theoretical predictions match firms' self-reported vulnerabilities to high interest rates in the WBES.

4.3.1 Operationalization and Method

To measure firms' domestic debt burdens, I use two different operationalizations. First, the share (percentage) of a firm's financing over the previous year that does not come from internal funds, retained earnings, equity, sale of stocks, or foreign banks is used to get a general measure of its dependence on domestic debt financing.[18] The second measure is the logarithm of the ratio of a firm's value of debt relative to its value of assets.[19] The higher a firm's debt/asset ratio, the more vulnerable it should be to interest-rate increases and high interest rates more generally. The extent to which a firm is interested in making new investments is measured somewhat crudely with a dummy variable for firms in the manufacturing sector, because manufacturers typically need to make investments more frequently than, for instance, firms in the service sector.[20] Finally, the domestic orientation

---

[18] WBES question 27.
[19] WBES question 38.
[20] WBES question IV.

of firms is measured with the export variable used earlier – the percentage of a firm's sales generated from exports. The higher this figure, the lower the firm's vulnerability to high interest rates should be.

As before, I add country-level data taken from Dreher and Walter (2010) to the dataset. Because the analyses investigate the determinants of vulnerability to high interest rates, I use information on yearly nominal interest rates for 1998, the year preceding most of the data collection efforts in the WBES survey. To examine the effects of both the level and the change in interest rates, I use the level of nominal interest rates and the year-on-year change in the nominal interest rate, relative to its previous year's level. Higher values on both variables denote high interest rates and a tightening of monetary policy, respectively. Consequently, I expect these variables to be positively associated with concern about high interest rates. To gauge the effect of monetary policy on firms' vulnerabilities to high interest rates, I additionally include interaction terms in which I interact firms' debt exposures and investment interests with both indicators of the country's monetary policy. The expectation is that the effect of high interest rates or a monetary tightening on concern about high interest rates should be magnified when firms are highly leveraged or operating in the manufacturing sector. In statistical terms, this means that I expect both the constituent terms and the interaction terms of these variables to yield positive and statistically significant regression coefficients.

As control variables, I include the same variables as in the analyses of concern about the exchange rate: dummy variables for foreign ownership, public ownership, and firm size as well as countries' real per capita GDP (logged). The countries included in the analyses and the descriptive statistics for all these variables are listed in Appendixes A and B.

As in the analyses of exchange-rate vulnerability, I use multilevel regression techniques to assess whether domestic debt and investment interests increase firms' vulnerabilities to high interest rates. More specifically, I estimate random intercept ordered logit models, with firms nested in countries.

4.3.2 Results

Table 4.2 presents the results of analyses of firms' concerns about high interest rates. The first two columns focus on the effects of nominal interest rate levels, whereas columns three and four present the results for interest-rate changes. The results support the prediction that firms burdened with high levels of domestic debt are more concerned about high interest rates. Both debt-based financing and a high ratio of debts over assets strongly increase the

Table 4.2. *Determinants of self-reported vulnerability to high interest rates*

	Interest rate level		Interest rate change	
	Model 1	Model 2	Model 3	Model 4
Nominal interest rate	0.011	0.003	0.013	0.006
	(0.01)	(0.01)	(0.01)	(0.01)
Year-on-year change in	0.012	0.018[+]	0.014	0.016
nominal interest rate	(0.01)	(0.01)	(0.01)	(0.01)
% debt-based financing	0.403***		0.353***	
	(0.12)		(0.08)	
Debt financing x	−0.004			
nominal interest rate	(0.00)			
Debt financing x			−0.013*	
interest rate change			(0.01)	
Debt/Assets (logged)		0.032***		0.016**
		(0.01)		(0.01)
Debt/Assets x nominal		−0.002**		
interest rate		(0.00)		
Debt/Assets x interest				−0.003**
rate change				(0.00)
Manufacturing sector	0.051	0.052	0.183**	0.176**
	(0.09)	(0.09)	(0.06)	(0.06)
Manufacturer x	0.008*	0.007*		
nominal interest rate	(0.00)	(0.00)		
Manufacturer x interest			0.007[+]	0.007
rate change			(0.00)	(0.00)
% Exports	−0.060	−0.083	−0.060	−0.081
	(0.11)	(0.11)	(0.11)	(0.11)
Foreign-owned firm	−0.396***	−0.367***	−0.393***	−0.367***
	(0.08)	(0.08)	(0.08)	(0.08)
Publicly owned firm	−0.132	−0.177*	−0.117	−0.168[+]
	(0.09)	(0.09)	(0.09)	(0.09)
Large firm	−0.144	−0.242**	−0.141	−0.235**
	(0.09)	(0.09)	(0.09)	(0.09)
Medium-sized firm	0.013	−0.019	0.019	−0.011
	(0.07)	(0.06)	(0.07)	(0.06)
Real GDP per capita	−0.000***	−0.000***	−0.000***	−0.000***
	(0.00)	(0.00)	(0.00)	(0.00)
Number of firms	5439 (53)	5646 (51)	5439 (53)	5646 (51)
(countries)				
BIC	11551.8	12132.5	11560.6	12135.2

(*continued*)

Table 4.2. (*continued*)

	Interest rate level		Interest rate change	
	Model 1	Model 2	Model 3	Model 4
Country-level variance	0.479	0.418	0.480	0.427
Reduction in country-level variance	51.35%	57.59%	51.22%	56.70%
Intraclass correlation	0.1271	0.1127	0.1274	0.1148

Notes: Random-intercept multilevel ordered logit regression models. The dependent variable is the extent to which high interest rates pose an obstacle to the operation and growth of a firm's business, ranking from (1) no obstacle to (4) major obstacle. Values in parentheses are standard errors. Cutoff points are not reported. The proportional reduction in country-level variance is estimated relative to a model that only contains the individual-level variables.
†p ≤ .1; *p ≤ .05; **p ≤ .01; ***p ≤ .001

odds of expressing concern about high interest rates. Unexpectedly, this positive effect tends to be somewhat less pronounced in countries with tighter or tightening monetary policy, as the small negative coefficients on most of the interaction terms of the monetary policy indicators with the debt variables infer. One possible explanation for this finding is that when interest rates are high or on the rise, this turns into a more general problem for all firms, so that the difference between debt-laden firms and the average firm becomes less pronounced. The constituent terms on the interest variables do suggest that high interest rates and interest-rate increases raise the level of concern with the interest rate across the board, just as the descriptive evidence presented in Figure 4.2b indicate, although these effects are mostly not statistically significant.

Tight monetary policy also hurts firms' propensity to invest. This dynamic becomes evident in the regression analysis, which shows that firms in the investment-intensive manufacturing sector feel particularly vulnerable to internal adjustment. Manufacturers are more likely than firms in other sectors to report high interest rates as an important obstacle to their business, and this propensity to see interest rates as a problem increases when monetary policy tightens – irrespective of whether the tightness of policy is measured in terms of nominal interest rates or the change in the nominal interest rate.

In line with the argument about the heightened vulnerability of domestically oriented firms to domestic economic conditions, export-oriented firms feel less vulnerable to high interest rates than firms whose revenues come mainly from the domestic market. Similarly, foreign-owned firms are significantly less likely to worry about high interest rates than domestic firms, probably because these firms tend to be less dependent on domestic economic conditions and are likely to have access to funding outside the country. Because the last section showed these firms to worry more about the exchange rate, this finding supports the argument that international investors are less concerned about domestic policy autonomy than about exchange-rate stability (Frieden 1991b). Moreover, publicly owned, large-, and medium-sized firms are less likely to worry about domestic interest rates than small and privately owned firms.[21] Finally, firms tend to show less concern about tight monetary policy in countries with a higher level of development.

The main conclusion from this part of the analysis is that just like external adjustment, internal adjustment hurts some firms more than others. Manufacturing firms and firms holding larger quantities of domestic debt are particularly concerned about high interest rates. However, the analysis has also made clear that in line with the classic arguments about the widespread pain of internal adjustment (Eichengreen 1992; Simmons 1994), high and rising interest rates are painful to firms in general. Firms operating in countries where interest rates were high were much more likely to view this macroeconomic environment as a serious impediment to their business operations. Akin to external adjustment, internal adjustment has thus the potential to raise significant opposition from the corporate sector.

4.4 Firms' Overall Vulnerabilities to Macroeconomic Adjustment

The analyses so far have shown that firms differ widely in their vulnerabilities to internal and external adjustment and that these vulnerabilities are associated with certain firm characteristics, such as their export orientation or the composition of their balance sheets. This finding is in line with this book's main argument that the distributional consequences of macroeconomic adjustment are strong and play an important role in the politics of adjustment. However, as the next chapter will discuss in more detail, what matters most for governments confronting the task of responding to balance-of-payments problems is the overall vulnerability profile of the country's electorate to different types of adjustment. It thus makes a difference whether voters and their employers are less vulnerable to depreciation

---

[21] Results are robust to controlling for the exchange-rate regime. Both fixed and, to a lesser extent, intermediate exchange-rate regimes are associated with more concern about high interest rates, which mirrors the logic implied by the Unholy Trinity that in countries with an open capital account and fixed exchange rates, monetary policy must be used for the purpose of stabilizing the currency.

than internal adjustment, or more vulnerable to a tightening of domestic economic conditions than a depreciation of the currency. One group that is particularly important politically consists of those voters and firms who are vulnerable to both external and internal adjustment, because this group is likely to oppose any type of adjustment. If this group is large, policymakers face strong incentives not to adjust at all and to delay the implementation of painful (although necessary) reforms.

To improve our understanding of this demand-side pressure facing governments, this last part of the firm-level analysis examines the determinants of firms' overall vulnerabilities to macroeconomic adjustment. Even though it concentrates on firms, this research strategy allows me to generate insights into the more general distributional politics of adjustment. First, the insights on the determinants of firms' vulnerability profiles can be applied to voters' direct vulnerabilities to adjustment. Second, because the analysis covers an important component of voters' vulnerabilities – their indirect, employment-specific exposure to adjustment – gaining a better understanding of how balance sheet and competitiveness concerns shape firms' overall vulnerabilities contributes to our understanding of voters' overall vulnerabilities.

The theoretical expectation for the determinants of a firm's overall vulnerability to macroeconomic adjustment is that the same firm-level characteristics that influenced a firm's vulnerability to external and internal adjustment, respectively, will matter for its overall vulnerability as well. As a consequence, I expect firms' export orientation, foreign-currency borrowing, general indebtedness, and propensity to invest to influence their overall vulnerability to adjustment. Firms with large-scale borrowing in foreign, but not domestic, currency should be much more concerned overall about external than internal adjustment. Both export- and domestically oriented firms with low levels of foreign, but high levels of domestic, debt should feel much more vulnerable to internal adjustment than external adjustment. Finally, domestically oriented manufacturers that have borrowed heavily in both domestic and foreign currency should exhibit the highest level of overall vulnerability to both depreciating exchange rates and rising interest rates.

4.4.1 Operationalization and Method

The dependent variable for this final part of the analysis is a firm's overall vulnerability to adjustment. This vulnerability is measured with the nominal variable combining firms' vulnerabilities to the exchange rate and the interest rate introduced earlier (see Figure 4.1, panel (3)). The variable classifies firms into four categories based on whether or not the exchange rate and/or high interest rates pose a major obstacle for the operation and growth of the firm's business. As a result, firms can be unaffected by either form of adjustment (category 1) vulnerable only to external, but not internal adjustment (category 2) vulnerable only to internal, but not external adjustment (category 3), and vulnerable to both types of adjustment (category 4).

To explain the variation in vulnerability profiles, I combine the explanatory variables used in the preceding analyses. To gauge firms' vulnerabilities to external adjustment, I focus on firms' levels of export orientation and financing from foreign banks. Vulnerability to internal adjustment is proxied with a dummy variable for firms in the manufacturing sector and the percentage of domestic debt-related financing in a firm's balance sheets. These firm characteristics are then interacted with the country-specific extent of exchange-rate adjustment and the interest-rate level over the past year.[22] The control variables are the same as in the preceding analyses.

Because the dependent variable is a nominal variable, I use hierarchical multinomial logit regression models to analyze the determinants of firms' overall vulnerabilities to adjustment. This means that the effects of the firm-specific and country-specific characteristics on firms' vulnerability perceptions are jointly but separately evaluated for each category of the dependent variable. For this purpose, one category has to be chosen as the base category, in relation to which the coefficients can then be interpreted. I choose the first category as base category – that is, low vulnerability to both external and internal adjustment. The regression coefficients presented in Table 4.3 consequently tell us how a given firm- or country-specific variable affects the likelihood that a firm will find itself in the respective vulnerability category relative to the likelihood that the firm exhibits a low level of overall vulnerability to any type of adjustment.

4.4.2 Results

The results for the analysis of the determinants of firms' overall vulnerabilities to macroeconomic adjustment are displayed in Table 4.3. They suggest

---

[22] Results are robust to using interest-rate changes rather than interest-rate levels and the debt-over-asset ratio rather than the percent of debt-related borrowing.

Table 4.3. *Determinants of firms' overall vulnerability to adjustment*

	Not vulnerable to adjustment	Only vulnerable to external adjustment	Only vulnerable to internal adjustment	Vulnerable to both internal and external adjustment
Nominal interest rate		0.028*	0.019	0.031*
		(0.01)	(0.01)	(0.01)
Nominal interest rate		0.001	0.013	0.013
change		(0.01)	(0.01)	(0.01)
Exchange rate		0.343	−0.765+	−0.134
depreciation		(0.45)	(0.45)	(0.44)
% of output exported		0.671**	0.077	0.377+
		(0.25)	(0.18)	(0.21)
% of financing from		1.718**	−0.104	1.162*
foreign banks		(0.60)	(0.54)	(0.54)
% exported x foreign		−3.095*	−0.166	−2.168*
financing		(1.23)	(0.97)	(1.08)
% exported x		−0.333	−0.043	−0.667
depreciation		(0.51)	(0.58)	(0.51)
% foreign financing x		1.437	1.473	1.712
depreciation		(1.52)	(1.52)	(1.48)
Manufacturing sector		0.194	0.038	0.014
		(0.20)	(0.13)	(0.16)
Manufacturing x		−0.001	0.011*	0.009+
interest rate		(0.01)	(0.01)	(0.01)
% debt-based financing		−0.259	0.189	0.475*
		(0.25)	(0.16)	(0.19)
Debt financing x		−0.001	−0.004	−0.005
interest rate		(0.01)	(0.01)	(0.01)
Foreign-owned firm		0.275+	−0.394***	−0.203
		(0.15)	(0.11)	(0.13)
Publicly owned firm		−0.378+	−0.043	−0.249+
		(0.19)	(0.12)	(0.14)
Large firm		−0.440**	−0.226+	−0.426"
		(0.19)	(0.13)	(0.15)
Medium-sized firm		−0.227+	−0.076	−0.054
		(0.14)	(0.09)	(0.10)
Fixed exchange-rate		−0.456	0.605	−0.480
regime		(0.48)	(0.42)	(0.44)
Intermediate exchange-		−0.687*	0.112	−0.418
rate regime		(0.30)	(0.27)	(0.28)

	Not vulnerable to adjustment	Only vulnerable to external adjustment	Only vulnerable to internal adjustment	Vulnerable to both internal and external adjustment
Real GDP per capita		−0.000**	−0.000***	−0.000***
		(0.00)	(0.00)	(0.00)
Constant		−1.181**	0.310	0.118
		(0.40)	(0.36)	(0.37)
Number of firms (countries)	5057 (53)			
BIC	11860.435			
Country-level variance	0.69			
Reduction in country-level variance	55.46%			
Intraclass correlation	0.17			

Notes: Multilevel random-intercept multinomial regression model. The dependent variable measures a firm's overall vulnerability to adjustment, with values denoting that the firm (1) is not vulnerable to any type of adjustment, (2) is only vulnerable to external but not internal adjustment, (3) is only vulnerable to internal not external adjustment, and (4) is vulnerable to both internal and external adjustment. Values in parentheses are standard errors. The proportional reduction in country-level variance is estimated relative to a model that only contains the individual-level variables.
$^{\dagger}p \leq .1$; *$p \leq .05$; **$p \leq .01$; ***$p \leq .001$

that, as expected, the same factors that were important for explaining firms' specific vulnerabilities to external and internal adjustment, respectively, also matter for explaining their overall vulnerabilities to macroeconomic adjustment. Exporters are significantly more likely to feel vulnerable only to the exchange rate or to both the exchange and the interest rate when the exchange rate is appreciating, but this concern decreases when the exchange rate depreciates or when the negative effect of appreciating exchange rates is offset by exporters' debt obligations to foreign banks. As expected, firms that have borrowed abroad are more likely to report high levels of vulnerability to any type of adjustment that includes a depreciation of the currency, and this likelihood is higher in countries in which the exchange rate has depreciated over the course of the past year. For firms with a strong domestic orientation, depreciation tends to increase the likelihood that they do not feel exposed to any type of adjustment.

Manufacturers are more likely to express vulnerability to any adjustment strategy involving internal adjustment, and this vulnerability is higher in national contexts characterized by high interest rates. Firms that finance larger portions of their operations with borrowing are significantly more likely to report to be vulnerable to both types of adjustment. Moreover, high nominal interest rates and a tightening of monetary conditions decrease the likelihood that a firm is not vulnerable at all, and a depreciating exchange rate decreases the likelihood that a firm is concerned only about the interest rate. Interestingly, high interest rates increase concern about the exchange-rate or both exchange-rate and monetary policy among nonmanufacturers and firms with low levels of bank debt.

To facilitate the interpretation of these results, Figures 4.4 and 4.5 illustrate the effects of different levels of depreciation and nominal interest rates on the likelihood that firms will consider themselves vulnerable to different types of adjustment strategies. For this purpose, both figures distinguish between a firm that my theoretical argument would consider barely vulnerable to any type of adjustment (a nonmanufacturing sector exporter with no foreign and low levels of domestic bank financing, left-hand panels) and a firm that it would consider highly vulnerable to any type of adjustment (a nonexporting manufacturer with substantial foreign and domestic bank financing, right-hand panels).[23]

The graphs show that with regard to external adjustment (Figure 4.4), firms with a vulnerability profile exhibiting low exposure to both external and internal adjustment are increasingly unconcerned when the exchange rate depreciates. In contrast, firms with a high overall vulnerability to both types of adjustment become increasingly worried about both exchange and interest rates in such a context. These findings are in line with expectations. Regarding internal adjustment, Figure 4.5 shows that the proportion of firms feeling concerned about both types of adjustment grows with higher nominal interest rates for both types of firms. As expected, however, this concern is much more intense for vulnerable firms than for firms with a relatively sheltered vulnerability profile. Interestingly, higher interest rates increase the concern about both the exchange and interest rate much more than concern about the interest rate only. One possible explanation for this finding is that very high interest

---

[23] All other variables are held at their mean or median. Thus, these firms represent small, private, domestic firms in a country with a flexible exchange-rate regime and a real GDP per capita of US$8,209.

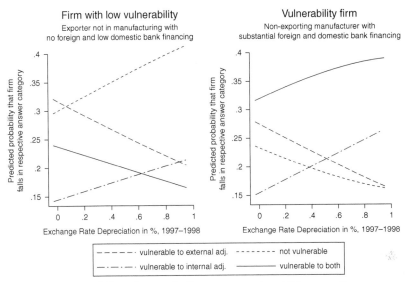

Figure 4.4. Effect of external adjustment on vulnerability perceptions.

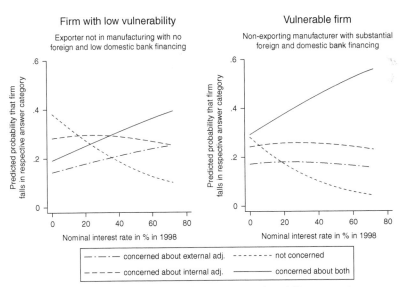

Figure 4.5. Effect of internal adjustment on vulnerability perceptions.

rates may be required to defend the exchange rate against speculative pressure.

The results of this final analysis indicate that the distributional considerations found to be important drivers of firms' specific vulnerabilities to external and internal adjustment, respectively, also matter with regard to overall vulnerabilities. Balance sheet concerns in particular are influential determinants of firms' vulnerabilities to external and internal adjustment, and that holds for both the currency denomination of liabilities and the overall dependence on borrowing. Importantly, a substantial number of firms (21%) report that they are vulnerable to both internal and external adjustment. This poses considerable problems for national policymakers: Whether they let the exchange rate depreciate or tighten monetary policy, these firms will be hurt. They will thus be opposed to depreciation but also opposed to stabilizing the exchange rate through monetary tightening. The next chapter will discuss that this aversion to any type of adjustment can create powerful incentives for policymakers to delay adjustment, even though such delay increases the risk of experiencing a severe financial crises.

4.5 Conclusion

This book argues that both the choice of adjustment strategies to macroeconomic problems and the timing of the implementation of such strategies are influenced by how they affect the electorate. Both internal and external adjustment strategies have significant distributional consequences, which drive voters' policy preferences and, more importantly, their willingness to reelect the incumbent. As the next chapter will discuss, these electoral consequences influence policymakers' decisions about how and when to adjust the country's macroeconomic policies.

The last two chapters have empirically examined the microfoundation of this argument. Whereas Chapter 3 focused on voters, this chapter used firm-level survey data to investigate the distributional implications of exchange-rate and monetary policy adjustment on firms' business operations. The findings show that firm-level characteristics such as firms' export orientation and financial structures are important determinants of their concern about external and internal adjustment of macroeconomic policy. The results also imply that a substantial proportion of firms are vulnerable to both tight monetary policy and exchange-rate depreciation and are hence likely to oppose any policy adjustments in these fields. Overall, the analyses in both chapters underline that both external and internal adjustments have significant distributional implications.

Two main insights follow from these analyses. First, by providing detailed information on firm characteristics, such as their export orientation, production sector, and balance sheet composition, the WBES data is indeed useful in illustrating the complex and interrelated effects of external and internal adjustment. Although the analysis here focused on firms, the insights can be used to further our understanding of such policy changes on individual voters as well. For one, this is because the effects of adjustment on firms indirectly impinge on voters through the employment-specific and aggregate economic effects. Second, the findings presented here once more provide strong evidence that balance sheets matter. In financially open economies, the effects of exchange-rate and monetary policy are no longer confined to issues of competitiveness and the investment climate but can turn into life-or-death issues when balance sheets are vulnerable to changes in these policies. Voters and firms who have borrowed in foreign currency are therefore particularly concerned about and hurt by external adjustment, whereas those who are indebted in domestic currency are harmed by and worried about a tightening of monetary policy. While political economy research so far has mostly overlooked this issue, the results call for a closer attention to balance sheets, in particular because voters' balance sheets increasingly exhibit such vulnerabilities as well.

Overall, the findings presented in the last two chapters support the book's argument that macroeconomic adjustment has significant distributional consequences, which depend on voters' and firms' specific vulnerabilities to exchange-rate depreciation on the one hand and interest-rate increases (and other forms of internal adjustment) on the other. The microlevel analyses presented in these chapters consequently provide a sound microfoundation for the argument that voters' direct and indirect vulnerabilities to macroeconomic adjustment influence the incumbent's decision calculus regarding potential policy responses to balance-of-payments problems. How this plays out at the macro-level is the topic of the next three chapters in this book. They examine how distributional and electoral considerations shape policymakers' choices and timing of macroeconomic policy responses and analyze the adjustment experiences of four countries affected by the Asian financial crisis of 1997–8 and various Eastern European countries affected by the ongoing global financial crisis.

Table 4.4. *Appendix A: Descriptive statistics*

	N	Mean	Std. dev.	Min	Max
Dependent variables					
Concern about exchange rate	6591	2.60	1.18	1	4
Concern about high interest rates	6347	3.23	1.05	1	4
Major obstacle to business operations	6347	2.47	1.19	1	4
Policy variables					
Depreciation (exchange-rate change)	6591	0.20	0.33	−0.03	2.44
Nominal interest rate	5792	21.69	17.91	2.48	74.60
Nominal interest rate change	5687	3.43	13.70	−63.95	34.98
Vulnerability characteristics – external adjustment					
% of output exported	6591	0.13	0.27	0	1
% of financing from foreign banks	6591	0.03	0.12	0	1
Vulnerability characteristics – internal adjustment					
Manufacturing sector	6123	0.39	0.49	0	1
% debt-based financing	6523	0.43	0.39	0	1
Debt/Assets (logged)	6203	−0.96	5.36	−20.72	18.53
Control variables					
Foreign-owned firm	6591	0.17	0.38	0	1
Publicly owned firm	6591	0.11	0.31	0	1
Large firm	6591	0.17	0.37	0	1
Medium-sized firm	6591	0.42	0.49	0	1
Fixed exchange-rate regime	6591	0.09	0.29	0	1
Intermediate exchange-rate regime	6591	0.31	0.46	0	1
Real GDP per capita	6591	8208.87	6584.42	471.56	32300.17

Table 4.5. *Appendix B: List of countries included in the analyses*

Albania	El Salvador	Peru
Argentina	Estonia	Philippines
Armenia	France	Poland
Azerbaijan, Rep. of	Georgia	
Bangladesh	Germany	Portugal
Belarus	Guatemala	Romania
Belize	Haiti	Russia
Bolivia	Honduras	Singapore
Bosnia and Herzegovina	Hungary	Slovak Republic
Brazil	India	Slovenia
Bulgaria	Indonesia	Spain
Cambodia	Italy	Sweden
Canada	Kazakhstan	Thailand
Chile	Kyrgyz Republic	Trinidad and Tobago
China, P.R.: Mainland	Lithuania	Turkey
Colombia	Malaysia	Ukraine
Costa Rica	Mexico	United Kingdom
Croatia	Moldova	United States
Czech Republic	Nicaragua	Uruguay
Dominican Republic	Pakistan	Venezuela, Rep. Bol.
Ecuador	Panama	

FIVE

Interests, Elections, and Policymakers'
Incentives to Adjust

What explains the substantial differences in how and when governments respond to balance-of-payments problems? The first part of this book argued and showed empirically that the two available strategies for macroeconomic adjustment – internal and external adjustment – have very different distributional consequences for voters. Depending on their specific vulnerability profile, some voters are more vulnerable to internal adjustment, others will be hurt more by external adjustment, and yet others are vulnerable to any type of adjustment so that they will be hurt by any economic policy correction intended to rebalance the economy. This raises the question, how do these distributional effects of macroeconomic adjustment influence policymakers' decisions on how and when to address imbalances in their country's balance of payments?

To answer this question, the second part of this book analyzes how the vulnerability profiles of voters in the aggregate shape policymakers' choices of adjustment strategies and under which circumstances they create incentives to delay a serious adjustment of the country's economic policies. Building on the characterization of the distributional effects of macroeconomic adjustment developed in the previous chapters, I argue that when a majority of constituents are more vulnerable to exchange-rate changes than a contraction of the domestic economy, internal adjustment becomes more likely, and vice versa. Moreover, specific vulnerability profiles in the electorate can create incentives for policymakers to avoid timely adjustment, especially when they command sufficient funds or can acquire such funds from external sources to finance the current account deficit. Under these circumstances, policymakers tend to have a strong incentive not to implement painful policy adjustment in the short run. Moreover, elections frequently (although not always) aggravate these incentives to not adjust in time, especially when the median voter exhibits high vulnerabilities to both external and internal adjustment and when it appears likely that adjustment can be successfully avoided before the election. This implies that the incentive to delay adjustment will often be particularly high when elections are close, whereas policymakers have more incentives to focus on the long-run effects of their policies and to implement painful adjustment early on when the next elections are far away. Unlike other explanations in the literature, however, the argument also suggests that upcoming elections can sometimes create incentives to adjust sooner rather than later: When macroeconomic conditions deteriorate so strongly that it becomes unlikely that adjustment can be postponed until after election day, policymakers have incentives to implement adjustment quickly, rather than letting the situation get worse and future adjustment get even more costly.

Delaying adjustment may seem politically advantageous to policymakers under certain conditions, but economically, this strategy frequently fails in the long run. Because the decision to delay adjustment usually allows the imbalances to deteriorate further, the amount of adjustment required at a later point in time tends to be much higher. Oftentimes, the internal adjustment required in such situations is very costly, so that voters are hurt less by a devaluation than a drastic tightening of monetary policy and severe budget cuts. This explains why phases of delayed adjustment often end with a major crash of the currency.[1]

Overall, this chapter shows that voters' individual vulnerabilities to different types of macroeconomic adjustment can have far-reaching consequences for national policy decisions about the type of adjustment strategies and the speed with which these policies are implemented. Chapters 6 and 7 illustrate this argument empirically by looking at two prominent cases of recent balance-of-payments crises: the Asian financial crisis of 1997–8 and the ongoing global financial and economic crisis, which started in 2007.

5.1 To Adjust or Not to Adjust? And If So, When and How? The Government's Decision Problem

How does the distribution of voters' direct and indirect vulnerabilities to macroeconomic adjustment influence policymakers' decisions about how and when to respond to balance-of-payments problems? Macroeconomic adjustment is needed when the economy faces balance-of-payments problems because the current account exhibits an unsustainable deficit. Such a deficit implies that the country imports more than it exports or, more

---

[1] For a related argument, see Walter and Willett (2012).

generally, that the country as a whole spends more than it earns. Current account deficits can emerge for a variety of reasons. On the one hand, they can be a symptom of structural or macroeconomic weaknesses, such as a loss in export competitiveness, a large and persistent fiscal deficit, or a high level of consumer demand that exceeds the country's production capacity. Such weaknesses can arise, for example, when labor productivity declines relative to other countries, or when large capital inflow "bonanzas" (Reinhart and Reinhart 2008) lead to real appreciation, strong increases in aggregate demand, and bubbles in the receiving country (Cardarelli et al. 2009). Current account deficits that are caused by such fundamental imbalances are unsustainable in the long run. Even though it is possible to finance them through capital inflows or by selling foreign currency reserves for some time, in the long run the imbalance in the balance of payments caused by the current account deficit will have to be redressed. As we have seen, this can be achieved through external and internal adjustment of macroeconomic policy, or a combination of both types of adjustment strategies.

However, current account deficits can also emerge because of more transient shocks, such as a sudden and temporary increase in the price of some important imported good (such as oil) or a temporary fall of the world market price of an export commodity that is central for a given country. Such deficits are not caused by fundamental economic problems. Accordingly, to avoid disruptions of the economy, in these situations it is usually advisable for the authorities to finance such temporary current account deficits and the resulting pressures on the currency by intervening in the foreign exchange market, rather than implementing destabilizing economic reforms such as a significant adjustment of macroeconomic policies.[2] Such intervention, for example in the form of sterilized foreign reserve sales, allows the central bank to offset the reduction in the demand for domestic currency and the resulting downward pressure on the exchange rate, without changing the money supply. As a result, it enables policymakers to keep the exchange rate, the interest rate, and other economic policies unchanged. Of course, this policy requires that the authorities have enough foreign currency reserves at their disposal or can procure enough funds from other sources (such as the IMF or other countries) to counterbalance the pressure on international financial markets.

---

[2] Such sterilized intervention, which means that the transactions in the foreign exchange market have no consequences for the domestic money supply and therefore do not affect domestic interest rates, is not necessary when enough private capital flows into the country to balance the current account deficit. However, when macroeconomic problems grow more severe, such capital inflows are often reversed.

Balance-of-payments problems thus sometimes require substantial macroeconomic adjustment, whereas at other times it is better not to adjust but to ride out exchange market pressures through sterilized foreign exchange interventions. Unfortunately, it is often quite difficult to identify immediately whether an emerging imbalance merely reflects a temporary deviation from the equilibrium path or the beginning of a more serious deterioration of fundamentals that requires an adjustment of macroeconomic policy. For example, despite considerable efforts to identify early warning indicators for currency crises, the main insight from this only moderately successful research program is that deteriorating fundamentals do not always result in crises and that the emergence of strong speculative pressure is not easy to predict (e.g., Kaminsky et al. 1998; Berg et al. 2005). As a result, policymakers face high levels of uncertainty about whether painful macroeconomic adjustment is necessary or not.

Notwithstanding this uncertainty, policymakers have to decide how to respond to the current account deficit once it has emerged. Because policymakers do not know for certain whether the imbalance is a signal of deeper economic trouble or just a transitory disturbance, they are confronted with the following two questions. First, should they adjust immediately or should they not adjust but intervene in the foreign exchange market instead? Second, if they decide to adjust, which adjustment strategy should they choose: internal or external adjustment (or a combination of both)?

Figure 5.1 depicts the different policy options at the government's disposal. Once balance-of-payments problems emerge, policymakers can either decide to adjust their economic policies immediately with a predominantly internal adjustment strategy, which involves tightening domestic economic conditions, or a predominantly external adjustment strategy in the form of a depreciation of the currency, or they can decide not to adjust but to finance the deficit with sterilized reserve sales instead. However, the decision to forgo adjustment will only successfully resolve the balance-of-payments problems if the economic problems are in fact transitory and not a manifestation of more fundamental economic problems. If the latter is the case, the strategy of not adjusting will not be successful in the long run, forcing policymakers to adjust at a later point in time, often in the context of an economic crisis. Because delay aggravates the underlying economic problems and therefore increases the extent of economic adjustment required in the future, the costs of adjustment will then be greater than if the government had adjusted economic policy immediately after the problems started to emerge.

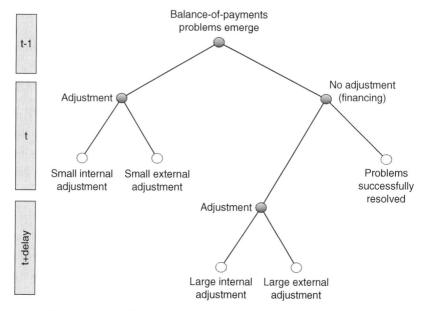

Figure 5.1. Possible policy responses to balance-of-payments problems.

5.2 The Voter's Viewpoint: Policy Outcomes and Vote Choice

Assuming that incumbent governments care about reelection, policy-makers' decisions about which of these different policy options to pursue depend to an important degree on how they expect voters to react to the implementation of each policy option and on how this reaction will affect their vote share in the next election. Building on the insight provided in the first part of the book, which showed that macroeconomic adjustment can directly and indirectly affect voters to a significant degree, this section argues that the electorate's vulnerability profile with regard to external and internal adjustment influences how the incumbent's management of the balance-of-payments problems will be received by voters and, consequently, the vote share the incumbent government can expect to receive at the next election.

Voters need to make up their mind about whether they should reelect the incumbent in the next election or vote for the opposition instead. A crucial criterion for this decision is the expected performance of each possible future government, as voters are typically interested in electing those parties and politicians into office who will best serve them and the country as a whole. Whereas it is often difficult to gauge how the current opposition will perform once in office, voters have more information about the quality of the current government. Its actions in the past provide voters with important clues about how they are going to act in the future, so that the government's performance while in office usually serves as a useful guide about the government's expected performance if it were elected for another term in office. Voters therefore often vote retrospectively – that is, they evaluate the government based on its past performance (Key 1966; Fiorina 1981).[3]

One of the most important issues that voters focus on when evaluating the incumbent's past performance is the economy, as the literature on economic voting has forcefully demonstrated (for recent overviews over the literature, see Duch 2007; Lewis-Beck and Stegmaier 2007). Even though the importance of the economy in determining voters' ballot choices varies across political contexts (see, for example, Powell and Whitten 1993; Anderson 2000; Hellwig and Samuels 2007; Duch and Stevenson 2008; Hellwig 2008), one of the stylized facts that have emerged from this research is that economic changes on average explain about one-third of the change in the incumbent's vote share (Lewis-Beck and Paldam 2000). The economy seems to be even more important electorally in economically less developed countries, possibly because economic fluctuations tend to be more pronounced in these countries (e.g., Lewis-Beck and Nadeau forthcoming). For example, one author finds that in Eastern Europe, the economic vote explains about 50 percent of the variance in vote shares (Roberts 2008).

Not surprisingly, the economy tends to be a particularly salient issue when elections take place during recessions and economic crises (Soroka 2006). For example, both popular commentary and empirical studies suggest that the 2008 presidential elections in the United States were largely decided by the rapidly worsening economic situation, which hurt presidential candidate John McCain, who represented the incumbent party, and helped the challenging opposition candidate Barack Obama into office (e.g., Holbrook 2009; Scotto et al. 2010). Similar evidence for the relevance of economic voting during economic crises exists for other elections, such as the Korean presidential elections in 1997 (Haggard and Mo 2000), the 2009 parliamentary elections in Iceland (Hardarson and Kristinsson 2010) or the German

---

[3] There is also evidence that voters sometimes vote prospectively (MacKuen, Erikson, and Stimson 1992). However, taken as a whole, the empirical evidence suggests that voters weigh their retrospective evaluations of the economy more heavily for their voting decision than for prospective expectations (Lewis-Beck and Stegmaier 2000). Given the poor track record of short-run economic forecasting, giving primary emphasis to retrospective evaluations is not an irrational behavior.

federal elections in 2009 (Beckmann et al. 2010).[4] This is, of course, not to say that the economy is the only thing voters take into account when casting their ballot. Ideology, a candidate's charisma, and noneconomic issues usually also play an important role. Nonetheless, the economy tends to be one of the most important determinants of citizens' voting decisions, and recent research suggests that it plays a particularly important role for voters who are vulnerable to certain economic policies and developments (e.g., Dorrussen and Taylor 2002; Singer 2010b, 2012). In what follows, I therefore abstract from noneconomic determinants of the voting decision and focus on how policymakers' responses to balance-of-payments shocks ceteris paribus affect their reelection chances.

I consequently assume that voters evaluate the incumbent's performance based on how their personal economic situation as well as their employer and the national economy as a whole have fared under the incumbent government's rule.[5] Because the first part of the book argued and showed that voters' vulnerabilities to specific macroeconomic policies determine their assessment both of aggregate economic conditions as well as their personal economic situation, I also assume that the indirect effects of different adjustment strategies on voters' employers or their regional economy are at least equally important for their voting decision as the direct effects on purchasing power and voters' personal balance sheets (see also Kinder and Kiewit 1979; Pattie, Dorling, and Johnston 1997).

Voters' propensities to cast their vote for the incumbent are therefore related to their overall vulnerabilities to the government's macroeconomic policies. Voters who are hurt by the government's policies are less likely to reelect the policymakers who have inflicted this pain on them (see also Singer and Gélineau 2012; Walter 2012). The probability that a voter will reelect the incumbent consequently depends on the direct and indirect effects of the government's macroeconomic policy response implemented to redress the balance-of-payments problem on that voter. The more negatively the voter is affected by these choices, the lower the probability that the voter will vote for the incumbent. The incumbent government therefore needs to pay attention to which groups of voters each available policy option would potentially hurt and how sizeable these groups are.

---

[4] However, economic crisis does not always lead to political turnover. See the discussion in Pepinsky (2012) and the case study evidence in Chapter 7.

[5] This assumption of retrospective voting (Fiorina 1981) is a standard assumption in many political economy models, such as the class of opportunistic political business cycle models (Nordhaus 1975; Rogoff and Sibert 1988; Rogoff 1990).

The more vulnerable voters are to external adjustment, the less likely they will be to reelect an incumbent who has devalued the currency. Likewise, voters vulnerable to internal adjustment will be increasingly unlikely to reelect the incumbent the stronger the incumbent's efforts at implementing internal adjustment measures have been. And because the pain increases in the extent of the adjustment, adjustment that comes after a period of delay will result in a lower propensity to reelect the incumbent than early adjustment would. The aggregate distribution of vulnerabilities among the country's voters thus ceteris paribus determines the vote share the government can expect to receive in the next election.[6]

Both external and internal adjustment will typically cost the incumbent at least some votes, because the policies necessary to resolve balance-of-payments problems are always painful to at least some voters. However, at least in the early phase, governments also have the third policy option of not adjusting in response to emerging balance-of-payments problems and of financing the current account deficit through sterilized foreign reserve sales instead. Such sterilized intervention usually has no immediate effect on voters but carries the risk that more far-reaching adjustment policies will be required to rebalance the economy at a later point in time.

Rational voters should recognize this risk and anticipate that earlier adjustment is better than later adjustment. Consequently they should punish, rather than reward, policymakers who delay needed adjustment when macroeconomic fundamentals are bad. Nonetheless, such informed behavior rarely materializes. Instead, voters are often more likely to punish incumbents who implement adjustment policies than those incumbents who avoid adjustment in the short run, even if such a course of action is unsustainable in the long run (Walter and Willett 2012). An example for such seemingly shortsighted behavior is the electoral success of the radical left party Syriza in the May and June 2012 Greek elections, which took place in the midst of the deep balance-of-payments crisis that has engulfed Greece since 2009. This party campaigned on a platform of not implementing any further painful internal adjustment measures while at the same time promising to retain membership in the euro (and hence not to implement external adjustment either). Although this strategy was economically

---

[6] This abstracts from the role of political parties and the fact that they typically depend on different parts of the electorate (e.g., Oatley 1999; Bearce 2003). If different political parties draw on subsets of the electorate with different vulnerability profiles, the model suggests that there should be partisan differences in the choice of adjustment strategies. However, given the diverse composition of voters' vulnerabilities to internal and external adjustment, clear partisan patterns of overall vulnerability are likely to be rare.

infeasible in the long run, the party gained 26.9 percent of all votes in the June 17, 2012 elections on this platform of no adjustment.

Two factors contribute to this type of shortsighted behavior: first, rational inattention to and rational ignorance about the true state of the economy, and second, the importance of uncertainty, discounting, and the role of the political opposition.[7] Because human beings are characterized by a limited capacity for processing information, it is impossible for them to consider all available information for every decision they have to take. Rather, rational voters allocate their processing capacity to their most pressing problems, while devoting less attention to issues deemed less important (Sims 2003). Because the cost of acquiring information about every aspect in their lives would be much larger than the potential benefits such information would bring, voters therefore choose to remain "rationally ignorant" about less important issues (Downs 1957). Both theories of rational inattention and rational ignorance imply that most individuals are likely to devote limited attention to the government's management of the economy as compared with, say, their personal life. As a result, it is unlikely that a majority of voters will accurately and intensively evaluate to which extent the country's balance of payments is experiencing problems and how likely it is that these shocks signal fundamental economic problems that will ultimately require macroeconomic adjustment. In line with this prediction, empirical evidence suggests that voters tend to have limited knowledge about the state or the workings of the economy (Nannestad and Paldam 1999; Achen and Bartels 2004). This tendency not to pay much attention to macroeconomic developments tends to be particularly strong during extended periods of macroeconomic stability. For example, Carlson and Valev (2008) present survey evidence that in Romania, respondents' attention to and knowledge about the workings of the country's fixed exchange-rate regime decreased the longer the regime was in place: Even though the fixed exchange rate became less sustainable over time, respondents professed increasing levels of confidence in its stability and feasibility the longer the regime had been in place. Rationally inattentive or ignorant voters are consequently unlikely to pay much attention to difficult-to-observe macroeconomic policies such as sterilized foreign reserve sales, in particular because such sales have little immediate effects on their personal economic situation. Voters are thus likely to equate the government's decision

---

[7] The discussion here assumes rational voters. Much research has also emphasized the cognitive limitations of individuals that are likely to reinforce the short-term bias of voters (for a discussion, see Walter and Willett 2012).

not to adjust as a continuation of the status quo and hence an indication that the economy is stable.

However, even if we assume that voters pay attention to economic developments and make use of all available information, the uncertainty surrounding the source of a country's balance-of-payments problems may still lead them to discount that delaying adjustment in the short run can cause more pain in the long run. As we have seen, when the first signs for balance-of-payments problems emerge, it is usually unclear whether these problems are temporary imbalances, which are best addressed by financing the deficit, or indicators of more fundamental problems that require serious internal or external adjustment. As a consequence, every government that decides to adjust immediately inflicts pain on voters, even though there is a possibility that this pain is unnecessary. Voters vulnerable to the type of adjustment implemented then feel this pain, but cannot know for sure whether this pain today really precludes bigger pain tomorrow (in which case they would approve of it), or whether it is unnecessary because the balance-of-payments problems could have been resolved through temporary reserve sales (in which case they would disapprove of it). Voters thus cannot observe the counterfactual of what would have happened had the government not adjusted immediately. This increases myopia among the electorate (Healy and Malhotra 2009). In addition, the political opposition is likely to emphasize the fact that any adjustment that has been implemented may not have been necessary but could have been addressed through other means instead.[8] As a result, it is difficult for voters to ascertain what the appropriate policy response is and to evaluate the government accordingly. High levels of uncertainty also encourage discounting of the future, which increases the weight voters place on their current, as opposed to their future, economic situation. Under these circumstances, it becomes increasingly rational for voters to retrospectively focus on the incumbent government's past behavior and to take the voting decision based on the effects of the government's policies that have materialized until election day. They consequently do not pay much attention to what the best course of macroeconomic policy would be at any given point in time, but focus more on the policy outcomes they can easily observe.

Voters' inattention to and uncertainty about the true state of the economy changes, however, when an economic crisis erupts or major

---

[8] Because voters can confidently hold misinformed views, such statements by the opposition, even if false, can have powerful effects (Kuklinski et al. 2000).

adjustments in macroeconomic policy are implemented. Under these unusual circumstances, voters have more incentives to pay attention to macroeconomic policy and are consequently likely to display a deeper understanding of these policies and their effects. Moreover, the true state of the economy is revealed to them, so that uncertainty about the best course of action is substantially reduced. Similarly, once adjustment policies are being implemented, voters can easily observe whether and how much they are being hurt or helped by these policies. Thus, even if their understanding of the workings of the economy is limited and they spend little time considering which policy option would be best (or least painful) for them ex ante, voters can easily observe the consequences of the government's policy decisions ex post.

Because voters' propensities to reelect the incumbent depend on their retrospective assessments of the governments' economic policies, the demands on their understanding of the workings of the economy and their ex ante development of policy preferences are relatively small. Thus, these vulnerabilities can translate into voting decisions without demanding from voters to undertake a detailed and explicit analysis of their vulnerability profiles ex ante and to judge the government's policies against these profiles. Whether a government wins or loses votes at the polling booth consequently depends not so much on whether or not a policy choice carries the risk of a large and painful adjustment in the future but on whether or not the government has imposed costs on the voters up to the day of the election. This also means that voters' evaluations of the government's decision not to adjust are largely independent of whether the absence of any adjustment results from a sound economy, merely transitory economic problems, or a fundamental disequilibrium that will require painful adjustment in the future.

One important implication of this retrospective behavior with its focus on past, rather than future, policy outcomes is that voters who are vulnerable to both internal and external adjustment will be more likely to reelect an incumbent who chooses not to adjust the country's macroeconomic policies than one who implements painful adjustment. As a consequence, voters vulnerable to adjustment tend to reward policymakers for not adjusting, even though this policy path may aggravate the existing balance-of-payments problems and necessitate even bigger – and consequently more painful – adjustment in the future. This shortsighted behavior is not unique to economic policy outcomes but occurs in other policy areas as well. For example, regarding natural disaster policy, Healy and Malhotra (2009) show that American voters do not reward policymakers for investing in disaster preparedness projects but do reward the delivery of ex-post disaster relief spending.

For policymakers faced with macroeconomic problems, this means that voters do not necessarily have to understand their vulnerabilities to the possible policy responses to these problems in detail ex ante. Rather, for distributional considerations to influence the incumbent's policy decision, it suffices that the incumbent knows that voters will punish her ex post for the pain inflicted on them by way of her policy choice. And because each voter's vulnerability profile determines the effect of each policy choice on the voter's utility, it demands little from voters to observe these effects ex post. For this reason, voters' vulnerability profiles have important implications for policymakers' incentives on how to address emerging balance-of-payments problems.

5.3 How the Electorate's Vulnerability Profile Affects Policymakers' Choices about the Speed and Type of Adjustment

Whether the incumbent is reelected or not is of course not the choice of one individual voter but that of the electorate as a whole. What matters for policymakers therefore is the aggregate effect of their policy choices on the vote share they can expect to achieve in the next election. Faced with the emergence of balance-of-payments problems, policymakers consequently base the decision of whether and how to adjust their macroeconomic policies on a comparison of the expected vote shares associated with the different policy strategies.

The vote share the incumbent government can expect to receive in the next election directly depends on whether and how policymakers have adjusted in response to the economic shock. The nature and the extent of this effect depends on the distributional effects of the implemented policy and hence the aggregation of voters' vulnerabilities to internal and external adjustment. The larger the group of voters that is being hurt by the implemented policy, the lower the vote share the incumbent government can expect to achieve in the next election. Policymakers know that their potential vote share depends on the distributional effects of their policies. To maximize their electoral chances, they will therefore choose their response to economic shocks with an eye to the type of vulnerability dominant among voters.

When making their decision, policymakers hence need to evaluate a number of questions: Which groups are directly and indirectly affected by their policies; are these effects positive or negative, strong or weak; and how large – and hence electorally influential – are the different groups of voters?[9] Even though incumbents are ultimately interested in the aggregate effects of their different policy options, they need to understand the subnational variation to gauge the aggregate effects. In addition, policymakers also need to gauge how likely it is that the emerging problems signal a fundamental economic disequilibrium or only represent transitory economic problems and how likely it is that adjustment can be postponed until after the next election. Based on all this information, policymakers need to infer whether their voters are on average helped or hurt by macroeconomic adjustment and to which type of adjustment they are, in the aggregate, more vulnerable. Although policymakers are thus ultimately interested in the aggregate effects, a more detailed understanding of the distributional effects of the individual policy options helps policymakers to correctly identify the aggregate vulnerabilities of their electorate. This need for information also explains why interest groups (such as trade unions, business associations, etc.) play an important role in the domestic politics of macroeconomic adjustment, as much previous research has documented (e.g., Frieden 1991b; Walter 2008). Interest groups can gauge the potential effects of different adjustment strategies on their businesses and members quite well and can therefore provide the government with detailed information about the indirect vulnerabilities of voters. As a result, their concerns are likely to be heard and considered even by a government that is only motivated by maximizing votes.

Overall, the aggregate vulnerabilities in the electorate, which vary both over time and across countries, determine how voters evaluate the government's handling of balance-of-payments problems. Because governments are aware of this, these distributional considerations affect both the speed of adjustment and the choice of adjustment strategy.

5.3.1 The Timing of Adjustment

When faced with balance-of-payments problems, governments first have to decide whether to implement any policy adjustments to address these problems or whether to avoid adjustment by financing the deficit instead. To reach this decision, policymakers weigh the vote shares that each strategy is expected to generate against each other. They thus compare the expected vote share associated with an immediate (external or internal)

---

[9]   The electoral influence of different groups of voters will also depend on national electoral and party systems.

adjustment with the vote share that they can expect if they choose not to adjust immediately. This latter expected vote share is a weighted average between the vote share that results from successfully staving off speculative pressure through sterilized foreign reserve sales and the expected vote share associated with adjusting after a period of initial delay. The weight is determined by the probability that the economy experiences fundamental problems that will require either internal or external adjustment in the future.

If a majority of voters are likely to benefit more from policy adjustment than from the status quo, then a quick adjustment of macroeconomic policies is likely. In this situation, avoiding adjustment through a financing of the deficit prolongs a situation that is suboptimal for a majority of voters, whereas adjustment on average increases voters' utilities. For example, in highly export-oriented countries plagued by an overvalued exchange rate, depreciations can have more positive effects than the status quo because they stimulate export performance and growth, from which voters indirectly benefit. This implies that governments in such countries should be more likely to quickly adjust (through a depreciation of the exchange rate) than governments presiding over countries where voters are more vulnerable to macroeconomic adjustment.

In the more common scenario, the consequences of adjustment are likely to be negative for most voters, at least in the short run. Because any adjustment definitely decreases the vote share when voters are at least somewhat vulnerable to both types of adjustment, whereas most voters do not invest energy in discerning the probability of adjustment at a later point in time, governments can expect to receive more votes if they do not adjust before election day. Although the costs of adjustment become larger the longer adjustment has been delayed, elections therefore create strong incentives for opportunistic policymakers to delay an adjustment of economic policies. The political costs of adjustment are particularly high when voters exhibit high levels of direct and indirect vulnerabilities to both external and internal adjustment. For example, in a country with a large nontradables sector in which foreign-currency liabilities are widespread among individuals and firms and whose private sector is highly indebted and highly dependent on government spending, policymakers have a strong incentive to pursue a wait-and-see strategy, rather than implementing adjustment policies quickly. In contrast, when voters are vulnerable to adjustment, but this vulnerability is not particularly large, incumbent policymakers have more of an incentive to implement adjustment quickly rather than waiting and letting vulnerabilities grow so that an adjustment at a later point in time will cost them significantly more votes than adjustment today.

An electorate highly vulnerable to both internal and external adjustment can hence create considerable incentives for policymakers to delay a necessary adjustment of their economic policies. However, not adjusting only yields the highest vote share if the status quo can be maintained at least until election day. Whether this can be achieved or not, and consequently whether policymakers have incentives to delay adjustment or not, depends on four issues. The first two relate to the domestic environment: the nature of the economic problems and the electoral calendar. As many crisis episodes vividly illustrate, however, the decision about the timing of adjustment does not rest solely with national policymakers. Rather, two additional issues relating to the international environment – international financial markets and external actors such as the IMF – strongly influence policymakers' incentives to delay adjustment as well.

Domestically, the likelihood that the problems will escalate before the next election depends to a large extent on whether these balance-of-payments problems reflect merely a transitory economic shock or fundamental macroeconomic imbalances and how serious these fundamental problems are. The more fundamental the problems, the higher the probability that a serious financial and economic crisis will erupt before the election, making it impossible for the authorities to further avoid adjustment. In addition, the likelihood that adjustment can be delayed until after the elections depends on the closeness of the next elections. Because maintaining the status quo for another month is typically more feasible than avoiding adjustment for another year, incumbent governments have less incentives to adjust when the next elections are scheduled for the near future. In contrast, when the next elections are far away, the more the likelihood increases that policymakers take a longer term perspective and implement adjustment measures in a timely manner. As a result, elections create political business cycle dynamics in the politics of internal and external adjustment: Adjustment is much less likely to occur shortly before and much more likely to occur shortly after elections have taken place (see also Walter 2009).[10] Elections thus increase the incumbent government's incentives to delay adjustment, even though this usually means that adjustment ultimately will be more painful than if it had been implemented right away.

---

[10] The literature on political business cycles shows that macroeconomic policy – monetary, fiscal, and exchange-rate policy – is strongly affected by the electoral cycle as policymakers set out to generate positive developments in the economy shortly before an election, at the expense of more negative developments in the long run (for example, Nordhaus 1975; Rogoff and Sibert 1988; Willett 1988; Alesina et al. 1997; Stein and Streb 2004; Blomberg et al. 2005; Walter 2009).

In addition, the probability that adjustment can be avoided until the next election depends on the pressure exerted by international financial markets and on the amount of financing available to the authorities. When financial markets begin to question the soundness of a country's macroeconomic fundamentals and the government's willingness to address the resulting economic problems, they usually begin to speculate against the currency. Much research on the dynamics of speculative attacks and currency crises has shown that speculative pressure is almost certain to emerge when a country's macroeconomic fundamentals deteriorate beyond a certain point (Krugman 1979). However, speculative pressure can also emerge if a country's fundamentals are merely mediocre rather than outright bad, especially when markets believe that governments would not be willing to tolerate the pain of withstanding speculative pressure on a currency but would rather let the economy adjust externally via a devaluation of the exchange rate (e.g., Obstfeld 1994, 1996). Self-fulfilling expectations (e.g., Sachs, Tornell, and Velasco 1996), contagion from other countries under speculative pressure (e.g., Gerlach and Smets 1995; Eichengreen, Rose, and Wyplosz 1996), and herding behavior (Morris and Shin 1998), can also lead to speculative attacks on currencies, and these can take governments by surprise. Irrespective of the source of speculative pressure, however, the government's ability to avoid adjustment is weakened when such pressure intensifies, because the financing needed for a successful pursuit of this strategy increases significantly. Stronger pressure from financial markets thus increases the risk that internal or external adjustment will have to occur just before the election. Moreover, speculative attacks on a country's currency can raise voters' awareness of the underlying problems and make the decision of whether or not to adjust economic policies a more salient issue. This can create incentives for incumbent governments to adjust economic policies in a timely manner even when elections are scheduled for the nearer future. Moreover, speculative pressure also creates incentives for policymakers to implement at least some reforms in an attempt to calm markets by signaling policy activity. Speculative pressure overall thus tends to decrease governments' incentives to delay adjustment.

Nonetheless, speculative pressure from financial markets does not always lead to immediate adjustment (Eichengreen 2003; Sattler and Walter 2009). Rather, policymakers can respond to this pressure with sterilized reserve sales and therefore avoid macroeconomic adjustment even in times of adverse market sentiments. Their ability to pursue such a strategy depends on the availability of funds to finance the deficit and fight off speculative pressure. Such funds can come from two possible sources: one domestic and one international. If governments have accumulated enough foreign currency reserves in the past, they can use these funds to stave off speculative pressure and to finance the deficit rather than adjusting their economic policies. A second possible source for such funds is international actors, such as other governments or international organizations such as the IMF. For example, during the Asian financial crisis, the U.S. government bilaterally supported the Korean government with substantial sums of money, while both the EU and the Nordic states, especially Sweden and Norway, gave bilateral support to the Baltic countries during the global financial crisis of 2008–10. The IMF also regularly lends funds to countries facing balance-of-payments problems. The willingness of international actors to loan governments money thus influences policymakers' abilities to delay adjustment and increases their incentives to do so. At the same time, these funds are usually subject to strict conditions, which typically include reforms leading to macroeconomic adjustment. For example, the IMF often requires recipient governments to adjust their exchange rate at least slightly, so that IMF programs tend to increase the speed with which external adjustment measures are implemented (Dreher and Walter 2010). Similarly, it usually requires internal adjustment in the form of structural reforms and fiscal consolidation measures. By acting as a scapegoat, such conditions can ease the political costs of adjustment to some extent and hence decrease the incentives to avoid painful adjustment (Vreeland 2003). Nonetheless, governments also often fail to fulfill all of these conditions (Dreher 2004; Stone 2008). In the meantime, they can still use the initial funds granted to delay any significant adjustment.

This discussion shows that the timing of adjustment is a highly political issue. Distributional and electoral considerations can significantly complicate the speedy and decisive resolution of balance-of-payments crises, especially when the electorate is vulnerable to any type of adjustment. When the domestic political costs of a speedy adjustment are very high, incumbent policymakers have strong incentives not to adjust, even if this means that more painful adjustment measures will have to be implemented in the future.

5.3.2 The Choice of Adjustment Strategies

Voters' vulnerabilities to internal and external adjustment also influence the type of adjustment strategies governments ultimately implement. When a majority of the electorate is vulnerable to interest-rate increases, cuts in public spending, tax increases, and structural reforms, but less vulnerable to external adjustment, a depreciation of the exchange rate is likely to be the preferred adjustment strategy. For example, the government of a country characterized by a large, export-oriented manufacturing sector, high levels of unemployment, and low levels of investment should be more likely to adjust to macroeconomic imbalances externally than internally. Conversely, when a majority of voters are more negatively exposed to depreciation than a tightening of fiscal and monetary policy and structural reforms, governments are more likely to pursue a predominantly internal adjustment strategy. As we have seen in Chapter 2, such a situation is particularly likely when the private sector holds a lot of foreign-currency denominated debt.

Finally, when the electorate is vulnerable to both external and internal adjustment, the choice between the two adjustment strategies becomes more difficult. In these cases, any type of adjustment decreases the incumbent's vote share relative to the status quo. As we have seen, policymakers therefore often have incentives to delay adjustment. However, when the balance-of-payments problems persist, policymakers eventually will be forced to address these problems. They will then also carefully assess voters' direct and indirect vulnerabilities and choose their adjustment strategies with the goal of minimizing the (already large) costs to the electorate. In these situations, governments are unlikely to pursue purely external or purely internal adjustment strategies. Rather, they will implement policy mixes, which typically emphasize one type of macroeconomic adjustment more than the other. An example is a devaluation of the currency coupled with structural reforms in the labor market or fiscal consolidation coupled with a widening of the exchange-rate band. The relative weight placed on external versus internal adjustment in such mixed strategies is, however, once more influenced by the distributional concerns highlighted in the first part of this book.

Like the timing of adjustment, the choice of adjustment strategies is similarly influenced by the international context, in particular international financial markets and international political actors. Because speculating against a country' currency is easier than betting on the implementation of a diverse set of internal adjustment measures, speculative pressure on countries' exchange rates increases the likelihood of a devaluation and, hence, external adjustment. In contrast, international lenders, such as the IMF, often demand a combination of adjustment policies, such as a depreciation of the exchange rate, fiscal consolidation, and significant structural reforms. The willingness of national governments to comply with these demands, however, once more depends on the vulnerability profiles of their electorates. Although the conditionality of international lending provides governments with the opportunity to blame international actors for the pain imposed on their voters, compliance is likely to be lowest in those reform areas, which impose the highest costs on voters and vested interests.

5.4 Conclusion

How do policymakers respond to the emergence of balance-of-payments problems, and how do the distributional consequences of macroeconomic adjustment affect this policy choice? This chapter has shown that the distribution of vulnerabilities in a country's electorate affects both the type of a country's adjustment strategy and the speed with which it is implemented.

When the electorate's vulnerabilities to internal or external adjustment are lower than their vulnerability to the continuation of the status quo, policymakers have incentives to quickly adjust their macroeconomic policies when imbalances emerge, choosing the reform strategy to which voters are least vulnerable.[11] In contrast, when a majority of voters are vulnerable to any type of adjustment, the economic and political costs of adjustment are very high and weigh heavily in the government's decision calculus. Governments initially always have the option not to adjust and to finance the current account deficit instead, and they know that this is in fact the appropriate policy response when the economic shock is only transitory. Governments facing a highly vulnerable electorate also know that not adjusting is likely to yield a significantly higher vote share than any other policy response, although adjusting later will eventually result in higher electoral losses than early adjustment. Governments therefore need to gauge how likely it is that the economic shock is indicative of fundamental macroeconomic problems. When voters are very vulnerable to both types of adjustment and the likelihood that the country is experiencing serious economic problems is small or elections are scheduled for the near future, policymakers are most likely to refrain from implementing serious reforms. The ability to engage in such a strategy is constrained by the international context: Speculative pressure exerted by international financial markets and conditions imposed by international lenders limit a government's ability to postpone adjustment. The funds granted by international lenders, in contrast, increase a government's ability to continue a strategy of limited adjustment even under adverse financial conditions.

Overall, this chapter has argued that when constituents are highly vulnerable to both external and internal adjustment, when the authorities

---

[11] Unless it is very likely that these imbalances are only a transitory phenomenon.

command sufficient funds to intervene in international markets, and when they are confident that they can successfully stave off adjustment until after the next election, distributional concerns can create strong incentives for policymakers to avoid timely adjustment. The discussion also hints at why negotiations with international lenders are often heated and why conditions imposed by these lenders are sometimes not fulfilled.

Voters' individual vulnerabilities to different types of macroeconomic adjustment can thus have far-reaching consequences for national policy decisions about the timing and the type of macroeconomic adjustment governments implement. To assess the empirical relevance of these predictions, the next two chapters present case studies of such decisions taken by governments that faced two of the most prominent global financial crises in recent times: the Asian financial crisis of 1997–8 and the global financial crisis of 2008–10.

These two sets of crises constitute interesting cases for analysis for a number of reasons. First, they represent the two most serious global financial crises of recent times. Both crises swept throughout the world and caused serious financial and economic disruptions around the globe, and observers have pointed out that they exhibit important parallels (e.g., Aslund 2010). Comparing these crises, both in terms of their similarities and differences with respect to voter vulnerabilities and policymakers' responses to these crises, should help us gain a better understanding of the mechanics of these crises.

The two crises are particularly suited for such an analysis because governments implemented very different macroeconomic policies when balance-of-payments problems and speculative pressure on their currencies emerged, both with regard to the type of adjustment strategies and with regard to the speed with which policymakers chose to implement them. Whereas some countries such as Taiwan or Poland chose to rely predominantly on rapid exchange-rate adjustment, other countries such as Hong Kong or Latvia opted for internal adjustment and maintained exchange-rate stability. Moreover, the countries affected by these crises also differed with regard to the speed with which serious adjustment was implemented. Whereas some countries such as Taiwan or Estonia reacted quickly when pressures first emerged, other countries such as Thailand or Romania initially delayed their decision to adjust. This book has argued that such differences should be associated with different overall vulnerability profiles of these countries' electorates and with differences in electoral calendars. The variation in national policy responses to these crises thus presents a good testing ground for this argument.

Finally, both sets of crises share important similarities, but also exhibit some theoretically interesting differences. The cases are similar to the extent that in all countries studied, governments had to devise their macroeconomic policies amid bearish global market conditions and under pressure and scrutiny from international financial markets. Moreover, all of these countries are economically open economies, which enabled domestic economic actors to accumulate foreign-currency denominated positions in their balance sheets. Finally, although the level of democracy differs among these countries, all of them held elections at regular intervals and displayed comparable levels of civil liberties, thus enabling their citizens as well as interest groups to voice concern and to express their support for, or opposition to, certain adjustment strategies at the ballot box. However, the crises also differ significantly not only with regard to their cultural background but also with regard to one aspect that is important to the theoretical argument in this book. Whereas the countries studied in the context of the Asian financial crisis represent cases in which the private sector – banks and firms – had accumulated substantial amounts of foreign-currency denominated debt, the Eastern European countries studied in the context of the recent global financial and economic crisis represent cases in which not only the corporate and banking sector but also large numbers of individual voters had built up such debts. The Asian countries therefore constitute cases in which voters were mostly indirectly exposed to currency mismatches accumulated by firms and banks, whereas the European cases include countries in which voters were both directly and indirectly vulnerable to exchange-rate adjustments. The case studies of these two crises therefore complement each other in examining the importance of both types of voter vulnerabilities on policymakers' decisions.

Overall, the next two chapters will present evidence in favor of this chapter's argument that differences in the vulnerability profiles of national electorates can lead to very different policy responses to speculative pressure in countries affected by balance-of-payments crises.

SIX

Adjustment in the Asian Financial Crisis

The Asian financial crisis swept through Asia and several other countries, such as Russia and Brazil, in 1997 and 1998. The crisis began in Thailand, where the authorities floated their currency in July 1997 amid severe speculation against the country's currency, and then spread across the region. It almost immediately affected Malaysia, the Philippines, and Indonesia, whose currencies depreciated considerably in the wake of the crisis. Just as these currencies began to stabilize, however, a second wave of the crisis began to affect Taiwan, South Korea, Hong Kong, Singapore, and even as distant a country as Brazil. One of the main symptoms of the crisis in all of these countries was strong speculative pressure on national exchange rates. However, not all of these countries responded with an exchange-rate adjustment, and even among those countries that did depreciate, the speed with which this decision was taken varied widely. Different governments implemented very different macroeconomic policies when balance-of-payments problems and speculative pressures on their currencies emerged, both with regard to the type of adjustment strategies and with regard to the speed with which these were implemented.

Although much has been written about the causes of the currency and financial crises that swept through the region as the Asian financial crisis unfolded,[1] a related and equally interesting question is why the governments of the affected countries reacted so differently in response to the balance-of-payments pressures generated by the crisis. The previous chapter argued that voters' vulnerability profiles and electoral calendars play

This chapter is based on material also covered in Walter (2008).

[1] See for example, Furman and Stiglitz (1998), Radelet and Sachs (1998), Corsetti et al. (1999), Haggard (2000), Noble and Ravenhill (2000), Athukorala and Warr (2002), Willett et al. (2005), Satyanath (2006), and Pepinsky (2009).

an important role in this respect. It suggested that in situations in which a majority of constituents are more vulnerable to exchange-rate changes, internal adjustment becomes more likely, whereas a higher vulnerability to a tightening of domestic monetary and fiscal conditions as well as structural reform make adjustment via changes in the exchange rate more likely. Moreover, it argued that the distributional consequences of adjustment can create strong incentives for policymakers to delay any adjustment and to finance the balance-of-payments deficit instead. Elections can increase this incentive to delay adjustment in these situations, unless the probability is high enough that the efforts to avoid adjustment will break down before the next election has taken place.

To investigate to what extent this argument can explain the variation in crisis responses among countries affected by the Asian financial crisis, I examine voters' direct and indirect vulnerabilities to different strategies and governments' policy responses in four countries: Hong Kong, South Korea, Taiwan, and Thailand. These countries responded very differently to the speculative pressure they experienced on international markets, both with regard to the type of adjustment strategies and with regard to the speed with which these strategies were implemented. Whereas Taiwan, and after some delay South Korea and Thailand, relied predominantly on exchange-rate adjustment, Hong Kong opted for internal adjustment and kept its exchange rate stable. Moreover, Taiwan and Hong Kong reacted very quickly when pressures first emerged, whereas South Korea and Thailand substantially delayed their decision to adjust and subsequently experienced quite drastic financial and economic turmoil as their currencies collapsed.

These different policy responses present a series of puzzles: What explains the different degrees to which the authorities relied on internal or external adjustment and sterilized reserve sales? Why, despite a high level of foreign-currency reserves in both countries, did Taiwan choose to let its currency depreciate whereas Hong Kong chose to defend? Why were the authorities in Thailand and Korea willing to spend almost all their reserves in a desperate attempt to stabilize their exchange rates while at the same time strenuously resisting a significant increase in interest rates?

Despite these differences in policy responses, the countries also share a number of commonalities, which make them suitable candidates for comparison. First, all policymakers acted in the same context of a global financial crisis. Second, the authorities in all four countries had experience with intervening in the foreign exchange market and hence knew about the option of delaying adjustment through foreign reserves sales. Third, all four countries were export oriented and had begun liberalizing their capital accounts, allowing domestic economic actors to engage on international markets. Finally, all of these countries held elections at regular intervals and displayed comparable levels of civil liberties. The selected cases thus maximize variation in the type and speed of adjustment strategies implemented by the governments in these countries, while simultaneously allowing me to account for alternative explanations by holding these control variables constant.[2]

The qualitative case studies in this chapter are based on two main sources of information. First, they draw on thirty semi-structured expert interviews with central bankers, government officials, IMF staff, and academics, who had detailed knowledge about the vulnerabilities and preferences of voters, firms, and interest groups in these countries.[3] The second source of information consists of secondary literature, statistics, newspaper sources, and official documents, such as central bank and government publications and material from the archives of the IMF and the German Bundesbank.[4] The breadth of sources consulted allows me to compare the distribution of vulnerabilities in the four Asian countries and examine how these vulnerabilities influenced policymakers' decisions about the speed and type of adjustment to the speculative pressure that emerged in the context of the Asian financial crisis of 1997–8. As such, the analysis helps us to evaluate the usefulness of the theoretical argument proposed in this book.

The case studies show that the variation in policymakers' willingness to adjust to emerging pressure on their currencies in the four countries can indeed be traced back to differences in distributional concerns and the election cycle. In Taiwan, the low vulnerability of most Taiwanese voters to external adjustment and high vulnerability to domestic economic contraction, coupled with an absence of upcoming elections, allowed policymakers to let the currency depreciate early on. As a result, the country emerged as one of the countries least affected by the Asian financial crisis. In Hong Kong the central importance of exchange-rate stability trumped the electorate's vulnerability to interest-rate increases, allowing policymakers to

---

[2] Several other Asian crisis cases were not chosen because certain features made them unsuitable candidates for comparison. For example, Indonesia was excluded because of its authoritarian political regime and Malaysia because of its unorthodox strategy of imposing capital controls.

[3] Interviews took place between February and April 2006. Although the interviewed experts are not personally identified in the text to preserve their anonymity, their names and titles are listed in the appendix.

[4] Most of the information collected in the Bundesbank archive is confidential. The information was used to validate the information provided by interviewees and publicly available sources but is not cited directly.

quickly impose the painful consequences of internal adjustment, especially monetary tightening. In contrast to these two cases in which adjustment was implemented relatively rapidly, in Thailand and Korea large segments of the electorate exhibited high vulnerabilities to both depreciation and internal adjustment. Faced with demands to neither adjust internally nor externally in addition to upcoming elections, the authorities in both countries initially tried to stabilize the currency through the sterilized sale of enormous sums of foreign-currency reserves. When this strategy failed, both countries ultimately implemented a policy mix that relied predominantly on external adjustment in the form of major currency crashes. Overall, the case studies demonstrate that careful attention to the distribution of direct and indirect vulnerabilities of a country's electorate to different types of macroeconomic adjustment, as well as the electoral calendar, lead to a better understanding of how and when policymakers adjust macroeconomic policies in response to balance-of-payments problems.

6.1 Thailand: Delayed Adjustment and Exchange-Rate Crash

The Thai crisis represents a classic case of delayed external adjustment. The argument developed in this book posits that this should typically be the outcome in countries where a majority of voters is highly vulnerable to both external and internal adjustment. This section first reviews how the Thai authorities responded to the balance-of-payments problems that emerged in 1996 and then investigates the vulnerability profile of the Thai electorate. In a final step, the chapter examines whether and how policymakers took these vulnerabilities into account when crafting their policy response.

6.1.1 Thailand's Policy Response to the Asian Financial Crisis

Thailand had experienced high economic growth after it had begun to open up its economy to international trade in the 1980s. Growth was further fueled by capital account liberalization, which allowed large sums of foreign capital to pour into the country. The exchange rate was pegged to the U.S. dollar and provided stability, and the growing economy offered many business opportunities. Figure 6.1 presents the developments in Thailand's economy graphically. It shows how the baht–U.S. dollar exchange rate (black line) and the nominal interest rate (money market rate, grey line) evolved between the years 1990 and 2000. In the years preceding the crisis, the exchange rate remained stable, whereas the nominal

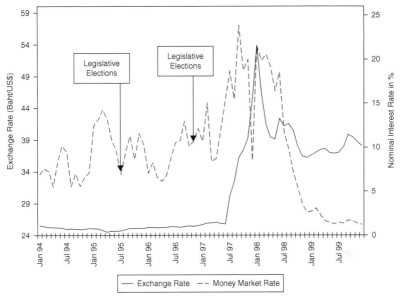

Figure 6.1. Exchange-rate and interest-rate developments in Thailand, 1994–1999.
Source: International Financial Statistics (IMF 2004)

interest rate fluctuated between 2.4 and 16.3 percent. Foreign reserves increased steadily during this time, a development that resulted from sizeable capital inflows.

Despite these positive developments, the economic situation in Thailand began to deteriorate in the mid-1990s. In the years leading up to the crisis, the current account deficit became persistent and grew substantially. It more than doubled in absolute terms, and in relative terms increased from −5.1 percent of GDP to −7.9 percent of GDP between 1993 and 1996 (IMF 1998d: 61). This development was accompanied by additional problems, such as a high external debt burden, a boom (and bubble) in the property sector, and serious weaknesses in the Thai financial system.

As markets became increasingly aware of these developments, speculative pressure emerged in the summer of 1996 on the long-standing peg of the Thai currency, the Thai baht, which had been pegged to the U.S. dollar at the same rate since 1984.[5] Rather than addressing the balance-of-payments problems in a determined manner, however, no serious policy adjustments were implemented. Although nominal interest rates were moderately

[5]   More precisely, the exchange rate was pegged to a basket of currencies, which was heavily
    dominated by the U.S. dollar.

increased in the summer and early fall of 1996,[6] they were substantially cut in spring 1997 (see Figure 6.1). Fiscal policy was somewhat expansionary and hence not suited to limiting the balance-of-payments problems (IMF 2000b: 57). Instead, the authorities began to heavily intervene in the foreign exchange market (Berg 1999: 19). For this purpose, the Bank of Thailand (BOT) – Thailand's central bank – engaged in significant (and mostly unreported) forward sales on the foreign exchange market beginning in October 1996 and introduced some capital controls designed to deter foreign speculators. These actions led to a depletion of foreign-currency reserves. Statistics from the Thai Central Bank indicate that approximately 90 percent of all foreign reserves had been turned into forward obligations by June 1997 (Nukul Commission 1998: 68).

However, Thailand faced fundamental balance-of-payments problems, manifesting themselves as a slowdown in export competitiveness, increased trade competition within the region, and a widening current account deficit, which could not be solved by simply selling foreign reserves but ultimately required that macroeconomic policy be adjusted either internally or externally. Nonetheless, even when speculative pressure escalated in May 1997, the authorities consciously continued not to implement any significant reforms but instead sold virtually all of their reserves in a desperate attempt to avoid a currency crash (Nukul Commission 1998: 80f.).[7] When reserves were exhausted, however, Thailand's authorities were forced to adjust: On July 2, 1997, they chose to float the currency and hence allowed the economy to adjust externally. As a result, the baht plummeted, losing over 50 percent of its value over the course of the following months (as the steep increase in the exchange-rate line in Figure 6.1 indicates) and calmed down only in mid-1998. Interest rates also increased substantially in late June during the last days of the defense and remained high as the IMF prescribed monetary and fiscal tightening as one of the conditions for its support program.

In sum, Thailand thus delayed adjustment as long as possible and then predominantly adjusted externally. Although the authorities tried to avoid internal adjustment, however, the IMF imposed conditions on the country, which eventually forced them to implement painful contractionary monetary and fiscal policies as well.

---

[6] Some studies even suggest that real interest rates did not consistently increase at all (e.g., Goldfajn and Baig 1998).

[7] The authorities imposed some capital controls for offshore market transactions, which led to an increase in offshore interest rates but allowed domestic interest rates to remain stable.

6.1.2 The Distribution of Vulnerabilities in Thailand

Why did Thai policymakers wait so long to adjust their macroeconomic policies? Why were they so reluctant to abandon the pegged exchange rate, and why were they even more reluctant to raise interest rates or tighten fiscal policy? The argument advanced in this book suggests that the vulnerabilities of Thai voters should have influenced these policy stances. The next section therefore examines the direct and indirect vulnerabilities of the Thai electorate to external and internal adjustment.

6.1.2.1 Vulnerability to External Adjustment

The first part of the book argued that external adjustment – that is a depreciation or devaluation of the national currency – can affect voters both directly and indirectly. Thai voters were no exception. They were directly vulnerable to changes in the exchange rate in terms of their purchasing power and, to a lesser extent, their balance sheets and indirectly vulnerable to the effects of a devaluation on their employers and general economic conditions.

The direct exposure of Thailand's voters to external adjustment was relatively limited. Because many Thai consumers were buying goods produced abroad, as the pegged and overvalued exchange rate had kept import prices stable and made imports relatively cheap, a devaluation of the baht was certain to reduce the purchasing power of Thai voters. However, the vulnerability of voters' balance sheets to external adjustment was fairly low because they had not borrowed heavily in foreign currency. Changes in the exchange rate therefore were likely to have little direct effects on their personal finances.

In contrast, voters' indirect vulnerabilities to external adjustment were substantial. In 1997, Thailand's industry was mostly capital intensive. The majority of exporters were producers of industrial goods, who imported almost half of the raw materials and other inputs.[8] They were hence vulnerable to devaluation because the increased prices of tradable inputs were likely to offset the competitiveness effects of a devaluation for their final products on world markets. Industries that produced highly price-sensitive products such as textiles, which had provided the growth impetus for many years but now faced increasing competition from Thailand's neighboring countries, were particularly vulnerable to higher input prices. Moreover, domestic market-oriented businesses were even more vulnerable to depreciation, because they

---

[8]   *Bangkok Post*, 17 February 1997 and 11 April 1997, and interview 24.

would face increased import prices, such as higher oil prices, without the benefit of an increased price competitiveness of their products (Hall 2005: 70). The only production sector that could hope to benefit from a devaluation was agricultural exporters, because these businesses only used a small portion of imported inputs. Nonetheless, for the average Thai business, a devaluation threatened to cause more harm than help. The Thai Banker's Association chairman Olarn Chaipravat therefore repeatedly warned that a devaluation might hurt rather than help most exporters.[9]

The effects of a potential devaluation on the balance sheets of Thai businesses caused even more concern than the relative price effects. The liberalization of Thailand's capital account in the early 1990s had led to considerable foreign capital inflows. Given the long-standing stability of the exchange rate, Thai banks and especially finance companies had borrowed substantially in foreign currency and re-lent these funds on the domestic market, taking advantage of the interest differential between international and domestic markets (Tsurimi 2000). This practice resulted in severe currency mismatches in the financial sector's balance sheets in which liabilities denominated in foreign currency were matched with assets denominated in domestic currency. Most vulnerable were the finance companies, which had borrowed abroad to channel these funds into unprofitable investments in the faltering domestic property sector. According to an IMF official, for them the stability of the baht was a "life or death issue," because a devaluation would have capsized their business model.[10] Big companies also borrowed substantially in foreign exchange and often did not hedge, making them highly vulnerable to external adjustment, although exporters with foreign-currency liabilities were to some extent "naturally hedged" through their export earnings.[11] Private sector short-term external debt amounted to almost US$38 billion in 1996 (IMF 1998d: 78), and foreign loans amounted to half of GDP (50.14%) in 1996 (Nukul Commission 1998: 19).

As a result, a minority of Thai voters – those working for banks, finance companies, or large corporate firms – exhibited a high employment-specific vulnerability to external adjustment. In addition, virtually all voters were very exposed to a second source of indirect vulnerability to depreciation. As financial intermediaries play an exceptionally important role in every

---

[9] *Bangkok Post*, 17 March 1997 and 2 July 1997.
[10] Interview 29.
[11] Interviews 24 and 29. In a survey of 1,200 Thai firms, Dollar and Hallward-Driemeier (2000) found that only 19% of Thai firms with substantial foreign-currency denominated debt had hedged some of their debt. Tsurimi (2000) likewise reports that more than 80% of the short-term foreign loans were said to be unhedged.

economy, the fact that these institutions were highly vulnerable to external adjustment consequently made virtually all Thai voters indirectly vulnerable to the adverse economic effects a devaluation would have on the financial sector, because it was likely that such an adjustment would result in a major financial crisis, with destructive consequences on the economy at large.

In sum, the Thai electorate exhibited a moderate direct vulnerability to external adjustment but was highly vulnerable to it in indirect terms. Some individuals, such as bankers or those highly involved in finance companies, were very vulnerable. Others, such as farmers, were less exposed to external adjustment. However, the general economic risks associated with a potential devaluation of the baht on aggregate economic activity meant that on balance, external adjustment would have serious adverse consequences for all voters.

6.1.2.2 Vulnerability to Internal Adjustment

Thai voters also had significant direct and indirect vulnerabilities to the monetary tightening and fiscal contraction associated with internal adjustment. Many Thai had borrowed money in baht, their domestic currency, mainly for mortgages used to finance housing. Private households were also saving money, most of it in domestic currency and invested in commercial banks, finance companies, the government's saving banks, and savings cooperatives (Kawai and Takayasu 1999: 38f.). Every Thai voter with savings or loans in the country's financial system hence had a direct interest in the interest rate, with net savers preferring higher rates and net borrowers, lower rates. Overall, however, this direct vulnerability to changes in monetary policy was not higher than in other countries, although it varied widely among the electorate. Voters' direct vulnerabilities to fiscal tightening were similarly moderate, because many of them did not rely heavily on transfers from the state, although they could always be hurt by increases in direct taxes such as the income or value-added tax. For example, in February 1997 the authorities discussed proposals to raise excise taxes on imported "luxury goods deemed unnecessary for daily life, including liquor, tobacco products, passenger vehicles and cosmetics."[12] These plans threatened to directly hurt the consumers of such products, most notably voters from the upper middle and upper class (and were subsequently discarded).

The indirect vulnerability of Thai voters to internal adjustment once more far outweighed their direct vulnerability to this adjustment strategy, particularly with regard to monetary tightening. Even though foreign investment in

---

[12] *Bangkok Post*, 4 February 1997.

Thailand was significant, the large majority of Thai firms still borrowed only in baht – but on an extensive scale (Dollar and Hallward-Driemeier 2000). With the ratio of private loans to GDP standing at 147 percent at the end of 1996, the Thai corporate sector was highly leveraged, making balance sheets very vulnerable to interest-rate increases (IMF 1998e). In fact, an IMF official concluded in retrospect that "the corporate sector would have been much more hit by an interest-rate shock than an exchange-rate shock."[13] This also posed problems for the financial sector, which feared that their outstanding loans might not be paid back if monetary policy was tightened. Monetary tightening was a particularly worrisome prospect for the finance companies, which not only had borrowed substantially in foreign currency but had also invested large portions of these funds in the once-booming property sector, which by 1997 had created vast amounts of empty property, estimated at 350,000 empty units in Bangkok and 850,000 nationwide.[14] Real estate firms, which were no longer able to find buyers for their property, faced significant problems to repay their debt, and these problems were apt to increase the higher interest rates were raised. Because this development occurred in a very lax context of financial regulation (Desai 2003; Satyanath 2006), it is not surprising that the ratio of nonperforming loans increased significantly, creating serious problems for many finance companies and banks, many of which would eventually go bankrupt.

Thai voters employed in the corporate and financial sector thus faced significant employer-specific risks. Moreover, the problems in the financial sector were of great concern to those voters who had invested money in the domestic financial system and therefore had much to loose from a banking and financial crisis, which threatened to eliminate their savings. More generally, because such crises tend to seriously depress economic growth, all voters were vulnerable to adverse developments in the increasingly fragile financial sector and the economy more generally. Internal adjustment in the form of fiscal tightening (such as plans not to invest in big infrastructure projects) equally implied a slowdown of economic activity, once more hurting the average Thai voter indirectly.

6.1.2.3 The Vulnerability Profile of the Thai Electorate

The discussion of Thai voters' vulnerabilities to external and internal adjustment has shown that when balance-of-payments pressures emerged in 1996, Thai voters were vulnerable to both external and internal adjustment.

---

[13] Interview 8.
[14] *The Economist*, 1 February 1997.

Although some individuals, particularly wealthy people with large property assets, significant stock market positions, or sizable outstanding loans denominated in foreign exchange, exhibited substantial direct vulnerabilities (Overholt 1999: 1024), the majority of Thais was predominantly indirectly vulnerable to macroeconomic adjustment in terms of their incomes and jobs. Despite this indirect nature, however, these vulnerabilities were substantial. The high exposure of Thai corporations and the financial sector to foreign-currency denominated and mismatched loans implied that external adjustment would cause many bankruptcies and a severe recession. Similarly, the high leverage of Thai businesses and the fragility of the financial sector meant that interest-rate increases would vastly increase the number of borrowers not able to repay their loans. This threatened to cause a financial crisis and a severe recession. Because more individuals and firms were vulnerable to interest-rate increases than a devaluation of the currency, this recession was likely to be even deeper than one caused by devaluation. Nonetheless, the overall vulnerability of the average Thai voter was high with regard to both types of adjustment. As discussed in Chapter 2, such a vulnerability profile should result in a strong preference for a continued financing of the adjustment rather than any serious adjustment of macroeconomic policies.

6.1.3 How Vulnerabilities to Adjustment Influenced Policy Choices in Thailand

Did this distribution of vulnerabilities affect actual policy choices in Thailand? The evidence suggests that Thai policymakers gave much thought to both the potential effects of a devaluation of the exchange rate and the effects of a tightening of monetary and fiscal policy. Highly aware of the fact that both types of adjustment would be very painful, they opted for the third option – financing of the deficit through sterilized reserve sales – as long as possible. Only when they had lost the option to further delay adjustment because they had run out of reserves did the authorities decide to adjust. In light of the somewhat higher vulnerability to internal adjustment, they then opted for external adjustment and let the currency float on July 2, 1997.

The question of whether the Thai exchange rate should be adjusted had emerged long before 1996, when the baht first came under speculative pressure. The IMF had raised the issue of introducing a more flexible exchange-rate arrangement with Thai officials as early as 1994 (IMF 1994). However, the Thai authorities argued that the stability of the exchange rate had served the economy well. When the worsening current account deficit led to increasing pressure on the currency in the summer of 1996, the authorities continued to oppose an adjustment of the exchange rate, largely because they feared the consequences such a move would have on relative prices and balance sheets. For example, in February 1997 a BOT official stated that "any policy to devalue the currency would cause more damage to the overall economy than could be offset by the gains expected from improved price competitiveness. Most importantly, devaluation would lead to inflationary pressure and more costly imports. At the same time, the private sector would find it more difficult to service overseas debts."[15] The large foreign debt held by large corporations, banks, and finance companies were of particular concern to Thai officials, because they feared the potentially detrimental effects a devaluation would have on their balance sheets and the private sector (Interviews 26 and 29, Nukul Commission 1998: 99; Overholt 1999: 1015; Hall 2005).

Policymakers were thus acutely aware of the high vulnerabilities of the electorate to these policy choices, especially those originating in the high risks a devaluation involved for Thai banks and finance companies. The financial sector has traditionally been one of the sectors with the greatest political influence and intense lobbying took place.[16] Given these potentially disastrous effects, policymakers were reluctant to adjust externally as long as they saw a chance in addressing the pressure on the baht through reserve sales. At the same time, the authorities were similarly reluctant to further increase interest rates or to cut spending because they feared the consequences for the highly indebted financial sector and the real economy.[17] The authorities did recognize the need to dampen aggregate demand and therefore proposed cuts in public expenditure of about 10 billion baht in February 1997 and moderately tightened monetary policy. However, the high interest rates (high for Thai standards, but low for crisis standards) repeatedly prompted business leaders to call for lower interest rates, calls that were echoed by several politicians, including Finance Minister Amnuay.[18] Fiscal tightening was equally not decisively pursued. After Amnuay had proposed significant budget cuts in early 1997, coalition politics and opposition from business leaders led to a reversal of these efforts to dampen aggregate demand through fiscal policies as a result of which Amnuay resigned on June 19, 1997 (Haggard and MacIntyre 2000:

---

[15] *Bangkok Post*, 19 February 1997.
[16] Interview 26, and Hall (2005).
[17] Interviews 5 and 27.
[18] *Bangkok Post*, 5 January 1997, 19 February 1997, 20 February 1997, 6 April 1997, 10 April 1997, and 25 April 1997.

53). Business leaders particularly emphasized the indirect economic vulnerability of Thai voters. For example, when the government announced spending cuts to tighten fiscal policy in spring 1997, the president of Siam City Bank and former chairman of the Thai Bankers' Association Som Jatusipitak warned that the cuts would increase unemployment in Thailand and therefore pleaded for a reconsideration of these plans.[19]

Overall, Thai policymakers were intensely aware of the pain decisive external or internal policy adjustments would cause the economy, specific groups of influential individuals, and voters more generally. In addition to these distributional incentives to delay adjustment, the fact that the Thai government consisted of a shaky coalition of six parties that threatened to collapse easily further discouraged policymakers from implementing far-reaching reforms that would impose such substantial pain on the electorate. Moreover, in the early phase, the incentives to delay reforms were exacerbated by electoral considerations, because national legislative elections were held in November 1996. Not surprisingly electoral and intra-coalitional politics further delayed action on the budget, the exchange rate, and other adjustment measures (Interview 7, Haggard 2000; Hall 2005: 76).

Given this high vulnerability to any type of adjustment and the politically difficult situation, Thai officials engaged in the third option of fighting against the speculative pressure on their currency with foreign reserve sales. To make sure that firms and voters would not experience any adverse affects from this strategy, the BOT engaged in a dangerous strategy of sterilizing its reserve sales through massive and secret swap transactions. These sales later strongly contributed to the crash of the currency. As the commission set up by the Thai parliament to investigate the causes of the crisis (the so-called Nukul Commission) notes, the explicit purpose of this strategy had been to maintain exchange-rate stability while simultaneously preventing interest rates from skyrocketing (Nukul Commission 1998: 64). In May 1997, when pressure intensified and it became increasingly clear that reserve sales were no viable long-term strategy, the option to stop sterilizing exchange market interventions was discussed but dismissed by policymakers, partly because this would have caused interest rates to rise substantially (Nukul Commission 1998: 78f.). Instead, the authorities decided to impose capital controls for offshore market transactions, which led to rising interest rates in offshore markets but allowed domestic interest rates to remain stable (Nukul Commission 1998: 80f.). In fact, a significant increase in interest rates was never seriously considered. Likewise, attempts to tighten

---

[19] *Bangkok Post*, 22 April 1997.

fiscal policy and to cut spending repeatedly proved politically infeasible. Interest rates were substantially raised only months later, when the IMF mandated these steps in return for its rescue package, even though Thai officials had fiercely argued against this move in the negotiations with the IMF (Blustein 2001).

Adjustment ultimately occurred in July 1997, after the authorities had used up all their foreign reserves and were therefore finally forced to choose between internal and external adjustment. Given that the vulnerability to internal adjustment was deemed even higher than the vulnerability to external adjustment, the authorities opted for the latter strategy and chose to float the baht on July 2, 1997.

6.1.4 Discussion

The Thai case shows how a high vulnerability to any type of macroeconomic adjustment in the electorate can create very strong incentives for policymakers to delay adjustment until it becomes inevitable because the country lacks funds to further finance the deficit. The high foreign-currency mismatches in important economic sectors coupled with the economy's high dependence on imported goods made Thai voters vulnerable to a devaluation of the exchange rate. At the same time, the negative effects an interest-rate increase and spending cuts would have had on growth and employment in Thailand made internal adjustment equally unpopular. As a result, the authorities tried to avoid adjustment through a strategy of selling reserves as long as possible. This fierce defense against speculative pressure cost the country almost all its foreign-currency reserves and in the end proved futile, forcing the authorities to adjust by letting the exchange rate float in July 1997. Thailand's behavior during the Asian financial crisis thus makes it a poster child of the dynamics surrounding delayed adjustment and crisis.

To be sure, distributional and electoral concerns were not the only considerations driving this behavior. The tight links between the business and political elites, or "crony capitalism," and distorted beliefs about the ability to stave off speculation through reserve sales were also important drivers of policymakers' crisis management (Haggard 2000). Many well-connected individuals, including many politicians themselves, were highly vulnerable to both changes in the exchange and the interest rate and hence lobbied intensively against adjustment. For example, many of the country's leading politicians had direct interests in finance and property companies (Overholt 1999; Haggard 2000). At the same time, the Bank of Thailand believed for a long time that its reserve sales would be successful, because they had staved of speculative pressure in this way in the past.[20] In addition, not all policymakers understood the severity of the situation but rather saw the speculation against the baht as a temporary problem.[21] Many policymakers thus underestimated the probability that the speculative pressure was indicative of fundamental problems that would have to be addressed eventually. Moreover, the extent of the reserve operations the BOT engaged in was only known to a few individuals, so that many policymakers learned about the true extent of the problem at a fairly late point in time (Nukul Commission 1998; Blustein 2001).

Nonetheless, the effects of different adjustment strategies on the electorate were an important concern for policymakers. In this respect it is noteworthy that upper- and middle-class voters were more vulnerable to either type of adjustment than poor voters. Because the latter are also those voters who tend to be more politically active and more likely to cast a vote, minimizing their pain was an important concern. It is not surprising that two months after the government decided to float the currency, a survey found that 94 percent of Thais distrusted Prime Minister Chavalit. His government collapsed two months later, paying a high political price for the pain caused by the massive external and internal adjustment imposed on the country by market forces and IMF conditionality.

Overall, the Thai case thus fits well with the prediction that in countries where a majority of voters are highly vulnerable to both external and internal adjustment, adjustment is likely to be delayed until it ends in a politically and economically costly crisis.

6.2 Taiwan: Speedy External Adjustment

The floating of the Thai baht in July 1997 sent shock waves across Asia. Indonesia and Malaysia were the first to be affected and eventually experienced massive depreciations of their currencies. In early fall 1997, another wave of speculative pressure hit previously unaffected countries such as Taiwan, South Korea, and Hong Kong. The authorities in each of these countries responded very differently to this pressure. In Taiwan, policymakers rather rapidly decided to stop intervening and to allow the exchange rate to adjust. This section argues and shows that this decision was influenced by the distribution of vulnerabilities amongst Taiwanese voters, who were on

---

[20] Interview 26.
[21] This is a frequent phenomenon, see Walter and Willett (2012).

average very vulnerable to internal, but much less vulnerable to external, adjustment.

6.2.1 Taiwan's Policy Response to the Asian Financial Crisis

As one of the four "Asian Tiger" economies, Taiwan, the Republic of China, had grown very quickly in the decades preceding the Asian financial crisis. Because exchange-rate stability was seen as one of the prerequisites for the successful performance of the export-oriented economy, the country's exchange rate had been very stable for years, despite an officially flexible exchange-rate regime (see Figure 6.2).[22] This stability was achieved by the central bank routinely intervening in the foreign exchange market with the explicit goal of counteracting exchange-rate fluctuations. This intervention was facilitated by the country's sizeable stock of foreign reserves, which had been built up as part of a comprehensive strategy of the Taiwanese government to prepare the country against serious external shocks, especially with regard to the country's precarious geopolitical situation.[23]

Taiwan's currency, the New Taiwan dollar (NT$), first came under speculative pressure in August 1997. These pressures emerged mainly because the large depreciations in other Asian countries such as Thailand, Indonesia, Malaysia, and the Philippines put competitive pressure on the exports of other Asian countries and because the ongoing crisis had generally increased financial markets' reservations about the viability of Asian currencies. In the case of Taiwan, the pressure thus emerged because markets expected that the crisis in Southeast Asia might lead to a reduction of Taiwanese exports or a depreciation of the Taiwanese currency, rather than because of serious macroeconomic imbalances in Taiwan's economy. In fact, in 1996 Taiwan had recorded a current account surplus of 4.1 percent of GDP (Corsetti, Pesenti, and Roubini 1999: 310), and Taiwan was just recovering from an economic slowdown, which had affected the economy in the early 1990s, when the Asian financial crisis hit in 1997.

Nonetheless, the pressure on the currency was severe and confronted the authorities with a choice between changing their macroeconomic policies to accommodate this pressure and responding to it through interventions on the foreign exchange market. The Taiwanese authorities initially decided

---

[22] Note that for ease of comparison the scales used in all graphs in this chapter are comparable in relative terms.

[23] In particular the conflict with the People's Republic of China. In 1996, Taiwan's foreign reserves were enough to cover 8.7 months of imports (Corsetti et al. 1999: 342).

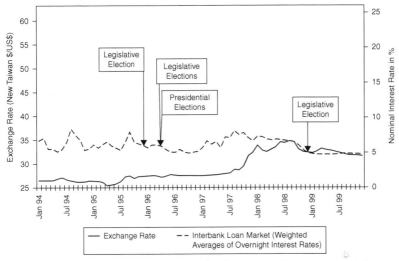

Figure 6.2. Exchange-rate and interest-rate developments in Taiwan, 1994–1999.
Source: Central Bank of China

on the latter option and spent several billion U.S. dollars in foreign reserves in the next two months in an attempt to calm markets through foreign reserve sales. These reserves sales were not fully sterilized and therefore led to some monetary tightening and moderate interest-rate increases, which began to noticeably hurt the economy and particularly the stock market in September 1997. As the pressure on the currency continued, the authorities faced the choice to further raise interest rates despite these negative effects or to stop defending the NT dollar. On October 17, 1997, they chose the latter option and allowed the exchange rate to depreciate. Over the course of the crisis, the NT dollar subsequently lost up to 21 percent of its value,[24] substantially less than other crisis countries such as Thailand, South Korea, the Philippines, or Indonesia. Notably, the decision to allow the exchange rate to adjust in response to market pressure was taken even though at this point the authorities still had the fourth largest foreign-currency reserves fund worldwide at their disposal (IMF 2006) and exchange-market pressure had increased but was not yet particularly severe.

Taiwan thus opted for external adjustment after a brief period of delay. The vulnerability argument predicts this outcome for countries in which a majority of voters are much more vulnerable to internal adjustment than to external adjustment. As we will see, Taiwan's export-oriented economic

[24] Compared to its pre-crisis level in January 1997.

structure in which most voters were not very vulnerable to exchange-rate changes but highly vulnerable to a slowdown in the domestic economy goes a long way toward explaining why the Taiwanese authorities showed such a low tolerance for enduring the pains of an exchange-rate defense.

6.2.2 The Distribution of Vulnerabilities in Taiwan

How were the vulnerabilities to internal and external adjustment distributed in Taiwan? This section investigates the direct and indirect vulnerabilities of the Taiwanese electorate at the eve of the Asian financial crisis.

6.2.2.1 Vulnerability to External Adjustment

When the Asian financial crisis hit the country, Taiwanese voters exhibited relatively low direct and indirect vulnerabilities to external adjustment. Of course, as consumers, a depreciation was bound to lower their purchasing power.[25] However, because imported consumer goods only made up 7.2 percent of households' consumption expenditures in 1996, voters' vulnerabilities to reductions in purchasing power was not too high.[26] This small share of imports in total consumption also reduced the risk that a depreciation would spark an increase in inflation rates, which had been very low in Taiwan anyway. Voters' direct exposures to balance sheet mismatches were even smaller, as Taiwanese households had hardly borrowed in foreign currency at all.

The indirect vulnerability of Taiwanese voters to external adjustment was equally low. Taiwan's economy is highly export oriented, with a technologically advanced industrial sector. In 1996, the year before the crisis hit, 96.2 percent of its exports were high value added and high-tech products in electronics or the IT industry (Euromonitor 1998; Chou 2001: 72). Taiwan's production sector is mainly composed of small- and medium-sized enterprises, which are more export oriented and more flexible than large firms (Yang and Shea 1999: 270). About one-half of Taiwan's exports go to Asia (Chou 2001: 55), and Taiwan's main international competitors are other Asian countries such as South Korea, Japan, or Singapore. This export

---

[25] In effect, Taiwanese imports of consumer goods markedly decreased in the years following the depreciation of the currency, by 12.6% between 1997 and 1998 and another 22.9% between 1998 and 1999 (Council for Economic Planning and Development 2002: table 3b).

[26] Author's calculations, based on data provided in tables 1-b, 11–8, and 3–16b in Council for Economic Planning and Development (2002).

structure meant that the large crisis-induced depreciations of other Asian currencies would hurt Taiwanese exporters if Taiwan kept its exchange rate stable, first, because the loss in purchasing power in these nations reduced their ability to buy Taiwanese products, and second, because the depreciations made Taiwanese products relatively more expensive on other markets (such as the United States or Europe) than the products sold by their Asian competitors. As in Thailand, there were concerns about the effect of a depreciation on the price of imports, particularly the price of oil, but the much higher value-added nature of Taiwanese exports reduced this negative effect and increased the potential benefits of a depreciation.[27] This meant that voters employed in Taiwan's export sector and related industries, who constitute a large proportion of the electorate, would gain, rather than lose, from external adjustment, even if exchange-rate volatility tends to be a disadvantage for international trade (Frieden 1991b). Moreover, the intense export orientation of the Taiwanese economy entailed that all voters would be indirectly affected from any positive or negative developments in the export-oriented sector, the central pillar of the general economy. In terms of competitiveness concerns, vulnerability to depreciation was consequently fairly low.

There was even less reason to worry about banks' and firms' balance sheet vulnerabilities to depreciation. Taiwanese companies had not borrowed substantial amounts in foreign currencies, and very few banks in Taiwan held substantial foreign-currency denominated positions (Yu 1999). Between 1993 and 1996, the external liabilities of Taiwan's private sector as a percentage of GDP only averaged 10.6 percent (Chu 1999: 186), and Taiwanese foreign assets greatly exceeded foreign liabilities in 1997, both in the banking and in the nonbanking sector (Corsetti et al. 1999: 339). With such a constellation, balance sheets would gain, rather than suffer, from a depreciation of the exchange rate. In contrast to the Thai experience, the average Taiwanese balance sheet was therefore not vulnerable to external adjustment.

Overall, the vulnerability of Taiwanese voters to external adjustment was consequently relatively low; in fact it might even have beneficial effects. In addition, Taiwan's current account surplus, low foreign debt, and other sound macroeconomic fundamentals, as well as the fact that the NT dollar had been allowed to depreciate in real terms in the early 1990s (Corsetti et al. 1999: 353), made a currency collapse of the proportions seen in the other Southeast

---

[27] Interviews 10 and 21.

Asian countries unlikely. This further reduced the potential negative effects of a depreciation and lessened the vulnerability to external adjustment.

6.2.2.2 Vulnerability to Internal Adjustment

In contrast to this relatively low vulnerability to external adjustment, the Taiwanese electorate exhibited a substantial vulnerability to internal adjustment. First, voters' balance sheets were much more vulnerable to interest-rate increases than to a depreciation of the exchange rate. A history of excess savings had enabled both individual Taiwanese and companies to borrow predominantly in domestic currency (Hsu 2001). This turned the domestic interest rate into the main determinant of the debt burden for borrowers, who were thus directly and negatively exposed to monetary tightening, although savers would directly benefit from higher interest rates. One in three Taiwanese had also invested in the country's stock market, which was dominated by private domestic investors and remained largely closed to foreign investors (Chu 1999). In 1997, Taiwanese individuals were responsible for 90.7 percent of the trading value on the Taiwanese Stock Exchange (Dunn and Soong 1998). These individuals were vulnerable to internal adjustment, because higher interest rates and a slowdown of economic activity were bound to take its toll on the stock market. Indeed, the Taiwan Stock Exchange's weighted index plunged by about a quarter between the end of August 1997 and mid-October 1997 after monetary conditions had tightened during the central bank's initial defense of the currency against speculative pressure, causing investors heavy losses.[28]

Second, Taiwanese voters faced indirect employer-specific risks if their employers experienced financing problems as a result of rising interest rates and the bearish developments on the Taiwanese stock market. Even though Taiwanese companies were much less leveraged than companies in Thailand or Korea,[29] interest-rate increases were bound to hurt firms that heavily relied on borrowed money and on financing through the capital market. Finally, internal adjustment measures, such as monetary and fiscal tightening, as well as the prospect that the NT dollar would be one of the very few Asian currencies not to depreciate, created the prospect of a

---

[28] The index fell from a peak of 10,116.84 points on 16 August 1997 to 7,618.45 points on 17 October 1997 (*China Post*, 19 October 1997), although this drop was much smaller than the collapse of the stock market in the early 1990s.

[29] In 1997, the average debt-to-equity ratio for listed companies in Taiwan stood at 78% (Perng 1999), with SMEs usually more leveraged than large enterprises (Yang and Shea 1999: 273). See also interviews 8, 10, and 21.

slowdown in the large export sector and were bound to slow down aggregate demand and growth, and all voters were indirectly vulnerable to such a negative development of the general economy.

Overall, the majority of Taiwanese voters were thus quite vulnerable to internal adjustment, both in direct and indirect terms.

6.2.2.3 The Electorate's Vulnerability Profile in Taiwan

Overall, the vulnerability of Taiwanese voters to internal adjustment far exceeded their vulnerability to external adjustment. The low level of vulnerability to external adjustment was based on the domestic focus of the Taiwanese financial market and the economy's strong export orientation. The emphasis on domestic sources of capital meant, however, that Taiwanese voters were more vulnerable to internal adjustment, in particular a monetary tightening and its effects on the country's stock market. Internal adjustment was bound to inflict pain on most Taiwanese both directly and indirectly, because it implied higher interest rates on outstanding debt, lower investments, and a significant loss in the value of the assets many Taiwanese had invested in the local stock market. Taken together, Taiwanese voters were hence much more vulnerable to internal than to external adjustment. The argument laid out in this book suggests that in such a setting, voters should exhibit a low tolerance for internal adjustment and little opposition to external adjustment, facilitating a timely response of exchange-rate adjustment.

6.2.3 How Vulnerabilities to Adjustment Influenced Policy Choices in Taiwan

To what extent did this distribution of vulnerabilities among the Taiwanese electorate shape the authorities' macroeconomic policy responses to the Asian financial crisis?

The public debate about how to respond to speculative pressure indicates that distributional concerns were high on the agenda of Taiwanese policymakers. When pressures first began to emerge, Taiwan's central bank, the Central Bank of China (CBC), initially judged it to be a transitory phenomenon, because models based on purchasing power parity considerations suggested that the NT dollar was not overvalued and because the economy was believed to be in a fundamentally healthy state.[30] High-ranking central bankers, such as CBC governor Sheu Yuan-dong and deputy governor

---

[30] Interview 20.

Hsu Chia-tung, and politicians, including premier Vincent Siew, therefore repeatedly stressed that in face of the speculative pressure on the NT dollar "maintaining financial market stability" was their policy priority.[31] Because this goal was defined as exchange rate, interest rate, and stock market stability, this meant that the authorities planned to confront speculative pressures by not adjusting macroeconomic policies. This decision was facilitated by Taiwan's enormous stock of foreign-currency reserves, which the country had built up in light of its difficult international diplomatic situation, which, among others, precluded an IMF bailout in the event of a financial crisis (Chu 1999: 192).[32] Stock analysts echoed the view that the pressure on the currency reflected a transitory problem and supported the central bank's strategy to defend the NT dollar. They argued that the crisis would not significantly affect the Taiwanese stock market because of its low foreign investor participation and the high level of foreign-currency reserves.[33]

It quickly became clear, however, that these prognoses had been overly optimistic. Despite attempts to sterilize the substantial reserve sales through various measures, monetary conditions tightened. Interest rates began to exceed the CBC's target range of 7 to 7.5 percent by a few tenths, and the CBC stated it was willing to let them rise to 10 percent.[34] Although the CBC was working hard not to tighten monetary policy too much, and although short-term interest rates remained low compared to those seen during other exchange-rate defenses – such as in Hong Kong a few weeks later where interest rates peaked at 280 percent or in Sweden in 1992 where short-term interest rates had climbed to almost 500 percent – these attempts to defend the exchange rate resulted in a credit squeeze. Coupled with the continuous outflow of foreign funds, the tight monetary conditions began to negatively impact the stock market in September 1997, a development to which many Taiwanese voters were quite vulnerable. Not surprisingly, this prompted a heated discussion about potential remedies and further measures that could be implemented to inject liquidity into the system.[35]

When monetary conditions tightened further despite such measures – actual market rates shot up to nearly 20 percent in October[36] – the continued defense of the NT dollar took an increasingly heavy toll on the stock

---

[31] *China Post*, 5 September 1997, 8 September 1997, and 9 October 1997.
[32] Given the diplomatic tensions with the People's Republic of China, Taiwan is not a member of the IMF.
[33] *China Post*, 2 September 1997.
[34] *China Post*, 10 October 1997.
[35] *China Post*, 10 September 1997, 11 September 1997, and 12 September 1997.
[36] *China Post*, 9 October 1997.

market, which lost about a fifth of its value between mid-August and mid -October. When the pressure on the currency intensified in October after Singapore had allowed its currency to depreciate, the public debate therefore increasingly centered on the costs and benefits of the exchange-rate defense, stressing in particular the trade-off between protecting the exchange rate or the stock market.[37] The goal of avoiding external adjustment at all costs was increasingly criticized. For example, on October 8, 1997, the leaders of the nation's major industry and commerce associations publicly called for an easing of the monetary conditions, a call which was echoed by stock buyers.[38] Irrespective the benefits of exchange-rate stability, they were not willing to bear the costs of internal adjustment and increasingly voiced their anger publicly.[39] At the same time, exporters, who were facing demands for price reductions similar to those seen in the export prices of other Southeast Asian crisis countries from their international customers, increasingly called for and lobbied the national parliament for a depreciation and an easing of monetary policy.[40]

How to respond to the macroeconomic problems that arose as a consequence of the Asian financial crisis thus increasingly became a matter of political significance. Opposition legislators demanded the resignation of CBC Governor Sheu because his policy of defending the NT dollar was causing economic problems.[41] The competitiveness of the export sector and the performance of the Taiwanese stock market, with its strong emphasis on individual and domestic investors, were major concerns for policymakers, and these concerns were amplified by the fact that local elections were scheduled for November 1997, a mere month in the future. The resulting political debates did not remain without any consequences and Premier Siew became actively involved in the decision-making process.[42] When additional measures designed to alleviate pressure on the stock market failed, the central bank, in a surprise move, ceased intervening on the foreign exchange market on October 17 and allowed the exchange rate to depreciate "in order to minimize the adverse impact on the real sector and on financial markets" (Chen 2000: 56).

---

[37] Interview 21, *China Post*, 6 October 1997 and 13 October 1997. The depreciation of the Singaporean currency was important because its export structure was very similar to Taiwan's and therefore increased competitive pressures on Taiwan (Corsetti et al. 1999).

[38] *China Post*, 9 October 1997.

[39] *China Post*, 24 October 1997.

[40] *China Post*, 6 October 1997, interview 20.

[41] *China Post*, 24 October 1997.

[42] Interview 22.

After the defense of the NT dollar was abandoned, the stock prices initially slipped further. However, the central bank and the government quickly implemented a number of policy measures to help shore up the stock market and the economy more generally.[43] In addition, the decision in favor of external adjustment allowed the central bank to ease monetary conditions, and several banks cut interest rates a week after the decision to let the exchange rate depreciate.[44] As a consequence of these measures and the improved competitiveness of Taiwanese exports, stock prices recovered in November 1997.[45]

6.2.4 Discussion

The Taiwanese experience shows how a low tolerance for painful domestic economic contraction in combination with a strong export orientation and a low exposure to foreign-currency borrowing can decrease the incentive for policymakers to delay adjustment and can increase the incentive to allow the economy to adjust externally. Even though the Taiwanese authorities acknowledged the benefits of currency stability, the high vulnerability of Taiwanese voters to high interest rates and a poor stock market performance quickly became the more salient concerns. As a result, policymakers abandoned their attempt to stabilize the exchange rate through reserve sales relatively quickly as soon as the issue of exchange-rate stabilization presented itself as a trade-off between exchange-rate stability and a falling stock market and a contraction of the domestic economy. Given that the electorate's vulnerability to internal adjustment by far exceeded its vulnerability to external adjustment and in light of upcoming local elections, the authorities, as predicted by the vulnerability argument, let the exchange rate depreciate after a relatively short defense.

6.3 Hong Kong: Immediate Internal Adjustment

Hong Kong's response to the speculative pressure on its currency that arose in the wake of the Asian financial crisis was rather different. Rather than letting the exchange rate adjust, the authorities vigorously defended the Hong Kong dollar (HK$) and immediately opted for internal adjustment,

---

[43] See, for example, *China Post*, 21 October 1997.
[44] *China Post*, 22 October 1997.
[45] Before falling again starting in April 1998, mostly in response to the general downturn in the region as the Asian financial crisis continued.

mainly through a tightening of monetary conditions. The vulnerability argument suggests that such a behavior should be most likely when a majority of voters are highly vulnerable to external adjustment and much less vulnerable to internal adjustment. To investigate whether Hong Kong's electorate exhibited such a distribution of vulnerabilities in 1997 and 1998, this section first reviews Hong Kong's policy response to the Asian financial crisis, then examines the vulnerability profiles of Hong Kong voters, and finally investigates to which extent distributional considerations influenced the decision-making process during the crisis.

6.3.1 Hong Kong's Policy Response to the Asian Financial Crisis

Hong Kong is one of the most economically open and globalized cities in the world. As Asia's most important financial center with a very open capital market, it is a highly service-oriented economy with most services located in the financial services sector. In 1997, manufacturing accounted for only 7.3 percent of GDP, whereas services made up 84.4 percent of GDP (Hong Kong Industry Department 1999). Hong Kong's currency board, through which the Hong Kong dollar has been pegged to the U.S. dollar at the rate of 7.8 HK$/US$ since 1983, plays a pivotal role for the economy, reducing volatility, uncertainty, and transaction costs.

During the course of the Asian financial crisis, the Hong Kong dollar experienced repeated bouts of speculative pressure. Particularly severe speculative attacks occurred in October 1997, after Taiwan had abandoned its exchange-rate defense, and in June and August 1998. Although these attacks were partly the result of contagion, they were not without a macroeconomic basis: Hong Kong's inflation rate had been higher than the U.S. inflation rate for years, which had led to an exaggerated price level in the economy. This was particularly visible in the property sector, where prices had boomed in the years preceding the crisis (Corsetti et al. 1999), and the trade balance, which had been negative for a number of years (IMF 2000a). The resulting balance-of-payments problems suggested that an eventual adjustment would be necessary and hence encouraged financial market actors to speculate against the currency.

During the entire crisis, the authorities made it clear, however, that exchange-rate stability was their top policy priority and ruled out the option of external adjustment from the start. As a result, the Hong Kong Monetary Authority (HKMA) allowed the mechanism of the currency board to play out fully: The speculative attacks consequently caused a fall in the money supply, which tightened monetary conditions. Interest rates were allowed to rise substantially, with the overnight Hong Kong Interbank Offer Rate HIBOR surging to a peak of 280 percent on October 23, 1997. This internal adjustment mechanism plunged the Hong Kong economy into recession and forced a downward adjustment of prices, especially in the real estate sector and the stock market. The authorities thus declined to resort to sterilized reserve sales, even though this would have been possible economically (but would have been against the rules of the currency board arrangement). The authorities thus implemented internal adjustment measures without any delay, foregoing any external adjustment.

Tight monetary policy constituted the authorities' main policy response to speculative pressure during the entire period of crisis, as Figure 6.3 shows. Only when speculators started to take advantage of the foreseeable effects of high interest rates on the stock market – playing both markets and making huge profits – the authorities intervened heavily in the stock market, although not the exchange rate or money market. This unorthodox move of buying up about one-third of Hong Kong stocks surprised markets and pushed share prices up. This move proved successful in alleviating some of the pain caused by internal adjustment and thus made the strategy of avoiding external adjustment politically feasible and successful – the peg of the Hong Kong dollar to the U.S. dollar still stands at 7.8 HK$/US$ today.

6.3.2 The Distribution of Vulnerabilities in Hong Kong

Why did policymakers in Hong Kong adjust so swiftly when pressures emerged on their currency, and why did they choose to adjust internally, rather than devalue the exchange rate? The vulnerability argument suggests that such action should most likely be taken when a majority of voters is very vulnerable to external adjustment, but much less vulnerable to internal adjustment. This section investigates whether the Hong Kong electorate exhibited such a vulnerability profile in 1997–8.

6.3.2.1 Vulnerability to External Adjustment

As an extremely open economy, the value of the exchange rate has a lot of relevance for Hong Kong's citizens. Any adjustment in the exchange rate therefore strongly affects voters in direct and indirect terms.

Hong Kong imports almost everything, even drinking water. The price of imported goods is therefore important to every individual living in the territory, making residents directly vulnerable to any depreciation-induced price increases in imported goods. During the crisis, Hong Kong people

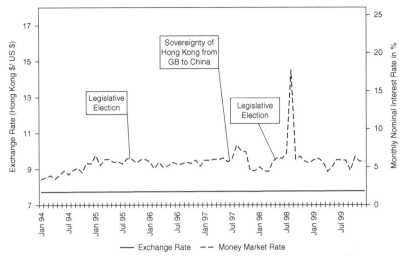

Figure 6.3. Exchange-rate and interest-rate developments in Hong Kong, 1994–1999.
Source: International Financial Statistics (IMF 2004)

were quite aware that their purchasing power was at stake, as they "vividly remembered how they rushed to the supermarkets to buy up everything" during the last major depreciation in 1983.[46] In contrast to voters' high level of vulnerability in terms of purchasing power, their direct exposure to devaluation through their balance sheets was more limited, because few individuals held unmatched foreign-currency loans. A majority of locals held most of their assets in Hong Kong dollars.[47]

In addition to these direct vulnerabilities to a devaluation of the currency, a large majority of Hong Kong voters exhibited a substantial indirect vulnerability to external adjustment. Given the importance of international trade for Hong Kong, maintaining international competitiveness is a central objective. Because the economy is highly service oriented and relies on the city's function as a key trading port, however, the vulnerability of Hong Kong's economy to external adjustment differs from that of the other three economies examined in this chapter. Whereas export-oriented manufacturing firms tend to be sensitive to real exchange-rate fluctuations, the service-oriented sector overall – with a few exceptions such as the tourism industry – is less sensitive to real exchange-rate movements. Instead, as a regional financial center, two alternative factors determine the international competitiveness of Hong Kong's economy: financial stability and

[46] Interview 11.
[47] *South China Morning Post*, 1 July 1997.

competitive domestic prices, such as wages and property prices. In this context, the currency board plays a pivotal role for financial stability in Hong Kong. Abandoning the exchange-rate link would seriously threaten this stability and would thus result in a marked loss, rather than gain, in competitiveness for Hong Kong's service sector, in which more than three-quarters of Hong Kong's working population were employed in 1997 (Hong Kong Industry Department 1999). In addition, it would seriously undermine the attractiveness of Hong Kong stocks and property as investment venues. As the fifth largest foreign exchange market worldwide (Jao 1997) and a major financial and trading center, exchange-rate stability is thus a major business requirement for Hong Kong.[48]

Giving up the currency board and devaluing the Hong Kong dollar would hence have brought competitiveness gains to some sectors, most notably the comparatively small tourism and manufacturing sectors, but would have had detrimental effects on the competitiveness of financial and trading services, the stock market, and the property sector, from which a majority of residents derived their income. Even for individuals working in those sectors for which external adjustment could have beneficial employment-specific effects, external adjustment consequently posed an indirect threat because it promised to lead to a significant downturn in the overall economy. This led to a very high level of indirect vulnerability to external adjustment among Hong Kong voters.[49]

In contrast, the balance sheets of Hong Kong businesses were only moderately vulnerable to a downward adjustment of the exchange rate. Hong Kong's business relations are based on the exchange-rate link, so that both the financial and the real sector had considerable foreign-currency liabilities. However, these were largely matched with foreign-currency assets (HKMA 1998). In late 1997, the IMF (1997: 14) therefore assessed the foreign-currency exposure of the banking sector as modest, because it "maintain[ed] a net positive open foreign currency position."

Nonetheless, the majority of voters in Hong Kong exhibited high levels of vulnerability to external adjustment. This vulnerability stemmed in a smaller part from their direct exposure, particularly in terms of their purchasing power, and more importantly from their very high indirect vulnerabilities, which arose as a consequence of the economy's general

---

[48] Interview 9.

[49] An additional factor was that Hong Kong SAR had just been handed back to China from British colonial rule and the Chinese government had openly declared that it supported the currency board arrangement (Yao 1998). Voters' indirect vulnerabilities were hence compounded by this "political" vulnerability to devaluation.

reliance on exchange-rate stability. This reliance resulted in very high employment-specific vulnerabilities to external adjustment for many voters, especially those employed in the financial services sector. In addition, voters exhibited a broader vulnerability to a general economic downturn and financial crisis, which were likely to engulf the territory in the wake of a depreciation of the currency.

6.3.2.2 Vulnerability to Internal Adjustment

Notwithstanding this high vulnerability to external adjustment, internal adjustment was bound to inflict pain on Hong Kong's electorate as well, both directly and indirectly. Compared to voters in Thailand, Taiwan, and South Korea, however, this vulnerability was less pronounced.

A majority of Hong Kong residents were directly vulnerable to interest-rate increases because they either held loans denominated in domestic currency or had invested in domestic assets. As these domestic loans mostly had variable interest rates (IMF 1997), large interest-rate rises were bound to increase the debt burden of these borrowers. Moreover, a majority of Hong Kong residents had not predominantly invested in regular interest-bearing deposits but rather in other domestic assets, most notably on the local property and the local stock market. Rather than regular interest-bearing investments, such investments do not benefit from an interest-rate increase. To the contrary, as intended by internal adjustment, property and stock prices fall in reaction to a tightening of monetary policy, and this fall tends to be substantial when it follows a boom phase. Hong Kong had seen sizeable asset price increases in the months before the crisis. In the first half of 1997, price increases in the property sector, which had long been one of the main generators of wealth in Hong Kong, had raised concerns about an emerging property bubble (IMF 1998a: 23). In addition, share prices peaked at an all-time high in August 1997. This suggested that the potential fall in housing and stock prices in response to an internal adjustment in terms of monetary tightening would be very painful to all those individuals who had invested in Hong Kong shares or who owned property in the territory. Given the high reliance of Hong Kong residents on such investments, it should come as no surprise that Hong Kong's experience from earlier economic downturns shows that sinking stock and property prices typically lead to a noticeable reduction in local consumers' purchasing power. The IMF (1998a: 19) reports that during the 1994 downturn of the Hong Kong economy, for example, purchases of durable goods and nonessential services in the territory declined considerably. Moreover, the competitiveness problems this strategy was likely to cause for the manufacturing sector and the tourism industry meant that voters employed in these sectors additionally exhibited a high indirect employer-specific vulnerability in terms of lower wages and the risk of job loss.

Voters were also indirectly vulnerable to internal adjustment, because the tightening of monetary policy and an associated bursting of the stock market and property bubbles were likely to lead to a general economic downturn. Certain voters, such as those employed in the construction and retail industries, faced serious employment-specific risks, as internal adjustment threatened their jobs, although most voters were more vulnerable to the general recession that was likely to be caused by internal adjustment. In contrast to many other Asian economies, however, three aspects made Hong Kong's economy much less vulnerable in this regard. First, companies in Hong Kong were less leveraged than their counterparts in the region (Carse 1998) The effects of interest-rate increases were therefore unlikely to disturb corporate balance sheets beyond repair. Second, the banking sector exhibited an unusually high level of capitalization and operated under a prudent and well-developed regulatory regime (Jao 1998; Satyanath 2006). This enabled the financial sector to endure very high interest rates and a serious drop in property and stock prices. Banks' profitabilities would suffer, but their solvency would not be threatened. Finally, the Hong Kong economy exhibits a high degree of flexibility. Its labor market, for example, ranks among the most flexible labor markets worldwide (e.g., Cunat and Melitz 2007, table 1). Because a high degree of flexibility facilitates asset price and wage deflation, internal adjustment was likely to successfully boost Hong Kong's competitiveness (IMF 1997: 10). Moreover, flexibility makes the process of internal adjustment "brutal, but blessedly quick."[50] Taken together, these three factors reduced the vulnerability of Hong Kong's voters to internal adjustment to a moderate level.

Voters' vulnerability to internal adjustment via fiscal retrenchment was less pronounced. Because the authorities stressed their intention to let adjustment work through the currency board mechanism (rather than fiscal policy) and because it had built up significant fiscal reserves in the past, which amounted to about one-third of the territory's GDP in 1997 (IMF 2000a), painful fiscal retrenchment was not a much discussed adjustment strategy in Hong Kong.

---

[50] *The Economist*, 1 November 1997.

6.3.2.3 The Vulnerability Profile of Hong Kong's Electorate

This analysis suggests that overall, the vulnerability of Hong Kong's voters to internal adjustment was lower than their vulnerability to external adjustment. The high dependence of Hong Kong's financial sector on the stability of the exchange-rate link, which provided the foundation of the territory's prosperity, meant that abandoning the currency board in favor of an external adjustment would have caused enormous economic and political costs. Voters were vulnerable to internal adjustment, too, because they had invested in domestic assets such as stocks and residential property in which prices were bound to decline in response to monetary tightening and because it was likely to induce a recession, but this vulnerability was less pronounced given several structural characteristics of the Hong Kong economy. Taken together, this resulted in a significantly higher overall vulnerability of the Hong Kong electorate to external adjustment as compared to internal adjustment.

6.3.3 How Vulnerabilities to Adjustment Influenced Policy Choices in Hong Kong

How did this vulnerability profile of the Hong Kong electorate affect how the authorities responded to the speculative pressure that first emerged in the summer of 1997? The following evidence suggests that they took these vulnerabilities seriously. Given the electorate's immense vulnerability to external adjustment, the first and foremost objective of policymakers in Hong Kong was to stabilize the exchange rate and to follow a path of internal adjustment, most notably in the form of monetary tightening. However, when the pain of internal adjustment grew excessively severe, the authorities devised an unorthodox strategy of stock market intervention to limit the cost of this adjustment strategy.

From the moment that Hong Kong began to experience pressure on its currency in July 1997, policymakers stressed their commitment to the currency board and the stability of the exchange-rate link and warned that this commitment might come at the cost of internal adjustment. For example, chief executive Tung Chee-hwa said that the authorities had "absolutely no intention of any kind to change the currency link. [...] But interest rates may have to go up."[51] This decision was not uncontested: Some business leaders, predominantly from the manufacturing and export-oriented

---

[51] *South China Morning Post*, 23 October 1997.

sectors, warned of the high costs of maintaining the peg.[52] The chairman of the Hong Kong General Chamber of Commerce, James Tien Pei-chun, suggested that the authorities should "rethink the peg," as the local tourism and manufacturing industries were suffering from the currency's strength against its regional rivals.[53] The sharp fall in the export of goods and the number of tourists caused by the currency defense shows that these reservations represented genuine concerns. Voters employed in these sectors were hurt particularly hard, as employment in registered private enterprises fell by 9 percent during the recession (IMF 2000a: 11). In contrast to these calls for external adjustment, however, representatives of the financial industry underlined the importance of the exchange-rate link as the "principal pillar" of Hong Kong's economic stability despite the problems caused by high interest rates.[54] For example, Hong Kong Bank's general manager Chris Langley argued for internal adjustment, saying that because the crisis had been inspired by a loss of competitiveness, there was a need for domestic adjustment, including wage restraint and property price deflation, rather than a need for abandoning the peg.[55]

Given their direct vulnerability to internal adjustment, it is not surprising that many voters had to take significant losses during the course of the crisis. As a result of the decision to adjust prices internally through interest-rate increases, both stock and property prices tumbled. By mid-1998, the Hang Seng index had lost more than half of its value relative to its peak in August 1997, and property prices had declined by an average of 40 percent (Ho 1998; Kalra, Mihaljek, and Duenwald 2000). *The Economist* reported that the fall in residential property prices had "wiped $170 billion from the wealth of Hong Kong's people [...] equivalent to half the deposits in the banking system,"[56] leaving many homeowners with loans bigger than the value of their property. In addition, wages fell and unemployment surged. In light of these numbers, it is not surprising that private consumption declined significantly. On the plus side, falling inflation rates and higher nominal interest rates benefited savers, who were able to enjoy positive real yields on their savings for the first time in nearly thirty years (Jao 1998: 164).

Nonetheless, in light of the electorate's overall vulnerability profile, which made internal adjustment the lesser evil than external adjustment, public

---

[52] *South China Morning Post*, 22 October 1997 and 23 October 1997.
[53] *South China Morning Post*, 23 October 1997.
[54] *South China Morning Post*, 23 October 1997.
[55] *South China Morning Post*, 25 October 1997.
[56] *The Economist*, 6 June 1998.

support for the currency board remained high.[57] Policymakers were hence able to follow through with their strategy of immediate internal adjustment even though legislative elections were held in May 1998. Given the difficulties of pursuing a reserve-financed strategy of delay under the rules of the currency board, these elections presented policymakers who were set on avoiding external adjustment with an additional electoral incentive to implement internal adjustment policies swiftly.

At the same time, however, the authorities were aware of the pain internal adjustment was causing local residents (e.g., Government of the Hong Kong SAR 1998; Yam 1998a). Although the defense of the currency board was widely supported, there was a lot of popular (as well as elite) pressure on the government to alleviate the pain caused by high interest rates (Lim 1999). In this regard, the Hong Kong government was in a more comfortable position than most other Asian governments because it had a large fund of fiscal reserves at its disposal. When yet another round of speculative attacks pounded the currency in the summer of 1998, speculators were simultaneously shorting both Hong Kong dollars and Hong Kong stocks in the knowledge that one of them must be losing in value in response, a behavior that became known as *cash machine* or *double play*.[58] As the authorities believed that this speculation was undertaken "with little regard to the economic fundamentals of Hong Kong and the extent of the market adjustments that [had] already taken place" and therefore presented serious risks of overshooting in the stock market (Yam 1998b), the financial secretary, following recommendations of the HKMA, decided to actively intervene in the stock market. In addition to new restrictions on speculative activity, the government consequently bought up large quantities of local stocks to prop up the stock market. HKMA chief executive Joseph Yam later justified this move by stating that "governments have a role in protecting the level of income and employment of their people" in the face of "manipulative speculative activities" (Yam 1998b). Despite criticism that this move might destroy Hong Kong's reputation as a free market economy,[59] it received widespread public support and successfully quenched speculation (Lim 1999).

The staunch defense of the currency board and the willingness to tolerate very high interest rates, coupled with the unorthodox move of stock market intervention, enabled Hong Kong to adjust successfully while maintaining

---

[57] Interviews 11 and 27.
[58] Interview 10.
[59] Interviews 10 and 11.

currency stability. In addition, by internally adjusting immediately after pressure emerged, the Hong Kong economy regained competitiveness quickly and began to recover in 1999.

6.3.4 Discussion

The case of Hong Kong demonstrates that a high vulnerability to external adjustment coupled with a moderate vulnerability to internal adjustment makes it politically feasible to actively defend a given exchange-rate peg and to accept internal price deflation as a consequence. Both policymakers and voters in Hong Kong were aware of the potentially disastrous consequences of giving up the country's currency board, which served as the foundation for the territory's role as a global financial center but had also resulted in the accumulation of severe vulnerabilities to external adjustment. As a result, the decision to defend the peg by allowing the currency board mechanism to fully play out received widespread support, even though many residents were hard hit by the stock and property market losses that resulted from this policy course. When the pain caused by interest-rate increases became too intense, the authorities found a way to relieve interest-rate pressures without compromising their commitment to the fixed exchange rate by intervening heavily on the stock market. Although this approach is unconventional and was only possible because of Hong Kong's extraordinarily high level of public funds, the stock market intervention is hence consistent with the argument advanced in this book.

6.4 South Korea: Delayed Adjustment and Exchange-Rate Crash

The Asian financial crisis began to cause problems in South Korea in the late summer and early fall of 1997. Similar to the Thai authorities, policymakers in Korea initially sought to offset this pressure through substantial foreign reserves sales and did not implement significant measures designed to foster internal or external adjustment. When speculative pressure intensified at the end of October and the authorities saw their foreign reserves dwindle, however, they abandoned the defense of the won and allowed it to depreciate sharply. Akin to the Thai response, the South Korean reaction to the Asian financial crisis can hence be classified as delayed devaluation. The vulnerability argument predicts that such delay should be most likely in countries where voters exhibit a high vulnerability to both external and internal adjustment. This section shows that the vulnerability profile of the

Korean electorate in 1997 matches this expectation and that, as in Thailand, distributional concerns prompted policymakers to delay an adjustment of macroeconomic policies. It also shows that South Korean officials additionally faced significant electoral challenges.

6.4.1 South Korea's Policy Response to the Asian Financial Crisis

As another one of the Asian Tiger economies, South Korea had wholeheartedly embraced the strategy of export-led growth and therefore placed great emphasis on its export industry with its particular focus on technologically advanced products with a high value added. As a result of this development strategy, the industrial structure in Korea was dominated by a few large, highly diversified, and politically influential conglomerates, the so-called chaebol, which play a leading role in the economy (Beck 1998). Overall, Korea's development strategy had been extraordinarily successful: Within a few decades, South Korea had turned from a developing country to a member of the Organization of Economic Co-operation and Development (OECD), which it joined in 1996.

Despite this remarkable economic success story, macroeconomic conditions in South Korea began to deteriorate in 1995.[60] The country had registered small current account deficits for most of the 1990s, but this deficit widened to 4.8 percent of GDP in 1996. In the same year, export growth fell and the growth rate of industrial production declined noticeably, the stock market dropped, the banking sector was burdened with nonperforming loans, and the Korean stock market price index fell by 26 percent year-on-year (Corsetti et al. 1999). Moreover, in early 1997 a series of corporate scandals and bankruptcies – the most prominent of which was the collapse of the Hanbo Steel Manufacturing Company in January 1997– shook the Korean economy (Kirk 1999). In the twelve months before the onset of the Asian financial crisis in early July 1997, six of the largest thirty chaebols went bankrupt. These problems suggest that the South Korean economy faced fundamental economic problems at the eve of the Asian financial crisis. Nonetheless, the government's response to these problems was only half-hearted. It ultimately did little

---

[60] An important reason for this deterioration was the economic slowdown in the Japanese economy and the related depreciation of the Japanese Yen. Because Japan is one of South Korea's main competitors, this led to a relative decline in Korean products' international competitiveness.

to address the misalignments in the economy (Haggard 2000; Haggard and Mo 2000).[61]

When the Korean won came under increasing speculative pressure in the wake of the spreading Asian financial crisis, the Korean authorities initially continued this course of marginal policy responses rather than implementing substantial internal or external adjustment policies. The exchange rate was allowed to depreciate slightly by an average of 1.1 percent per month between August and October 1997 and nominal (but not necessarily real) interest rates were marginally raised by an average of 0.7 percentage points per month over the same period.[62] More importantly, in a policy response that resembled the Thai strategy, the Korean authorities offset the bulk of speculative pressure through extensive foreign exchange market interventions, spending vast amounts of foreign reserves in the process (Berg 1999).

Even when speculative pressure intensified after the devaluation of the NT dollar and speculative attacks on the HK dollar took place in mid-October 1997, the South Korean authorities were reluctant to significantly adjust macro- or microeconomic policies. They particularly opposed a significant tightening of monetary policy, even if they proposed a new law to tackle financial sector problems. This law failed to pass the legislature, however, and consequently did little to ease speculative pressure on the currency. On November 17, 1997, faced with the increasing risk that the country would run out of reserves soon – some estimates suggest that reserves were almost certain to run out within days (Blustein 2001: 4) – the authorities abandoned their defense of the won. As a result, the currency depreciated sharply and lost about half of its value, as Figure 6.4 illustrates. Only four days later, South Korea announced that it would seek support from the IMF. In the negotiations with the Fund, one of the most contentious issues was the need for internal adjustment, in particular with regard to monetary policy and structural reform. The IMF wanted to see significant

---

[61] It should be noted that many standard macroeconomic indicators, such as inflation rates, monetary growth rates, or government budget deficits, did not flag the emergence of serious macroeconomic imbalances but suggested that the Korean economy was fundamentally healthy (Burnside, Eichenbaum, and Rebelo 2000). Some authors therefore see sudden shifts in market expectations and herding behavior of financial markets as the main cause of the crisis (e.g., Radelet and Sachs 1998). However, much other research suggests that severe structural and policy distortions and weak fundamentals, in combination with fragile investor confidence, played an important role in Korea's economic crisis (e.g., Corsetti et al. 1999).

[62] Some research indicates that real interest rates in Korea (and Thailand) did not considerably increase at all in this period (Goldfajn and Baig 1998).

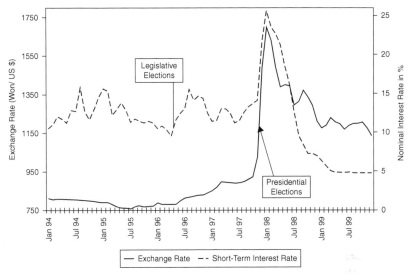

Figure 6.4. Exchange-rate and interest-rate developments in South Korea, 1994–1999.
Source: International Financial Statistics (IMF 2004)

interest rate increases, whereas the Korean officials tenaciously opposed this demand. However, they ultimately had to give in, because the IMF made tight monetary policy one of the conditions for their support package (Blustein 2001). As a result, even though the Korean authorities preferred external adjustment to a mixed adjustment strategy, Korean interest rates were significantly raised in December 1997, fiscal policies were tightened, and structural reforms were begun.

Overall, the Korean case thus shares many characteristics with the Thai experience. As in Thailand, the authorities spent almost all of Korea's foreign-currency reserves in an attempt to defend the pegged exchange rate. As in Thailand, the exchange rate plummeted after it was allowed to depreciate in mid-November 1997. In both countries, the authorities thus initially delayed adjustment and then chose external adjustment, while mostly forgoing internal adjustment (until the IMF required additional internal adjustment as a condition for its financial support). As such, both countries chose the suboptimal strategy of delaying adjustment as long as possible through massive sterilized foreign reserves sales until this strategy became infeasible, forcing the authorities to allow substantial adjustment to take place at a later point in time, which then put their economies in deep distress. As we will see, this resemblance of the two cases is not surprising when one compares the underlying vulnerability structure in both countries: In both Thailand and South Korea voters were highly vulnerable to both a loss in the currency's value and a tightening of monetary policy and other internal adjustment measures.

6.4.2 The Distribution of Vulnerabilities in South Korea

This section analyzes the vulnerability profile of the Korean electorate in the run-up to the Asian financial crisis.

6.4.2.1 Vulnerability to External Adjustment

Korean voters exhibited a modest direct vulnerability to a devaluation of the exchange rate, but were highly exposed to such an adjustment in an indirect way. As consumers, it was clear that devaluation would lead to a reduction in their purchasing power. However, the average Korean consumer did not consume particularly large quantities of imported goods – only 9.7 percent of all imported goods were food and consumer goods for domestic use in 1997 (IMF 1998c). This suggests that Korean voters' direct vulnerabilities to reductions in purchasing power was rather small. With respect to personal balance sheets, their direct exposure to devaluation was even smaller, as only a few Koreans had personally borrowed in foreign currency and held most of their assets and liabilities in domestic currency.

In contrast to their relatively low level of direct vulnerability to external adjustment, Korean voters' indirect vulnerabilities to a downward adjustment of the exchange rate was quite substantial. As in Thailand, this indirect vulnerability originated mainly in the balance sheets of the banking and corporate sector rather than competitiveness concerns. South Korea's economy is highly export oriented with a focus on technologically advanced, high value-added but price-sensitive products.[63] As discussed in Chapter 2, such a production structure typically means that devaluations increase the international competitiveness of export-oriented firms, although many Korean exporters were also sensitive to potential price increases in imported inputs associated with devaluation.[64] In fact, it has been argued that the overvalued exchange rate benefited large corporations and government enterprises and that these actors therefore lobbied for exchange-rate stability (Lee 1998).

---

[63] It thus has a similar export structure as Taiwan, which explains why Taiwan's decision to let its exchange rate depreciate on 17 October 1997 put Korean companies under significant competitive pressure.

[64] Interview 19.

Because almost a quarter of Korean employees worked in the manufacturing sector at the time of the Asian financial crisis (International Currency Review 1998: table 6), a considerable share of Korean voters were indirectly vulnerable to a devaluation in terms of their employers' competitiveness.

Compared with their indirect vulnerability to the effects of a devaluation on corporate and bank balance sheet vulnerabilities, however, these competitiveness effects were small. Korea's financial market liberalization in the 1990s had boosted borrowings from foreign banks. Taking advantage of the lower interest rates abroad and an overvalued exchange rate, Korean banks had borrowed substantially abroad, mostly on a short-term basis and re-lent these funds as won-denominated long-term loans (Blustein 2001; Chung 2004: 32). In 1996, short-term external liabilities of Korea's financial institutions amounted to US$78 billion, or 16 percent of GDP, whereas medium- and long-term external liabilities of financial institutions amounted to US$41.5 billion (IMF 1998c). The resulting currency and term structure mismatches, coupled with a relatively lax regulatory environment, made Korean banks extremely vulnerable to exchange-rate fluctuations (Satyanath 2006). Although the largest fraction of Korean borrowing from foreign banks was channeled through the domestic banking system, the chaebol also directly borrowed substantial amounts of money abroad. In 1996, short-term external liabilities (including trade-related credit) of domestic corporations stood at US$24.7 billion compared with US$17.6 billion in medium- and long-term external liabilities (IMF 1998c). Overall, Korean debt service plus short-term debt were almost twice as high as the country's foreign reserves (Corsetti et al. 1999: 337).[65] Importantly, most of these external liabilities were unhedged and therefore highly susceptible to exchange-rate changes.[66] Given the importance of the banking sector for the economy, the high exposure of Korean banks (and that of some chaebol) posed a major threat to the Korean financial system and the economy as a whole. As such, Korean voters faced not only employment-specific risks but also exhibited a very high vulnerability to the adverse general effects of external adjustment on the South Korean economy.

All in all, Korean voters therefore exhibited a high degree of vulnerability to external adjustment. Even though their direct vulnerability was

---

[65] The precise figure is 243.31% of foreign reserves. Blustein (2001: 130) reports that foreign debt totaled approximately US$115 billion.

[66] Interviews 7 and 17. To some extent the foreign-currency liabilities of export-oriented companies were naturally hedged, but given the amounts in which these companies had typically borrowed, these natural hedges were far from sufficient.

quite limited, their indirect vulnerability to a significant devaluation of the currency was substantial. The potentially disastrous consequences of devaluation for the financial sector and the resulting risks for aggregate economic activity in general meant that external adjustment would impose considerable pain on all Korean voters.

6.4.2.2 Vulnerability to Internal Adjustment

In addition to this high level of vulnerability to external adjustment, Korean voters were also very vulnerable to internal adjustment. As with their vulnerability to exchange-rate changes, the vulnerability to policies fostering internal adjustment was largely indirect and stemmed from the effects of such policies on employers and the general economic climate.

Korean voters' direct vulnerabilities to internal adjustment were limited. With 33 percent of GDP, the savings rate in Korea was very high (Corsetti et al. 1999). Even in the crisis year of 1998, about 69 percent of Koreans were savers (Hong, Sung, and Kim 2002). Of course, Koreans also owed debt, but data from the Korean household panel suggests that their balance sheets were on average quite balanced (Goh, Kang, and Sawada 2005). Given that social safety net programs in Korea were relatively limited before the crisis – public transfers only amounted to 3 percent of household income, and only 18 percent of households received such transfers (mainly pensions) before the crisis (Goh et al. 2005) – voters also were not too vulnerable to possible cuts in welfare programs.

Korean voters' indirect vulnerabilities to adjustment were substantial, however. With regard to employment-specific effects, both voters employed by small- and medium-sized enterprises (SMEs) and by the large chaebol faced significant risks. The liabilities of SMEs, especially in the nontradables sector, were almost entirely denominated in won, making these firms very sensitive to interest-rate increases,[67] but this vulnerability was by far exceeded by the chaebols' vulnerability to monetary tightening. The chaebol exhibited extraordinarily high debt-to-equity ratios, on average exceeding 400 percent for the top 30 chaebol. In the most extreme case, the Jinro chaebol, the debt-to-equity ratio amounted to a staggering 8,598.7 percent (Corsetti et al. 1999: 318). Most of this debt was short-term and denominated in won, making Korean companies extremely vulnerable to interest-rate increases (IMF 1998b). The roots of these high leverage ratios lay in

---

[67] Interviews 4 and 12. The crisis and eventual IMF-mandated interest increases led to many bankruptcies among SMEs (Kwon 2001).

lax financial regulation and close business–bank–chaebol relations. Political influence was pervasive in the Korean banking sector, and top posts were often filled by "de facto political appointees" (Kirk 1999: 123). Implicit government guarantees for corporate debt, direct government involvement in lending, and the expansion of the chaebol into the nonbanking financial sector were characteristic of this relationship and had fueled an investment boom prior to 1997 (Haggard and Mo 2000). As a result, lending decisions were frequently made for political reasons rather than prudent financial calculations. This development had not only significantly increased the indebtedness of Korean corporates but had also reduced loan quality and increased the amount of nonperforming loans. By 1996, 28.3 percent of manufacturing firms reported earnings that were lower than their interest costs (Chung 2004: 39). At the same time, although this organization of the economy was suboptimal, structural reforms intended to change these close ties between politics and large businesses were likely to be very costly politically.

Moreover, the high indebtedness of the corporate sector also affected the Korean economy more generally. The financial difficulties of the chaebol, which began in early 1997, coupled with the low loan quality led to serious concerns about bank solvency, especially as the government seemed increasingly willing to let poorly managed companies fail. Even though banks in theory could pass on higher interest rates to their customers, it was increasingly uncertain whether their borrowers would be able to repay their debt. As such, the high indebtedness of the Korean corporate sector and the high level of exposure among Korean banks to nonperforming loans created strong risks of financial collapse and a major economic crisis.

As a result, Korean voters were highly vulnerable to such a strategy in terms of the adverse employment-specific and general effects, despite their relatively limited direct vulnerabilities to the consequences of internal adjustment. Overall, their vulnerability to internal adjustment can hence be classified as very high.

6.4.2.3 The Vulnerability Profile of the South Korean Electorate

A comparison of the overall vulnerabilities of the Korean electorate to external and internal adjustment shows that voters were highly vulnerable to both types of adjustment. Even though their direct vulnerabilities were limited, their indirect vulnerabilities to the effects of both external and internal adjustment strategies on their employers and the economy as a whole were substantial. The high exposure to mostly unhedged and short-term foreign-currency debt by Korean banks and large chaebol implied that external adjustment was likely to cause a financial crisis and a severe recession. At the same time, however, the exceedingly high leverage of the corporate sector made internal adjustment equally likely to lead to a string of bankruptcies, a financial crisis, and a severe recession. Even though the corporate sector was more vulnerable to an interest-rate shock than an exchange-rate shock, both adjustment strategies were sure to cause major economic disruptions.[68] As in Thailand, Korean voters were hence caught between a rock and a hard place, because any type of adjustment was bound to cause them serious pain. I have argued that such a vulnerability profile should result in a strong preference for no adjustment. This in turn creates strong incentives for policymakers to delay reform, a strategy that can be successfully pursued in the short term by selling foreign-currency reserves.

6.4.3 How Vulnerabilities to Adjustment Influenced Policy Choices in South Korea

How did this vulnerability profile of the Korean electorate affect the macroeconomic policy choices of Korean policymakers during the Asian financial crisis? As in the other three cases discussed in this chapter, the evidence suggests that policymakers were quite aware of the distributional consequences of different policy strategies. As the vulnerabilities of Korean voters were mostly indirect in nature, the governments' considerations mostly focused on the potential effects of different adjustment strategies on the corporate and banking sector and aggregate economic activity. These considerations combined with electoral concerns to significantly affect policymakers' decisions in the run-up and the course of the Asian financial crisis.

When the first warnings about an overexpansion of the economy emerged in 1995, policymakers introduced some half-hearted measures to slow the boom but failed to implement more comprehensive and effective measures (Haggard and Mo 2000). One of the main reasons for this failure was a concern that such contractionary measures would hurt the economy, especially SMEs and their employees, who had not yet fully recovered from the previous economic downturn. Given that the viability of SMEs was a salient issue among the public, the government was unwilling to take strong stabilization measures, especially because elections for the National Assembly were scheduled for April 1996 (Haggard and Mo 2000). Rather than tightening monetary policy, interest rates were lowered in the months preceding these legislative elections (see Figure 6.4). Consistent with my argument,

---

[68] Interview 8.

electoral considerations hence incentivized policymakers to delay early macroeconomic adjustment.

By early 1997, when major corporate bankruptcies put the economic problems high on the political agenda, policymakers grew increasingly concerned about the viability of the corporate sector and the potential consequences a crisis could have on unemployment. Within the administration, there were debates about how the macroeconomic problems could best be addressed. Whereas some bureaucrats believed that a limited devaluation of the won would be beneficial, others opposed this proposal, citing foreign-currency debt and the importance of exchange-rate stability for trading relations as reasons for stabilizing the won.[69] The latter group prevailed, and the exchange rate remained stable until the fall of 1997 (see Figure 6.4).[70] When the pressure on the foreign exchange market began to intensify in the fall of 1997, the authorities were chiefly concerned with the possible impact of a devaluation on foreign liabilities, whereas competitiveness considerations were of "secondary- or third-order importance."[71] The preoccupation with foreign-currency debt became a major issue when it became increasingly difficult to roll over short-term debt denominated in foreign currency, making default a distinct possibility (Blustein 2001).

Nonetheless, even though it was aware of the potentially disastrous consequences of a devaluation, "the Korean government would never have dreamed of raising interest rates" either, because it worried about the corporate sector's high level of indebtedness.[72] This was not surprising because the corporate sector was very vocal about its distress: Vulnerable companies lobbied aggressively for government support (Haggard and MacIntyre 2000), the Federation of Korean Industries – the main representative of the chaebol – called for lower interest rates (Asia Pulse 1997), and banking institutions troubled with bad loans called for aid from the central bank (LG Economic Research Institute 1997). A Bank of Korea (BOK) official

---

[69] Interviews 12, 13, 14, 16, and 19. An additional reason was the concern that a depreciation would let Korean per-capita-GDP fall beyond the US$1,000/capita threshold, which had been a prerequisite for OECD membership that had just been achieved in the previous year (interviews 12 and 16).

[70] To some extent this lack of adjustment, especially in terms of the exchange rate, is surprising, because South Korea officially followed a managed float exchange-rate regime (Ghosh et al. 2003). The actual behavior of the exchange rate suggests, however, that it followed a much more rigid exchange-rate regime in the form of a de facto crawling peg (see Figure 6.4 and Reinhart and Rogoff 2004). See also the discussion in Walter and Willett (2012).

[71] Interview 8.

[72] Interview 17.

recalled that in light of the deteriorating situation, central bankers had been "afraid of the bankruptcies in the corporate sector."[73] As a result, rather than implementing policies that would have encouraged an internal adjustment of macroeconomic conditions, the BOK was willing to continue refinancing banks at a discount rate that was below what was needed to stop the speculative pressure.[74]

Unwilling to let the economy adjust externally through a substantial depreciation of the currency, and equally unwilling to let the economy adjust internally through a tightening of monetary conditions or contractionary fiscal policies, the Korean authorities decided not to adjust at all and to engage in massive sterilized foreign reserve sales instead. Even in November when the situation had deteriorated so much that initial negotiations with the IMF were being conducted, the minister of finance and economy Lim Chang Yuel told the IMF mission that a recession was unthinkable, saying that "the Korean people will not accept growth of less than five percent" (cited in Blustein 2001: 132).

This behavior of Korean officials is consistent with the prediction that in the face of high vulnerabilities of voters to both internal and external adjustment, policymakers are more likely to delay adjustment and to finance the deficit instead. In Korea, this problematic distributional setup was further complicated by a difficult political situation in which the authorities faced a number of problems (Haggard and Mo 2000). First, because of constitutional constraints, the Korean president Kim Young Sam was barred from reelection in the upcoming presidential elections scheduled for December 1997. This severely weakened the president by creating a lame duck status. Second, the ruling party was internally divided because of succession struggles and ultimately chose a candidate, Lee Hoi Chang, who desperately tried to differentiate himself from the president as the crisis progressed. Third, during the fall of 1997 when the crisis intensified and required close cooperation between the government and the central bank, this cooperation was severely hampered by an open conflict between the Ministry of Finance and Economy and the BOK about the creation of a new financial supervisory board.[75]

Finally, and most important in light of my argument, the fact that presidential elections were going to be held on December 18, 1997, itself influenced the incentives of policymakers of how to respond to the mounting

[73] Interview 19.
[74] Interview 5.
[75] Interview 14.

pressure on the Korean currency. As we have seen, the legislative elections of 1996 had provided strong incentives for policymakers to forgo early adjustment. Similarly, the upcoming presidential elections scheduled for the late fall of 1997 played an important role in shaping policymakers' responses to the growing speculative pressure. Both the pending elections and the high level of vulnerability of Korean voters to both external and internal adjustment initially created strong incentives to offset this pressure through foreign reserve sales rather than any substantial policy changes that would lead to painful macroeconomic adjustment. The authorities followed this strategy for several months. In mid-November 1997, however, the balance-of-payments pressures became so strong that they were increasingly difficult to contain through foreign exchange market interventions, especially because foreign reserves were dwindling rapidly. As such, it was increasingly unlikely that a major crash could be avoided until after the elections. As a result, the government decided to abandon the defense of the won on November 17, 1997, about one month before the scheduled date for the presidential election. In response, the currency began to decline rapidly and lost over half of its value over the next two months.

6.4.4 Discussion

Similar to the Thai experience, the Korean case demonstrates how a high vulnerability among the electorate to both policy options for adjustment can lead to delay and ultimately to a severe economic crisis. As in Thailand, the vulnerability of Korean voters was mostly of an indirect nature, resulting from employment-specific and general economic effects of both types of adjustment. The high exposure to foreign-currency denominated debt among Korean banks and the chaebol resulted in a high vulnerability to a devaluation of the currency, whereas the exceedingly high level of indebtedness of the Korean corporate sector meant that interest-rate increases would have devastating consequences as well. As a result, Korean officials delayed adjustment as long as possible and sold the majority of their foreign-currency reserves instead. When this strategy was no longer viable, adjustment became unavoidable. Given the vulnerability profile of the Korean electorate, with high vulnerabilities to both types of adjustment, it was clear that this decision was going to cause voters a lot of pain. As we have seen, their vulnerability to substantial interest-rate increases, fiscal tightening and structural reform nonetheless exceeded their vulnerability to a sizeable depreciation of the currency. As a result, internal adjustment presented an even less attractive option than exchange-rate adjustment. In this situation policymakers opted for a devaluation of the currency.

Because the prolonged defense had almost depleted the country's currency reserves and in light of the substantial foreign liabilities of the Korean private sector, however, the government also began negotiations with the IMF about a support package. These negotiations proved very difficult, because the IMF demanded that the Koreans follow a mixed strategy of both external and internal adjustment – devaluation coupled with sizeable increases in interest rates, cuts in government spending, and structural reforms.[76] Aware of the corporate sector's excessive vulnerability to monetary tightening, Korean officials tenaciously tried to avoid an IMF condition about higher interest rates (Blustein 2001). Given the IMF's insistence on this policy strategy, however, they ultimately had to accept monetary tightening in return for an IMF rescue package.

Korea thus implemented a combination of policies to which the Korean voters were highly vulnerable. Although these policies did lead to a rebalancing of the economy, it caused a lot of pain: As adjustment began to work, imports declined by 22 percent in 1998, whereas exports increased by 13.3 percent. At the same time, many firms went bankrupt, and unemployment more than tripled in comparison to 1996 (Bank of Korea 1999). Private consumption fell by over 10 percent in 1998, especially that of luxury and durable goods, which decreased by about two-thirds (IMF 2003; Goh et al. 2005). Nonperforming loans of banks and merchant banks amounted to 9.6 percent of nominal GDP in December 1997 (Park and Choi 2004: 53), and 14 merchant banks were closed between December 1997 and April 1998 (Berg 1999: 26).

Although the distributional argument can explain the delay and initial choice of adjustment strategy in Korea, the timing of adjustment presents somewhat of a puzzle, because it occurred only one month prior to the presidential elections. Elections usually create incentives to postpone adjustment until after election day. Why then did Korean officials decide to adjust prior to the election? As discussed in Chapter 5, policymakers' incentives to adjust are not only affected by the distributional consequences of adjustment but also by the likelihood that adjustment can be successfully delayed until after the election. The higher the risk that internal or external

---

[76] The IMF has been strongly criticized for this policy path, which deepened the recession and probably imposed more costs than would have been necessary (see for example Stiglitz 2002). For a detailed discussion of the politics surrounding the South Korean IMF package, see Copelovitch (2010b: 262–75).

adjustment will have to occur before the election and that delayed adjustment will be more costly the longer it has been put off, the weaker are the electoral incentives to avoid adjustment. Thus, even when the incumbent government faces a large group of voters vulnerable to adjustment, it can have an incentive to adjust before election day when speculative pressure becomes severe enough. In Korea, the rapidly intensifying pressure in the middle of the election campaign changed policymakers' incentives when it became clear that the country's foreign-currency reserves would not be sufficient to calm markets, so that monetary policy would either have to be significantly tightened or the exchange rate would have to be devalued substantially before the elections took place. Because every additional day of waiting further increased the costs of these two options, this encouraged the authorities to begin the adjustment process despite the upcoming elections.[77]

Not surprisingly, these developments had political consequences. The December 1998 elections were won by the opposition candidate Kim Dae Jung. Moreover, the crisis resulted in deep dissatisfaction of Korean voters with the political elite: In a 1998 survey, 64.8 percent of respondents said they believed that the crisis was rooted in the incompetence of politicians (Hayo 2005). This reinforces the notion that the politics of adjustment can involve substantial political risks for policymakers.

6.5 Conclusion

This book argues that the distributional consequences of macroeconomic adjustment affect both the types of adjustment strategies chosen and the speed with which policymakers respond to balance-of-payments problems. This chapter analyzed how distributional concerns and the timing of elections influenced exchange-rate and monetary policies in four countries affected by the Asian financial crisis of 1997–8: Thailand, Taiwan, Hong Kong, and South Korea. All four countries initially maintained exchange-rate stability when speculative pressure first emerged, but responded very differently when this pressure intensified as a result of the spreading regional crisis. These differences surface both with regard to the types of policies implemented to address the balance-of-payments problems and speculative

---

[77] This decision was further facilitated by the knowledge that the outgoing presidential administration, which was not standing for reelection, could be blamed for this decision. All presidential candidates, including the candidate from the ruling party, blamed the outgoing president for the crisis and demanded similar policy changes to ease the pain of the electorate.

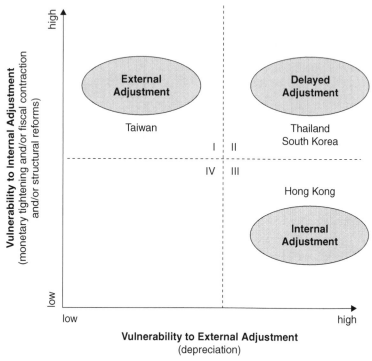

Figure 6.5. Summary of voters' overall vulnerabilities and policy responses.

pressures on local currencies, as well as the speed with which policymakers chose to implement reforms.

The case studies show that the variation in policymakers' willingness to adjust to emerging pressure on their currencies and their choice of adjustment strategies can be traced back to differences in the vulnerability profiles of their electorates. Figure 6.5 summarizes these vulnerability profiles for the four cases under study. In Taiwan, the low vulnerability of most Taiwanese firms and individuals to depreciation and their high exposure to interest-rate increases, coupled with an absence of upcoming elections, allowed policymakers to let the currency depreciate quite quickly. As a result, the country emerged as one of the countries least affected by the Asian financial crisis. In contrast, in Thailand and Korea large segments of the electorate exhibited high vulnerabilities to both devaluation and monetary tightening. Faced with demands to neither adjust internally nor externally, the authorities in both countries tried to stabilize the currency through the sale of enormous sums of foreign-currency reserves. When this strategy failed, policymakers in both countries ultimately implemented a mix of external and internal adjustment. As a result of the delay, the exchange rates crashed however. Finally, in Hong Kong the central importance of exchange-rate stability and the electorate's exceedingly high vulnerability to a devaluation trumped its vulnerability to interest-rate increases, allowing policymakers to impose the painful consequences of internal adjustment.

The case studies demonstrate that attention to the distribution of direct and indirect vulnerabilities of a country's electorate to different types of macroeconomic adjustment, as well as the electoral calendar, can improve our understanding of the politics of adjustment. In particular, they emphasize the relevance of foreign-currency denominated debt in the context of balance-of-payments crises. Vulnerability considerations particularly contribute to the understanding of the tragic cases of the Thai and Korean crises in which the authorities defended the currency for a prolonged period only to subsequently allow it to depreciate substantially – in the process causing their countries to fall into severe economic crises. The chapter hence shows that a correct specification of the relevant distributional consequences of different policy options complements and improves explanations focusing on the macroeconomic, institutional, and international decision-making context that delineate policymakers' abilities to implement different adjustment strategies.

Whereas the case studies in this chapter highlight the importance of indirect vulnerabilities of voters to the effects of government policies on their employers and the economy at large, the next chapter will show that such borrowing can also create substantial direct vulnerabilities in an electorate. It investigates the politics of adjustment during the global financial and economic crisis in eight Eastern European countries and examines policymakers' responses to the pressures caused by this crisis. As we will see, foreign-currency borrowing played an important role in this most recent crisis as well.

6.6 Appendix: List of Interviewees

Caroline Atkinson, Senior Deputy Assistant Secretary for International Monetary and Financial Policy, U.S. Treasury

Paul Blustein, Journalist, *Washington Post*

Jack Boorman, Director, Policy Development and Review Department, IMF

Michael S. F. Chang, Senior Specialist, International Funding Division, Department of Foreign Exchange, The Central Bank of China, Taiwan*

Robert Dekle, Economist, Asia and Pacific Department, IMF

Kokwang Huh, Director, International Department, Bank of Korea

Ho Lok Sang, Director of the Centre for Public Policy Studies, Lingnan University, Hong Kong*

Kang Kyong Sik, Minister of Finance and Economy, Korea

Kim Jung-Sik, Professor of Economics, Yonsei University, Korea*

Donald Kirk, Journalist, Korea

Timothy Lane, Policy Development and Review Department, IMF

Calvin Lin, Professor of Economics, Taichung National Institute of Technology, Taiwan*

James Lister, Director, Office of International Monetary Policy, U.S. Treasury

Min Sang Kee, Professor of Finance, Seoul National University, Korea*

Ekniti Nitithanprapas, Fiscal Policy Office, Ministry of Finance, Thailand*

Oh Jong-Nam, Executive Director, IMF*

Oh Jung-Gun, Deputy Director General, Institute for Monetary & Economic Research, Bank of Korea

Olarn Chaipravat, Chairman of the Thai Bankers' Association, Thailand

David O'Rear, Chief Economist for the Economist Intelligence Unit Asia, Hong Kong

David Robinson, Division Chief for Thailand, Asia and Pacific Department, IMF

Anoop Sing, Deputy Director, Asia and Pacific Department, IMF

Thitithep Sitthiyot, Ministry of Finance, Thailand*

Frank Tsai, Department for Foreign Exchange, Central Bank of China, Taipei, Taiwan

Wanda Tseng, Deputy Director, Asia and Pacific Department, IMF

Ya-Hwei Yang, Director, Center for Economic and Financial Strategies, Chung-Hua Institution for Economic Research, Taiwan*

Eddie Yue, Executive Director, Monetary Management and Infrastructure Department, HKMA, Hong Kong*

Titles were those held during the Asian financial crisis (current titles are denoted by an asterisk). Interview numbers in the text do not correspond to the order of names in this list. Three additional interview partners asked for full anonymity and are therefore not personally identified.

SEVEN

Adjustment in Eastern Europe during the Global Financial Crisis

The global financial and economic crisis, which began with trouble on the U.S. housing market in 2007 and spread throughout the world during the course of 2008, hit the transition countries in Eastern Europe particularly hard (EBRD 2009, 2010; Connolly 2012; Myant and Drahokupil 2012). Most of the economies in the region had boomed in the pre-crisis years. Annual GDP growth rates had averaged 5.7 percent across the region during the years 2000 to 2007 (Connolly 2012: table 1). At the same time, this boom had led to the accumulation of large balance-of-payments imbalances. All new EU member states in Eastern Europe exhibited current account deficits in 2007, most of these countries had experienced credit booms in the years preceding the crisis, and many exchange rates in the region were overvalued. As the crisis spread across the advanced economies, international financial markets became increasingly jittery. As a result, the crisis began to affect emerging markets as well, as a growing awareness of these macroeconomic vulnerabilities led to capital flow reversals and increasing balance-of-payments problems in these countries.

Despite similar macroeconomic problems and bearish conditions on financial markets worldwide, however, governments throughout the transition region responded quite differently to the crisis.[1] Whereas some countries, such as the Baltic states and Bulgaria, implemented far-reaching internal adjustment strategies but kept their currencies stable, other countries, such as Poland, immediately let their exchange rates depreciate without substantially altering more domestically oriented policies. Yet others,

---

[1] This chapter focuses on the first phase of the global financial and economic crisis from its beginning in Eastern Europe in 2008 until the first Greek bailout in May 2010. Financial problems in Eastern Europe intensified again after this date as a consequence of the eurozone crisis. However, because these are ongoing developments at the time of writing, they are not covered in this chapter.

like Hungary or Romania, opted for a mixed adjustment strategy in which domestic economic tightening was coupled with a more moderate adjustment of the exchange rate.

One explanation for this variation in policy responses that immediately comes to mind when looking at these countries is that the pattern of adjustment mirrors differences in these countries' exchange-rate regimes. Table 7.1 shows that those countries that followed very rigid exchange-rate regimes, such as a currency board (Estonia, Lithuania, and Bulgaria), or very tightly pegged exchange rates (Latvia), and at the same time had a clear exit strategy in the form of euro adoption, were the ones to successfully maintain exchange-rate stability and to adjust internally instead. In contrast, countries that had instituted more flexible exchange-rate regimes (such as the Czech Republic, Hungary, Romania, or Poland) allowed their exchange rates to depreciate in response to the balance-of-payments pressures.

Although this explanation certainly carries a lot of weight in explaining Eastern European crisis responses, it remains unsatisfactory in two respects. First of all, even though it can explain why some Eastern European countries chose internal adjustment over external adjustment, it fails to explain the variation in policy responses among countries with flexible exchange-rate regimes. Here some countries (the Czech Republic and Poland) fully relied on external adjustment, whereas others (Hungary and Romania) chose a mixed strategy, which combined elements of external and internal adjustment as well as central bank interventions on the foreign exchange market.

Second, and more importantly, this explanation assumes that fixed exchange rates are irrevocably fixed so that governments following such currency regimes in fact no longer have a choice between adjustment strategies. Yet, past experiences from other crises have shown that when faced with severe balance-of-payments pressures, even countries with seemingly irrevocably fixed exchange rates have nonetheless either considered or actually pursued external adjustment. The experience of Argentina, which abandoned its currency board and significantly devalued its currency amid a serious balance-of-payments crisis in 2001, is probably the best-known example for such a behavior. The most recent example is the experience of Greece and other countries in the eurozone periphery during the eurozone crisis. Here, external adjustment, which in this case would imply an exit from the euro and a reintroduction of a much depreciated national currency, has been seriously discussed as a possible adjustment strategy, especially because the internal adjustment measures required to rebalance these economies are proving increasingly

Table 7.1. *Selected macroeconomic indicators for eight Eastern European countries*

	Internal adjustment				External adjustment		Mixed adjustment	
	Bulgaria	Estonia	Latvia	Lithuania	Czech Republic	Poland	Hungary	Romania
Pre-crisis indicators								
Current account, % of GDP, 2007	−25.2	−15.9	−22.4	−14.4	−4.3	−6.2	−7.3	−13.4
Average real GDP growth, 2000–7 in %	5.5	8.4	8.8	7.5	4.4	4.1	7.6	5.7
Inflation rate 2007	7.6	6.7	10.1	5.8	3.0		7.9	4.9
Real wage growth 2007 in %	19.3	20.2	30.3	21.1	7.23	8.7	2.9	20.9
Credit growth, 2005–7 in %	21.3	14.6	21.0	28.0	14.0	12.0	11.0	31.0
Exchange-rate regime	Currency board	Currency board	Peg (±1% band)	Currency board	Managed float	Floating	Floating	Managed float
Crisis indicators								
Maximum depreciation in %	0	0	1.2	0	20.97	42.58	31.2	21.53
Unemployment rate in % (2007 ⇔ 10)	6.9 ⇔ 10.3	4.7 ⇔ 16.9	6.5 ⇔ 19.8	4.3 ⇔ 17.8	5.3 ⇔ 7.3	9.6 ⇔ 9.6	7.4 ⇔ 11.2	6.4 ⇔ 7.3
Real GDP growth rate, 2009 in %	−5.5	−14.3	−17.7	−14.8	−4.7	1.6	−6.8	−6.6
Real wage growth 2009 in %	14.4	−2.83	−4.67	−3.52	3.37	4.91	4.25	7.74
Credit growth, 2009 in %	5.3	11.88	15.6	11.8	3.36	1.61	−0.43	2.39
IMF involvement	–	–	SBA	–	–	FCL	SBA	SBA
Outcomes								
Current account, 2011 in % of GDP	1.9	3.2	−1.2	−1.7	−2.9	−4.3	1.6	−4.2

Notes and data sources: Current account data: Eurostat, accessed 20 July 2012; 2000–7 growth rates: Connolly 2012: table 1; Real GDP growth (percentage change relative to previous year): Eurostat, accessed 20 July 2012 (author's calculations); Inflation rate: Eurostat, accessed 15 August 2012; Real wage growth: IFS except those for Bulgaria: National Statistical Institute, accessed 22 August 2012; and Estonia: Statistics Estonia, accessed 22 August 2012; Credit growth (percentage of GDP): World Bank Development Indicators, accessed 22 August 2012; Maximum depreciation rate (typically between July/August 2008 and February–April 2009): Eurostat, accessed 15 August 2012. IMF involvement: SBA = Stand-By Arrangement, FCL = Flexible Credit Line. Unemployment rates: Eurostat, accessed 27 October 2012.

difficult to implement politically.[2] Thus, the choice between external and internal adjustment even presents itself to countries where this option officially no longer exists. This suggests that the exchange-rate regime by itself is an insufficient explanation for the variation in policy responses to balance-of-payments problems. Although it certainly heightens incentives to maintain exchange-rate stability, having a fixed exchange-rate regime is not a sufficient condition for internal adjustment. However, the fact that all four countries that successfully pursued internal adjustment during the 2007–10 global financial and economic crisis in Eastern Europe followed a fixed exchange-rate regime does raise the question of how such regimes increase the (political) incentives for internal adjustment.

Given that internal adjustment is not a foregone conclusion even in countries with fixed exchange-rate regimes, the variation in policy responses among Eastern European countries, in particular the successful completion of internal adjustment in the Baltic countries and Bulgaria, has puzzled many political economy scholars. This is because existing research in political economy argues that internal adjustment is exceedingly difficult to implement in democratic countries (Eichengreen 1992, 1996; Simmons 1994; Bearce and Hallerberg 2011). These studies contend that the measures required to lower relative prices through internal devaluation are so painful for virtually all citizens that they constitute a politically suicidal strategy to implement. In contrast, external adjustment is argued to hurt voters less and is therefore judged the politically more feasible strategy in the face of balance-of-payments problems. As a result, existing political economy models on the choice between external and internal adjustment strategies predict that democratic countries will invariably devalue their currency when confronted with serious balance-of-payments pressures.

Although these arguments were developed to explain the breakdown of the gold standard in the interwar years, they have been widely believed to hold in today's world as well. This is evidenced by the vivid debate, which was waged about possible crisis responses in the Baltic countries. For example, in June 2009, the economist Nouriel Roubini warned in the *Financial Times* that the Latvian strategy of pursuing internal adjustment would not be politically feasible in the long run because "a real exchange rate depreciation is necessary to restore [Latvia's] competitiveness; in its absence, a painful adjustment of relative prices can occur only via deflation and a fall in nominal wages that will take too long and exacerbate the recession....

---

[2] See, for example, Nouriel Roubini on 19 September 2011 (http://blogs.ft.com/the-a-list/2011/09/19/greece-should-default-and-abandon-the-euro/#axzz21AYnwudE).

But this is becoming politically unsustainable.... So it is a self-defeating strategy as long as the currency remains overvalued.... Devaluation seems unavoidable."[3]

Other well-known economists, such as Kenneth Rogoff or Paul Krugman, equally doubted Latvia's political ability to implement such drastic reforms of the domestic economy (for a more detailed criticism of this strategy, see also Weisbrot and Ray 2010).[4] Markets also questioned the ability of the Latvian government to pursue this strategy and bet on a significant devaluation of the currency (Kuokstis and Vilpisauskas 2010: 9). These doubts were shared by senior IMF officials, including IMF Chief Economist Olivier Blanchard (IMF 2012a), who initially harbored serious doubts about the viability of Latvia's strategy of maintaining the peg (Economist Intelligence Unit 2009b). This shows that at the outset of the crisis, devaluation was seen as a distinct and realistic policy option in at least one of the four countries that successfully pursued internal adjustment. The decision of the Baltic countries and Bulgaria to implement internal, rather than external, adjustment in response to the balance-of-payments pressures that emerged in 2008 and the successful implementation of this strategy have therefore puzzled many observers, including policy advisors and political economists.

Yet, this adjustment path appears much less surprising when viewed through the lens of this book's argument that a certain vulnerability profile in the electorate (i.e., one where vulnerability to external adjustment is very high) can create incentives for policymakers to adjust internally, rather than devalue the currency. I argue that the Baltic countries and Bulgaria exhibited such a profile, in particular a very high direct exposure of voters to foreign-currency denominated debt, which significantly raised the potential costs of a devaluation of the currency. This vulnerability profile explains why the governments of these countries were able to push through contractionary fiscal and nominal wage policies without serious public opposition.

To test this argument, this chapter investigates the experiences of the eight new EU member states that had not yet adopted the euro when the crisis hit the region (and hence had leeway in choosing between internal and external adjustment).[5] It will show empirically that the vulnerability profile of the

---

[3] *Financial Times*, 10 June 2009, Latvia's Currency Crisis is a Rerun of Argentina's.

[4] *Bloomberg*, 29 June 2009, Rogoff Says Latvia Should Devalue Its Currency, Direkt Reports, Paul Krugman, 23 December 2008, http://krugman.blogs.nytimes.com/2008/12/23/latvia-is-the-new-argentina-slightly-wonkish/

[5] The countries are Bulgaria, the Czech Republic, Estonia, Hungary, Latvia, Lithuania, Poland, and Romania. Slovenia and the Slovak Republic are not included because they had joined (Slovenia) or been accepted (Slovak Republic) into the eurozone by the summer of 2008.

electorates in the four Eastern European countries that successfully adjusted internally differed from voters' overall vulnerabilities in the two countries that adjusted externally (the Czech Republic and Poland) and those two countries that pursued more mixed adjustment strategies (Hungary and Romania). In the latter four countries, vulnerability to external adjustment was lower and vulnerability to internal adjustment higher than in the Baltic countries and Bulgaria.

7.1 Eastern European Responses to the Global Financial and Economic Crisis

In the years preceding the global financial crisis, most Eastern European economies had been booming. Successful economic reforms in the post-communist era, EU accession, and the prospect of euro adoption had led to high growth rates and rising per capita incomes. Much of this growth was driven by domestic consumption and to a somewhat lesser extent investment (Connolly 2012: 37–40) and occurred largely in the nontradables sector (Menkulasi, Miniane, and Poghosyan 2011). The capital required to finance domestic demand mainly came from abroad. After the countries in the region had liberalized their capital accounts in the 1990s, many foreign banks opened subsidiaries in these countries and began to lend freely to both firms and households (EBRD 2010). One of the consequences of this development was large capital inflows, which fueled credit booms and strong growth, particularly in the nontradable sector. Average wages doubled across Central and Eastern Europe and even tripled in Estonia and Latvia over the period of 2000–8 (Menkulasi et al. 2011). As a mirror image of these developments, current account deficits also grew. All countries in the region exhibited current account deficits in 2007, ranging from 3.3 percent of GDP in the Czech Republic to a deficit of about one-quarter of GDP in Bulgaria (see Table 7.1). By 2006, there were clear signals that the economy might be overheating in a number of countries in the region.[6]

Although growth had already started to slow before the onset of the crisis in Eastern Europe in 2008, the serious problems on international financial markets massively increased problems throughout the region. Eastern European economies were particularly hard hit by two major developments. First, the freeze-up of global financial markets, in particular after the Lehman Brothers bankruptcy in September 2008, and the financial problems of many European banks, which had vastly increased their presence

---

[6] See IMF article IV reports 2006 on Estonia, Latvia, and Lithuania.

in emerging Europe over the previous years, caused a sudden stop in capital inflows into the Eastern European economies. Second, the slowdown in economic activity throughout the world meant that export opportunities were declining. Both of these developments led to significant balance-of-payments problems: As the foreign capital needed to finance the current account deficits was drying up, the deficits widened because of the slowdown in export activity.

When the crisis hit, countries across Eastern Europe hence confronted significant and similar challenges, in particular the need to rebalance their economies. As deficit countries, they all faced a choice between internal and external adjustment when capital inflows stopped in the wake of the global crisis, worldwide demand for exports declined, and speculative pressure on their currencies emerged. However, despite similar problems and a common long-term goal for macroeconomic policy – euro adoption – these countries differed significantly in the adjustment strategies chosen to address the balance-of-payments problems they experienced in the context of the global financial crisis (EBRD 2009, 2010; Connolly 2012).

7.1.1 Internal Adjustment: The Baltics and Bulgaria

Four Eastern European countries – Estonia, Latvia, Lithuania, and Bulgaria – successfully pursued internal adjustment strategies in response to the global financial crisis that hit the region in 2008. Policymakers in all of these countries declared exchange-rate stability as the main goal of their crisis management, and all of them managed to reach this goal , as Figure 7.1 shows. To rebalance their external accounts and to stave off the speculative pressure that emerged in 2008 and peaked in early 2009, they instead implemented painful domestic reforms. Although this strategy caused severe recessions in the four countries, it ultimately allowed the authorities to stabilize their economies, all of which began to grow again in 2010 (2011 in Latvia).

The decision to pursue internal adjustment and to implement this strategy successfully is particularly notable in light of the fact that all four countries exhibited unusually large balance-of-payments imbalances on the eve of the global financial crisis. In 2007, current account deficits in the four countries ranged from 14.4 percent of GDP in Lithuania to 25.2 percent in Bulgaria (see Table 7.1). This suggests that a substantial adjustment in price levels was needed to restore international competitiveness and to rebalance the economy. Moreover, only one of the four

(1) Countries pursuing internal adjustment

(2) Countries pursuing external adjustment

(3) Countries pursuing a mixed adjustment strategy

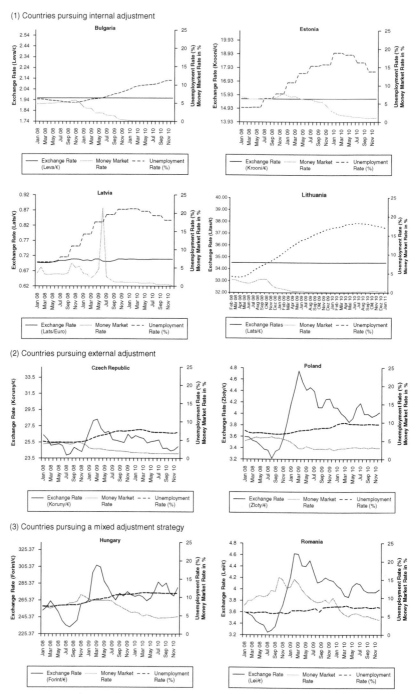

Figure 7.1. Exchange-rate, interest-rate, and unemployment-rate developments in eight Eastern European countries, 2008–2010.

countries – Latvia – turned to the IMF, so that the extensive adjustment policies implemented in the other countries cannot be explained by harsh IMF conditionality alone.[7]

To rebalance their economies, the authorities in all four countries implemented policies aimed at an internal devaluation of domestic prices, rather than allowing the economy to adjust externally through a devaluation of the currency. The emphasis of this adjustment strategy lay on fiscal consolidation and nominal wage adjustment. The countries implemented painful domestic reforms such as wage and expenditure cuts, substantial reductions in public sector employment, and tax increases. For example, in Latvia, the country that has been hardest hit by the crisis, the authorities cut public wages by about 25 percent (IMF 2012b: 11), significantly reduced public sector employment by about 20 percent or 14,000 jobs (Aslund 2010: 37), and cut public expenditures, such as pension and sickness benefits and education spending. Overall, fiscal adjustment in Latvia summed up to 16.6. per cent of GDP over the period 2008–11 (EBRD 2012: 136). Fiscal adjustment in the other Baltic countries was substantial as well and followed a consolidation strategy that was mainly expenditure based.[8] Bulgaria experienced a less severe crisis than the Baltic states, mainly because a large proportion of its capital inflows in the boom years had been foreign direct investments, which tend to be less susceptible to sudden stops and capital flow reversals (Aslund 2010). Nonetheless Bulgaria also implemented substantial fiscal consolidation measures to combat the balance-of-payments pressures that emerged during the crisis.

These measures successfully brought down labor costs and price levels more generally, which also led to depreciating (Baltics) or stagnating (Bulgaria) real exchange rates (IMF 2011: 10). This improvement in competitiveness and the sharp reduction in imports during the crisis led to adjustments of the current accounts in all four countries. After a low point in 2009, exports began to increase again in all four economies in 2010, a trend that continued throughout 2011 (Eurostat 2012). Nonetheless, the internal adjustment measures implemented by the authorities also caused a collapse in growth and massive increases in unemployment in these countries (see Table 7.1). Between 2007 and 2010, unemployment increased by almost

---

[7] In addition to the IMF, Latvia received funds from the EU, the Nordic countries, and the World Bank. It should also be noted that the Baltic states received bilateral support from the Nordic countries, especially Sweden and Norway, and that all countries benefited from the coordinated and continued commitment of foreign banks to their respective national subsidiaries.

[8] Rather than being mainly financed through tax increases and other revenue measures.

one-half in Bulgaria, doubled in Latvia, more than doubled in Estonia, and tripled in Lithuania. Although successful in terms of a rebalancing of the economy, the strategy of internal adjustment hence also imposed high social costs on citizens in these countries.

7.1.2 Mixed Adjustment Strategies: Hungary and Romania

Hungary and Romania pursued more mixed adjustment strategies in which they combined elements of external and internal adjustment and financing support from the international community (see Figure 7.1). These countries are particularly useful cases for comparison with the four internally adjusting economies, because they not only had equally experienced a boom phase in the years following EU accession and exhibited current account deficits by 2007 (see Table 7.1) but also faced similar problems on international financial markets when the global financial crisis intensified in the fall of 2008. Most notably, they also experienced a slowdown or sudden stop of capital inflows, speculative pressure,[9] and a difficult export environment as a result of the financial problems in the advanced economies, all of which resulted in serious balance-of-payments problems.

When the global financial crisis hit these economies, the currencies in both countries came under increasing pressure. After an initial phase of exchange-rate depreciation, during which currencies had depreciated despite significant efforts by the central banks to intervene on the foreign exchange market through reserve sales and interest-rate increases, the governments in both countries took more drastic steps to slow down the decline in their currencies' values. When their financing needs became more pressing, policymakers in both countries sought external sources of funding from the IMF and other sources. In Hungary, the governing Socialist Party, which had implemented some limited fiscal consolidation measures from 2006 onward, concluded an agreement with the IMF and the EU in October 2008, about a month after the forint had begun a free fall, in which it agreed to implement tough internal adjustment measures, most notably fiscal consolidation intended to reduce Hungary's high level of public debt. In return, Hungary received a US$25 billion package from the IMF, EU, and others, which allowed it to meet its financing needs and to

---

[9]   Speculative pressure in these countries was higher than in Poland and the Czech Republic, but lower than that experienced by the Baltic states. For example, although five-year CDS spreads significantly increased in both countries, the increase was lower than in the Baltic states and similar to the increase in Bulgarian spreads (Bakker and Gulde 2010: figure 17).

avoid a financial crisis.[10] Romania endured a longer decline of its currency before turning to the IMF in March 2009 but then equally committed itself to an austerity program designed to stabilize the currency and to rebalance the economy. In return, it received US$27 billion financing support from the IMF, the EU, the World Bank, and the EBRD.

Driven by the pressure on financial markets and program conditionality, both sets of policymakers thus began to adjust their fiscal policies. This was particularly important in Hungary, which had pursued unsustainable fiscal policies during the boom years and had therefore accumulated large fiscal deficits and a high level of public debt. The fiscal reforms adopted by Hungarian policymakers were aimed at cutting expenditures, mainly through wage cuts in the public sector, but also through the reduction of other public expenditures such as sick leave benefits or housing subsidies. Fiscal consolidation measures in Romania equally focused on expenditure cuts, in particular reductions in public wages and public employment. Moreover, structural reforms such as changes in the pension, education, and healthcare regimes and structural reforms regarding private debt were implemented by policymakers in both countries.

As in the four countries that adjusted internally, macroeconomic adjustment in Romania and Hungary was painful. Economic growth turned negative, unemployment rates and the proportion of nonperforming loans increased, and wages fell, even though these domestic repercussions were less severe than in the Baltic states. Overall, these developments caused strong reductions in domestic demand, even though they also resulted in lower production costs and hence improved levels of international competitiveness. By 2009, current account deficits had significantly decreased in both countries, and Hungary and Romania began to grow again in 2010 and 2011, respectively.

7.1.3 External Adjustment: Czech Republic and Poland

These experiences contrast with the responses in two other Eastern European countries, which predominantly followed external adjustment strategies: the Czech Republic and Poland. When the global financial crisis hit these economies, national policymakers let their exchange rates depreciate immediately. Between August 2008 and February 2009, the Polish

---

[10] Despite the program and the emphasis on fiscal consolidation, however, the authorities continued to pursue a more mixed adjustment strategy by letting the currency depreciate further.

zloty lost 32 percent and the Czech koruna 15 percent of their August 2008 values (see Figure 7.1).

When speculative pressure emerged on the Polish currency, national policymakers accommodated this pressure by letting the exchange rate depreciate, while pursuing countercyclical policies domestically. Rather than tightening domestic economic conditions, they combined this external adjustment with an expansionary monetary and fiscal policy stance. For example, the Polish central bank continued to cut interest rates in the fall of 2008 despite the depreciating exchange rate. This strategy was supported by a precautionary flexible credit line (FCL) agreed with IMF in April 2009, which can be offered to strongly performing economies with a solid record of timely and effective policy adjustments. This type of IMF program is different from traditional IMF programs in that it is available only to countries with very strong economic fundamentals and policy track records. FCLs are precautionary insofar as they are intended to provide a shield against speculative pressure for countries with solid fundamentals and therefore do not necessarily involve a disbursement of funds. Qualifying countries can apply for the FCL when faced with potential or actual balance-of-payments pressures, and subsequently have the flexibility to draw at any time within a pre-specified window on the credit line. The FCL worked well in Poland, which did not draw on these funds.[11]

The Czech Republic equally let its exchange rate depreciate when pressures emerged on international financial markets in the fall of 2008, although it declined less than the Polish zloty. Because the imbalances in the Czech economy were less pronounced than in other Eastern European economies, the extent of necessary adjustment was more limited. This allowed the Czech authorities to respond to the initial peak of the crisis with a fiscal stimulus package and an easing of monetary policy and to implement austerity measures for the government budget only in 2010. Growth picked up again in 2010 in both of these externally adjusting economies, and the current account deficits had decreased relative to their 2007 values.

7.1.4 Conclusion: Variation in Adjustment Strategies in Eastern Europe

This discussion shows that governments across Eastern Europe reacted quite differently to the balance-of-payments problems, which plagued their economies as a result of the global financial crisis, especially the sudden stop

---

[11] As most other Eastern European economies, Poland did receive additional support from the European Union.

in capital inflows that followed the Lehman Brothers collapse in September 2008. Whereas some countries followed internal adjustment strategies and others opted for external strategies, some chose more mixed strategies. Some countries relied on financing support by the IMF, the EU, and other sources, others implemented their anti-crisis strategies without major external funding support. Finally, the consequences of the crisis also differed widely: Although unemployment increased in almost all countries at least temporarily, the extent of job losses and wage reductions varied significantly.

7.2 Vulnerabilities to Internal and External Adjustment across Eastern Europe

How can this variation in policy responses to the global financial and economic crisis among new EU member states be explained? Did the electorates in the countries that chose to adjust internally exhibit different vulnerability profiles than those in externally adjusting countries and those that chose more mixed strategies? This book's argument suggests that distributional concerns are an important determinant of the choice of adjustment strategy. We consequently should observe different vulnerability profiles in the three groups of countries discussed in this chapter. This section therefore looks at the vulnerability profiles of the electorates in the eight Eastern European countries under study, considering both voters' direct and indirect vulnerabilities.

7.2.1 Direct and Indirect Vulnerabilities to External Adjustment

When the global financial crisis hit Eastern Europe with full force in the fall of 2008, voters in the eight different countries varied considerably in their exposure to external adjustment.

In terms of direct vulnerabilities to external adjustment, exposure to losses in purchasing power and personal balance sheets dominated. As in East Asia, Eastern European voters were vulnerable to depreciation-induced losses in purchasing power. For example, food represents about a third of total household consumption in the new EU member states. Because it is imported in large quantities in these countries, a depreciation exposes households, especially poorer ones, to a significant reduction in purchasing power. Figure 7.2, Panel A, shows that this is particularly true in the Baltic states, where an average 9.2 percent of all imported goods are food imports, whereas it constitutes a less pressing concern in the remaining countries,

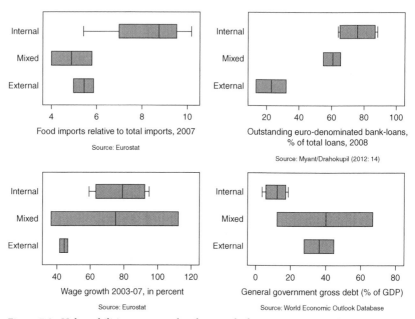

Figure 7.2. Vulnerabilities to external and internal adjustment, by type of chosen adjustment strategy.

where food (and fuel) imports constitute a much lower share of GDP (see also Tiongson et al. 2010: 39ff).

In most countries, however, voters' vulnerabilities to depreciation-induced price shocks were a second-rate concern in comparison with personal balance sheet vulnerabilities to external adjustment. After the Eastern European economies had opened their financial accounts in the process of transition, foreign capital had flown into these countries, and these capital inflows had accelerated sharply with EU accession. This resulted in substantial credit growth, a trend that was particularly pronounced in the four new EU member states that had fixed their exchange rate to the euro. In the Baltics and Bulgaria, credit to households grew on average by 46 percent per year over the period 2003–8, which compares to an average growth rate of 25 percent in the Czech Republic, Hungary, and Poland – a statistically significant difference (Mitra, Selowsky, and Zalduendo 2010: 50).[12] Much of this credit was denominated in foreign currencies, mainly euro and Swiss francs, and much of it was

---

[12] Nonetheless, household indebtedness in the new EU member states is lower than in the old member states.

unhedged.[13] The growth in foreign-currency loans was related to the growing presence of foreign-owned banks in Eastern European financial sectors and the fact that interest rates on local currency loans were typically much higher than interest rates for euro- or Swiss franc-denominated loans (Bakker and Gulde 2010). However, Figure 7.3, Panel B, shows that the prevalence of foreign-currency denomination varied widely across the region. Again, the Baltic republics recorded the highest level of foreign-currency lending to households. In these countries, well over one-half (Lithuania) or even three-quarters (Estonia and Latvia) of all bank loans to households were denominated in foreign currency (Tiongson et al. 2010: 27). Foreign-currency denomination in household lending was also high in Romania and Hungary. In the latter country, household debt in foreign currency stood at 25 percent of GDP (EBRD 2010: 172), whereas it was much lower in Poland and Bulgaria. The Czech Republic stands out on the other extreme, as Czech households accumulated virtually no foreign-currency debt during the boom phase. Instead, residential deposits in foreign currency approximately equaled foreign-currency denominated loans to residents, making Czech individuals much less vulnerable to currency movements (Bakker and Gulde 2010: 38).[14]

Overall, this discussion shows that Eastern European voters exhibited substantial direct vulnerabilities to external adjustment. Voters from poorer households were mainly exposed to depreciation-induced price increases in imported food and fuel, whereas many voters from middle- to high-income households were vulnerable in terms of foreign-currency denominated debt in their personal balance sheets. The direct vulnerabilities to external adjustment were particularly high in the three Baltic states, and much less pronounced in the Czech Republic, Hungary, and Poland. Bulgarian and Romanian voters exhibited intermediate-level direct vulnerabilities to external adjustment. Despite this variation, one aspect is particularly striking when looking at Eastern European voters' direct vulnerabilities to external adjustment: Compared to voters in the East Asian countries discussed in the previous chapter, the direct exposure of private citizens to exchange-rate changes was much higher in the Eastern European economies.[15]

---

[13] Because remittance flows also decreased as a consequence of the global economic downturn, many households additionally saw a reduction of this source of foreign-currency revenue (World Bank 2011).

[14] For a discussion about why foreign-currency lending to households did not take off in the Czech Republic, see Mitra et al. (2010: Box 1.3)

[15] For a detailed discussion of household vulnerabilities and transmission channels of the global financial crisis in Eastern Europe and Central Asia, see Tiongson et al. (2010).

Eastern European voters also exhibited substantial indirect vulnerabilities to external adjustment, both in terms of their employment-specific vulnerabilities and their vulnerabilities to the aggregate macroeconomic effects of external adjustment more generally. Once more, however, the level of these vulnerabilities varied considerably across countries.

The vulnerability of Eastern European firms to external adjustment was mainly related to the potential effects of a depreciation on their international competitiveness and their financial situation. During the pre-crisis boom phase, competitiveness had deteriorated in all eight countries. Between 2003 and 2008, real effective exchange rates increased most in Latvia and Bulgaria, followed by Lithuania, Romania, Estonia, and Poland, and finally the Czech Republic and Hungary, where competitiveness had deteriorated only slightly (Bakker and Christiansen 2011: 17). Given this reduced level of competitiveness, exporters in all countries were likely to benefit from external adjustment, especially because the simultaneously occurring slowdown in global demand caused by the global financial crisis constituted a major challenge for exporters across the region. As discussed in Chapter 2, the beneficial effect of depreciation tends to be largest for exporters (and indirectly their employees) producing highly price-sensitive goods, such as primary or standardized goods, and less pronounced for exporters of complex products, such as machinery (Frieden 2002). Looking at the share of primary and resource-based exports of total industrial exports, one can observe a large divergence in export structures across Eastern Europe. Surprisingly, the Baltic countries and Bulgaria export a much higher share of price-sensitive products – almost one-half (46.6%) of all industrial exports – than the four countries that chose mixed or external adjustment strategies, where this share only amounts to about one-quarter (23.8%).

However, this potentially beneficial effect of external adjustment for exporters was counteracted by two other characteristics of firms in these countries: a heavy reliance on imported inputs and a high exposure to foreign-currency denominated debt. First, it is frequently pointed out that the import content of exports is particularly high in the Baltic states and that the increased cost of imported inputs was therefore likely to offset potential competitiveness gains achieved by an exchange-rate devaluation (e.g., European Commission 2009a: 83; Purfield and Rosenberg 2010: 12). Second, and more importantly, firms that had borrowed in foreign currency faced significant risks in the event of a devaluation. Similar to households, foreign-currency lending had increased substantially during the boom phase in Eastern Europe, although there was again a lot of cross-country variation in the prevalence of such lending. Firm exposure to foreign-currency debt ranged from relatively low levels in the Czech Republic, where foreign-currency denominated loans amounted to only 13 percent of total bank loans in 2007 (most of it corporate loans), to a very high level in the Baltic Republics and Bulgaria, where the majority of bank loans was denominated in foreign currency (Myant and Drahokupil 2012: table 5). Corporate borrowing in foreign currency was sometimes substantially higher than household borrowing. For example, in Bulgaria, the foreign-currency debt of the nonfinancial corporate sector stood at 80 percent of GDP in 2010, compared to foreign-currency denominated household debt of about 10 percent of GDP (IMF 2010a: 7). Moreover, in some countries, such as Romania, firms had not only borrowed from banks but had directly borrowed abroad, so that the statistics on bank loans underestimate the full extent of exposure of corporate balance sheets to a depreciation of the currency (IMF 2010c: 11–12). For voters working in firms exposed to such foreign-currency risk, their indirect vulnerability to depreciation was considerable. Overall, this type of vulnerability to external adjustment was highest in the countries with fixed exchange-rate regimes – that is, the Baltics and Bulgaria. It was lower, although still substantial, in Hungary and Romania and comparatively low in Poland and the Czech Republic.

The three groups of countries also differed considerably in terms of the general economic effects that an external adjustment strategy was likely to bring about. First, given that balance sheet vulnerabilities to depreciation differed so widely across Eastern European countries, the effects of external adjustment on aggregate economic activity and growth were likely to vary as well. In the Baltics, particularly Estonia and Latvia, where foreign-currency denomination of private debt was most widespread, a devaluation was expected to lead to widespread bankruptcies, a significant increase in nonperforming loans, and a substantial reduction in domestic demand. It was feared that these developments would have severe negative feedback effects on the financial sector (as well as on foreign parent banks) and the economy as a whole (Purfield and Rosenberg 2010). This was compounded by the fact that imbalances were exceptionally high in these countries, so that a substantial downward adjustment in the exchange rate would have been needed to rebalance the economy. Given the relatively high level of foreign-currency lending in Bulgaria, Hungary, and Romania, the vulnerability of these economies to external adjustment was also high. In contrast, fears about the financial effects of external adjustment and its consequences for the real economy were much more muted in the Czech Republic and Poland, where the level of foreign-currency lending was significantly lower than the Eastern European average.

Second, for the Baltics and Bulgaria, external adjustment would have implied an official change of the exchange-rate regime and the abandonment of their near-term goal of euro adoption. This goal not only served as a credible exit strategy from the fixed exchange-rate regime but also was widely supported not only by politicians and the publics at large, but also by EU officials.[16] Because economic activities had been based on the assumption of exchange-rate stability for over a decade, economic actors not only in these countries, but also abroad – most notably the parent banks of many financial institutions in Eastern Europe – had developed significant vulnerabilities to a devaluation in these economies. Banks with a home base in the Nordic countries were particularly exposed and therefore opposed devaluation. This created additional opportunity costs for an external adjustment strategy. Moreover, the choice to abandon the fixed exchange rate in one country was also likely to create serious contagion risks, particularly for the other three countries with fixed exchange rates. For example, the Economist Intelligence Unit concluded in several country reports on Bulgaria, Estonia, and Lithuania in early 2009 that their currency arrangements were essentially robust but would be seriously threatened if Latvia devalued its currency (e.g., EIU 2009a, 2009b, 2009c). The decision to pursue external adjustment in one country might therefore have had serious consequences across the region, with negative feedback effects on the devaluing country. Taken together, the indirect vulnerability of voters in the Baltic republics and Bulgaria to the general economic effects of external adjustment were therefore very high.

Voters' indirect vulnerabilities to the effects of external adjustment on general economic activity were also high in Hungary and Romania, where a high proportion of private sector credit was denominated in foreign currency. However, it was lower than in the countries with fixed exchange rates, because external adjustment did not involve the negative consequences of abandoning an exchange-rate regime.

In contrast, Czech and Polish voters were much less vulnerable to the general economic effects of external adjustment. Their flexible currencies had been appreciating for a long period of time, inflation had been well-contained, and euro adoption was not an immediate priority. In addition, the comparatively low exposure of firms and households to

---

[16] Nonetheless, the desire to join the euro was not so large as to trump any other considerations, as the decision of all three fixed exchange-rate countries except Estonia (which joined EMU in 2010) to postpone euro introduction in light of the euro crisis, demonstrates.

foreign-currency debt also lessened the potential financial consequences of external adjustment in these countries.

In sum, both the direct and indirect vulnerability of Eastern European voters to external adjustment varied considerably. Individuals who relied heavily on the consumption of imported products, particularly food, and those repaying foreign-currency denominated debt exhibited the highest direct vulnerability to a depreciation of their country's currency. Directly vulnerable individuals were concentrated in the Baltic states, whereas direct vulnerabilities were on average much lower for Czech and Polish voters. In Bulgaria, Hungary, and Romania, voters' direct vulnerabilities were located somewhere between these extremes.

Moreover, individuals working for firms exposed to foreign-currency risk and firms in the nontradables sector exhibited high levels of indirect, employment-specific vulnerability, whereas this type of vulnerability was lower for individuals working in the export sector and in firms holding only domestic-currency debt. Again, this type of vulnerability was most prevalent in the Baltics, although it was also considerable in Bulgaria, Hungary, and Romania. Employment-specific vulnerability to external adjustment was on average much lower in the Czech Republic and Poland. Finally, voters' indirect vulnerabilities to the effects of external adjustment on aggregate economic conditions also varied widely. This type of vulnerability was highest in the Baltics and Bulgaria, intermediate in Hungary and Romania, and low in the Czech Republic and Poland.

Taken together, this analysis of voter vulnerabilities to external adjustment suggest that on balance, external adjustment would have had the most serious adverse consequences for voters in the Baltic states, followed by Bulgaria. Hungarian and Romanian voters exhibited a somewhat lower but still substantial overall vulnerability to external adjustment, whereas the vulnerability of Czech and Polish voters to external adjustment was relatively limited.

7.2.2 Direct and Indirect Vulnerabilities to Internal Adjustment

Voters' direct and indirect vulnerabilities to internal adjustment also differed across Eastern European countries.

Voters' direct vulnerabilities to internal adjustment mainly came from two sources: the effects of higher interest rates on their personal finances and the effects of higher taxes and lower transfers on their disposable income. An increase in domestic interest rates is particularly painful for highly leveraged individuals holding domestic-currency denominated debt with adjustable interest rates. Because such loans tend to be quite common in the new EU member states (Beck, Kibuuka, and Tiongson 2010: footnote 3 and table 1), voters' vulnerabilities to monetary tightening were therefore particularly high in countries where virtually all (Czech Republic) or a large majority (Poland) of household loans were denominated in local currency. Direct vulnerabilities were lower in countries where only a minority of household debt was denominated in domestic currency (as in Estonia and Latvia, and to a lesser extent in Bulgaria, Lithuania, Hungary, and Romania). Moreover, among the eight countries studied in this chapter, Poland also had the highest share of households with bills in arrears, suggesting that Polish voters were particularly exposed to a tightening of conditions on domestic credit markets (Beck et al. 2010: 24). In addition, a large proportion of household debt in Eastern Europe was mortgage debt. Individuals who had taken out loans to buy a house or apartment were not only vulnerable to higher debt-servicing costs, but also, as all other homeowners, faced the risk of asset-price deflation on the real estate market, which is a typical feature of internal adjustment. In the worst case, they would pay more to service loans for real estate with decreasing value.[17] Overall, this suggests that voters' direct vulnerabilities to monetary tightening were highest in the Czech Republic and Poland, where domestic-currency lending dominated, and lowest in Estonia and Latvia, where foreign-currency lending was the norm. The remaining four countries represent an intermediate category with respect to voters' direct vulnerabilities to monetary tightening.

Voters were also directly vulnerable to the direct effects of fiscal consolidation. For example, all countries in the sample increased value-added and/or excise taxes in an effort to increase public revenues (Darvas 2010; Bakker and Christiansen 2011). Such increases in consumption taxes decrease voters' disposable incomes and hit poorer voters disproportionally hard, because they spend a higher portion of their income on food and other consumption goods. Moreover, fiscal consolidation is often associated with reductions in social transfers, such as health benefits, pensions, or family allowances, and the Eastern European states were no exception. Again, poorer voters tend to be more vulnerable to such reductions. In general, voters' vulnerabilities increase as tax increases and expenditure cuts become larger. Voters in countries with very high imbalances were thus particularly vulnerable to the potential costs of internal adjustment.

---

[17] Because richer households are more likely to hold debt and to own housing, these direct risks were more concentrated among more well-off voters.

In addition to these direct vulnerabilities, Eastern European voters also exhibited considerable indirect vulnerabilities to internal adjustment, both in terms of their personal employment situation and the consequences on the economy more generally.

Employment-specific risks associated with internal adjustment existed both for employees in the public and the private sector. Public sector employees were particularly vulnerable to fiscal consolidation and structural reforms, because an important aspect of such measures tends to be a reduction of public wages and employment. As a result, internal adjustment leads to significant job losses in the public sector and substantial wage reductions for those public employees who can keep their jobs. Public sector employees therefore exhibited a very high employment-specific vulnerability to internal adjustment.

However, Eastern Europeans employed in the private sector were vulnerable to internal adjustment as well. The tightening of fiscal and monetary policies associated with internal adjustment, and the downturn in growth this usually entails, creates a difficult business environment for private sector firms. Not only does this adjustment strategy typically lead to a reduction in domestic demand and economic activity. It also puts a strain on firms' balance sheets, because higher interest rates make financing more expensive and because higher taxes and lower subsidies reduce firm profits. Because domestic-currency loans were most common in the Czech Republic and Poland, highly leveraged firms in these countries were most vulnerable in this regard. Moreover, in economically difficult times firms typically try to reduce labor costs, either by cutting jobs altogether or by reducing wage costs through a variety of measures including lower wages and benefits or a reduction in the hours worked. The latter option seems to have been the most prevalent response to the crisis in Eastern Europe. For example, in Bulgaria, six times more workers reported lower earnings than a job loss in 2009, and in Romania, this number stood at three times as many workers (World Bank 2011: 21–2). Moreover, part-time employment increased in almost all countries across the region, with the Baltic economies recording a particularly steep increase of over 20 percent (World Bank 2011: 24).

Job loss and wage reductions during crises are typically most widespread in economies and industries, which have shown signs of overheating in the pre-crisis period.[18] Economies and industries typically record disproportionally high wage increases during the boom period, which exceed

---

[18] Typically nontradables industries, such as construction or the retail sector, experience the largest booms.

productivity gains. This is particularly problematic when an industry expands in an unsustainable manner (as, for example, the construction sectors in the Baltics and Romania did), so that many of the jobs lost during the crisis will not be recovered once the economy stabilizes. Figure 7.2, Panel C, shows that there is considerable divergence in the pre-crisis developments in wage growth across the eight countries studied in this chapter. Whereas wages grew across all eight countries in the pre-crisis period, wage growth was particularly large in Romania and the four countries with fixed exchange rates. At the same time, however, such large pre-crisis wage increases to some extent shelter workers from wage reductions during the crisis, because these wage cuts start from an elevated level.[19] Thus, whereas workers in the Baltics, Romania, and Bulgaria, especially those working in industries with particularly high pre-crisis wage growth such as construction, were most vulnerable to falling wages and increases in unemployment during the adjustment process, they enjoyed higher "buffers" to tolerate wage cuts than workers in countries such as Hungary and Poland, where wages had increased to a much lesser extent prior to the crisis.

Although virtually all workers in Eastern Europe in both the public and private sector thus exhibited employment-specific vulnerabilities to internal adjustment, the degree of these vulnerabilities varied. They were particularly large for workers in the public sector and for workers in industries and firms with a high exposure to the risks of fiscal and monetary tightening, such as firms highly leveraged in domestic currency and firms in overheated economic sectors. In addition, voters' employment-specific vulnerabilities to internal adjustment are conditioned by the characteristics of national labor markets, above all the degree of labor market flexibility. On flexible labor markets, wages adjust more quickly than on inflexible markets and workers are more likely to lose their jobs in an economic downturn. On the plus side, however, they are also much more likely to find reemployment quickly when the economy stabilizes. In this context, many observers have emphasized the high level of labor market flexibility in the Baltic states (e.g., IMF 2009a; Purfield and Rosenberg 2010; Masso and Krillo 2011), although labor market flexibility across all the eight countries examined in this chapter is notably higher than average labor market flexibility in the old EU member states (Gwartney, Hall, and Lawson 2011). In the most frequently used data on labor market flexibility (Gwartney et al. 2011), Bulgaria and the Czech Republic top the list, followed by Latvia and Hungary, although other measures rank the Baltic labor markets among the most flexible in the new EU member states (IMF 2009a: 17).

---

[19] See Levasseur (2012: 135) for a similar point.

Another determinant of Eastern Europeans' vulnerabilities to internal adjustment was the effects of internal adjustment on the economy in general. These effects varied widely across the three groups of countries. First, given that the Baltic states and Bulgaria exhibited the most pronounced imbalances (see Table 7.1), the necessary macroeconomic adjustment was largest in these economies, amplifying the negative effects on domestic economic activity, domestic demand, and domestic labor markets that were to be expected from this adjustment strategy. This increased the indirect vulnerability of voters in these countries to internal adjustment. Second, even though the large imbalances meant that large-scale fiscal consolidation and structural reform would be needed, the positive news was that the countries following fixed exchange-rate regimes had shown better fiscal policy discipline in the pre-crisis period than most of their counterparts with more flexible exchange-rate regimes (Aslund 2010: 56). Bulgaria and Estonia even exhibited surpluses in their budget balances between 2000–8, which was unprecedented among other EU transition economies (IMF 2010b: 35). As a result, the internally adjusting economies in the Baltic states and Bulgaria as well as the mixed-strategy-pursuing Romania exhibited significantly lower levels of public debt at the eve of the crisis (see Figure 7.2, Panel D), which provided some buffer for the fiscal consolidation process in these countries. The fiscal situation was much more strained in the externally adjusting economies and Hungary. Finally, the countries also faced different international environments. As discussed, economic policy in the Baltics and Bulgaria had long been geared toward the widely supported goal of euro adoption and had created high stakes in the continuation of the fixed exchange-rate regime for both domestic and foreign actors. Most directly affected were the Nordic countries, where banks had an unusually high exposure to the Baltic financial sector, and the EU, whose officials worried about contagion effects. As a consequence, these external actors made it clear that they had a strong preference for internal adjustment and would be willing to support this choice financially. This commitment reduced the potential costs of internal adjustment for this group of countries to some extent. Although the other group of countries also benefited from international coordination and support, this was not tied to the goal of immediate exchange-rate stabilization.[20]

Overall, this suggests that although the vulnerability of voters in the Baltics and Bulgaria to the general economic effects of internal adjustment

---

[20] For example, key public and private sector stakeholders, including foreign parent banks, coordinated their crisis responses in the Vienna Initiative. One goal was to prevent a mass withdrawal of funding from the emerging European economies.

were high given the large-scale imbalances in their economies, the low level of public debt and the international support for this type of adjustment strategy mitigated this vulnerability to some degree. By the same token, the significant need for rebalancing in Hungary and Romania and less international support for an internal adjustment strategy, coupled with relatively high levels of public debt (especially in Hungary) and an overheated economy (especially in Romania), equally led to a high vulnerability to internal adjustment in these countries. Although the imbalances were less pronounced in the Czech Republic and Poland, voters in these countries also exhibited considerable indirect vulnerabilities to the aggregate economic effects of internal adjustment. These were rooted in the adverse effects of tight monetary policy on growth prospects in countries that relied mostly on domestic-currency lending, considerable levels of public debt, and limited international support for internal adjustment.

This discussion has shown that the direct and indirect vulnerability of Eastern European voters to internal adjustment varied considerably, although the overall picture that emerges is less clear than the vulnerability structure for external adjustment. Direct balance sheet vulnerabilities were concentrated in the Czech Republic and Poland, where the majority of household and corporate loans were tied to domestic interest rates, and were comparatively low in the Baltic states, where most household lending was tied to foreign interest rates. Voters' employment-specific vulnerabilities to internal adjustment were high in all eight countries under study, despite considerable subnational variation in labor market risks. With regard to the general economic effects of internal adjustment, the need for extensive fiscal consolidation and structural reform in the Baltics and to a lesser extent in Bulgaria and Romania was counterbalanced by their low levels of public debt and (except in the case of Romania) the international support for an internal adjustment strategy. It was significantly higher in the Czech Republic, Hungary, and Poland. Taken together, this analysis of voter vulnerabilities to internal adjustment suggests that on balance, all voters across Eastern Europe exhibited some vulnerability to internal adjustment, which was more moderate in the Baltics and Bulgaria than among Czech, Hungarian, Romanian, and Polish voters.

7.2.3 Vulnerability Profiles in Eastern Europe

When the global financial crisis hit Eastern Europe in 2008, governments charged with the task of rebalancing their economies and reducing their current account deficits confronted electorates with very different vulnerability profiles. Despite a high level of within-country variation in voters' vulnerabilities, three clusters can be identified. The largest group consists of the Baltic states (Estonia, Latvia, and Lithuania) and Bulgaria, where electorates overall exhibited moderate vulnerabilities to internal adjustment but very high vulnerabilities to external adjustment. Overall, this vulnerability profile suggests that internal adjustment should be the preferred adjustment strategy in these economies. In a second group of countries, comprised of the Czech Republic and Poland, voters' vulnerabilities to internal adjustment were very high, whereas their vulnerability to external adjustment was limited. As a result, the expected adjustment strategy in these countries is a strategy that mainly relies on exchange-rate depreciation. The final group of countries comprises Hungary and Romania. The electorates in these countries exhibited substantial vulnerabilities to external adjustment but equally substantial or even higher vulnerabilities to internal adjustment. This suggests not only that we should observe some delay in the decision to implement serious macroeconomic adjustment in these countries but also that both exchange-rate depreciation and internal adjustment measures should constitute important elements of the adjustment strategy eventually implemented.

7.3 The Distributional Politics of Adjustment to the Global Financial Crisis

The predictions about the effect of different vulnerability profiles on national crisis management developed in the previous section correspond quite well with the eight new EU member states' actual policy responses to the 2008–10 global financial crisis. To examine this finding more closely, the remainder of this chapter concentrates on the causal mechanism between national vulnerability profiles and the choice of adjustment strategies. For this purpose, it examines the distributional struggles and politics surrounding the macroeconomic adjustment processes between 2008 and 2010.

7.3.1 Strong Support for Painful Reform: The Baltics and Bulgaria

As discussed, policymakers in the Baltic states and Bulgaria implemented some of the most far-reaching macroeconomic and structural reforms seen in recent years. In fact, in a review of the Baltic adjustment experience, two IMF officials conclude that the fiscal consolidation implemented by the Baltic states "was unprecedented by historical and international standards" (Purfield and Rosenberg 2010: 18), and one that resulted in an economic contraction that was equally unprecedented.

Despite these very painful consequences, the decision to maintain exchange-rate stability at the price of serious internal adjustment enjoyed strong popular and political support in all four countries. In all Baltic states there was a large-scale political consensus to maintain the fixed currency arrangements, which was shared by a majority of voters, who were judged "likely [to] turn against any government that would devalue" (Kuokstis and Vilpisauskas 2010: 7). Even in Latvia, the hardest hit of these countries, almost two-thirds of respondents of an opinion poll conducted in August 2009, at the peak of the crisis, said that they wanted their currency's peg to the euro to remain unchanged (Aslund 2010: 35). The same applies to Bulgaria, where the currency board enjoyed "tremendous support" among the population even at the height of the crisis and whose continuation was supported by all political parties (EIU 2009b: 11).

This is not to say that the path of internal adjustment was politically easy. In January 2009, riots erupted in the capitals of both Latvia and Lithuania in the aftermath of initially peaceful demonstrations against austerity measures and the government more generally. In most countries, the coalition partners in government fought over the specific measures to be implemented in the context of the internal adjustment strategy, even if the strategy itself was never substantively questioned. There were also occasional discussions about the merits of defending the currency board arrangements in light of the enormous cost this strategy was imposing on the domestic economies, although the authorities tried to limit such critical discussions.[21] Nonetheless, although external adjustment was discussed as a distinct policy option in international policy circles, this option was ruled out, or not even considered, by most domestic analysts (Kuokstis and Vilpisauskas 2010: 5). In light of the extent of adjustment necessary and the immense pain imposed on the domestic populations in the course of its implementation, this low level of public debate on exchange-rate policy is striking. Overall, "the currency board [politically] remains a sacred cow in each of these countries, ardently supported by a large popular majority" (Aslund 2010: 54).

How can we explain this high level of support for the painful internal adjustment path pursued in the Baltic states and Bulgaria? Policymakers

---

[21] For example, in Latvia former Prime Minister Andris Skele, a member of the co-governing People's Party, called for a devaluation because he deemed the social costs of fiscal consolidation as too high (EIU 2009c). In early 2009, a singer and an economist had been charged by Latvian authorities for critical comments about the sustainability of the exchange-rate regime. In Bulgaria, two government officials were forced to resign after being strongly criticized for perceived lack of commitment to the currency board in early 2010 (EIU 2010).

and observers repeatedly emphasized two main issues when explaining the rationale for the choice of internal adjustment: One of the most important points, mentioned over and over again, was the high level of foreign-currency borrowing in these countries and the high vulnerability to devaluation this created for households and firms (e.g., Marer 2010; Purfield and Rosenberg 2010; Masso and Krillo 2011: 6). For example, in a public debate about macroeconomic adjustment in the Baltics, the director of the Lithuanian central bank's economics department Raimondas Kuodis reiterated that his position regarding devaluation was "no, no, and no" because "a substantial devaluation would lead to the bankruptcy of many."[22] In discussions (Lithuania) and negotiations (Latvia) with the IMF, the authorities stressed the risk that corporate and household debt burdens would rise quickly with a devaluation as one of the main motivations for continuing their exchange-rate regimes (IMF 2009b: 9f; 2009c: 12). The second frequently mentioned reason for choosing internal over external adjustment was the international dimension of this decision. Not only did this strategy entail a credible exit strategy in the form of euro adoption,[23] but external adjustment also carried large contagion risk across the other fixed exchange-rate regimes. These issues raised the opportunity cost of external adjustment, because the EU, which feared spillover effects to all Eastern European countries, and the Nordic countries, whose banking sectors had large stakes in the Baltic financial system, emphasized their strong preference for exchange-rate stability (IMF 2009b: 10; 2012a). This was particularly important for Latvia, which depended on international financial support. Summing up these two main issues, the governor of the Latvian central bank Ilmars Rimsevics was reported in February 2009 as saying that devaluation "would swell debt, cause a 'tremendous' loss of confidence and prompt Estonia and Lithuania to follow suit." [24] Two additional points in favor of internal adjustment were often raised in the debate: The first was the unclear effect of devaluation on exports. Given the high level of imported inputs in the production of exports and the depressed economic situation on the countries' main export markets, which were suffering from the Great Recession, it was argued that devaluation would only produce small gains in competitiveness (e.g., EIU 2009d; Purfield and Rosenberg 2010: 12). Making this point forcefully, Estonian Deputy Central Bank

---

[22] Baltic Management Institute, http://www.bmi.lt/en/news-and-events/news/113/?print=1
[23] An issue that was especially important for the Baltic states, which saw euro adoption also as a way to consolidate their independence from Russia.
[24] www.bloomberg.com Baltic Currency-Peg Defense Cuts Reserves Amid Slump (Update 1), 23 February 2009.

Governor Marten Ross remarked that "devaluation would not solve any competition issues."[25] Another issue frequently mentioned was the high level of labor market flexibility in these countries, which was likely to facilitate adjustment, especially the downward adjustment of wages, and hence would speed up the pace of adjustment.

Overall, this suggests that policymakers in the Baltics and Bulgaria were acutely aware of the significant direct and indirect vulnerabilities of their electorates to external adjustment. In light of this situation, they chose the lesser evil of internal adjustment, although they knew that this alternative adjustment strategy would be painful as well. This becomes clearest in the case of Latvia, which bargained hard with the IMF for being allowed to retain its fixed exchange rate. In the staff report for Latvia's request of an IMF Stand-By Arrangement (SBA), the IMF emphasized that "the authorities' unequivocal commitment to the exchange rate peg has determined their choice of program strategy. Though this commitment augurs well for program ownership, the authorities also recognize that their choice brings difficult consequences, including the need for fiscal tightening and the possibility that recession could be protracted, perhaps more so than if an alternative strategy had been adopted" (IMF 2009b: 9).

How did these policy decisions affect politics and the political fate of decision makers in these countries? The argument presented in this book suggests that despite the severe pain imposed by policymakers on their electorates in these four internally adjusting countries, the political costs associated with this strategy should be lower than the political costs that would likely have been associated with external adjustment. In recognition of their extraordinarily high level of vulnerability to external adjustment, voters should therefore limit their punishment of the government for the harsh economic crisis.

Of course it is difficult to establish a counterfactual to the policy path chosen by these countries. However, it is striking that although political tremors affected all four countries, no government pursuing serious internal adjustment was completely ousted from power. Even though changes in the government occurred, it was typically more reform-minded politicians who were voted into office (see also EBRD 2010). In Estonia, the ruling three-party coalition broke apart in May 2009 after the Social Democrats left the coalition to protest the postponement of an increase in unemployment benefits in light of deep structural labor market reforms and rising unemployment rates. Prime Minister Ansip continued to implement harsh

---

[25] Ibid.

internal adjustment with a center-right minority government until the next regularly scheduled elections in 2011, in which the government was reelected with a strengthened mandate. In Lithuania, the Social Democratic government, which had pursued procyclical fiscal policies in the boom phase and had neglected to react swiftly to the mounting imbalances in the economy, was voted out of office in October 2008. The new center-right government, which called itself a "coalition for change" (EIU 2008b) and was headed by an "ultimate fiscal hawk" (Aslund 2010: 37), almost immediately designed a package of anti-crisis measures concentrated on balancing the budget and cutting public spending. Although the country was shaken by a day of anti-austerity rioting one month later and although the government faced a drop in popularity, it continued its adjustment path and remained in government throughout the crisis (Krupavicus 2011).[26] Moreover, Lithuanians elected a candidate who openly supported the government's internal adjustment program in the May 2009 presidential elections (Krupavicus 2010). In Latvia, the most notable event was a large protest march ending in riots in January 2009 in which 10,000 people protested against the austerity measures but also voiced their dissatisfaction with Latvian politics more generally. This event resulted in the resignation of the prime minister and his cabinet, which had led a fragile coalition government even before the crisis began. Although this event has been classified as a case of government turnover (Pepinsky 2012), it was in fact more a major reshuffling of the cabinet. The new cabinet included four of the former coalition partners, seven of the former government's ministers and an equally center-right orientation. It is therefore perhaps not surprising that the new government was as intent as the old one on implementing the painful internal adjustment measures needed to rebalance the economy. Although it lost one of its coalition partners in March 2010, it governed until the regular October 2010 elections, after which Prime Minister Valdis Dombrovskis continued to govern, albeit with somewhat different coalition partners (Bloom 2011).[27] In terms of public protests, with the exception of the January 2009 riots, there were relatively few and only fairly small protests against the anti-crisis measures in Latvia. Given the magnitude of fiscal consolidation and structural reform in this country, the Latvian case is hence particularly notable for its comparatively low level of political change

---

[26] The center-right government did, however, lose the October 2012 parliamentary elections.

[27] The election campaign had been dominated by the economy and relationships with Russia.

and public opposition in this country. In Bulgaria, regular elections were held in July 2009. The incumbent government, headed by the Socialists, was resoundingly defeated and a new government headed by the center-right Citizens for European Development of Bulgaria (GERB) was elected. The campaign had been characterized by two main topics, the fight against corruption and the fight against the economic crisis in which the GERB proposed a much more austere policy geared toward internal adjustment than the outgoing government, including cuts in public administration, fiscal consolidation, and a reduction in the government's role in the economy (EIU 2009a; Aslund 2010: 42).

In sum, policymakers in all four internally adjusting countries faced political difficulties, public protests, and electoral challenges. Yet, given the size of reforms and the harshness of their consequences for the domestic economies, conventional political economy approaches would lead us to expect much more far-reaching difficulties, protests, and election outcomes. The experience of these countries thus supports this book's argument that it can be politically advisable to implement painful internal adjustment policies when the alternative would impose even higher costs on national voters.

7.3.2 A Mixed Bag: Hungary and Romania

In contrast to the four countries that implemented internal adjustment strategies, Hungary and Romania pursued more mixed strategies, combining elements of both internal and external adjustment. This choice is not surprising if one considers the vulnerability profiles of the electorates in these countries, which exhibited high levels of vulnerability to both internal and external adjustment.

In both countries, the high level of foreign-currency denominated debt was an important factor for the governments' decisions not to pursue a purely external adjustment strategy but to implement internal adjustment measures as well (and through this decision to receive external funding from the IMF and others). In Hungary, the impact of the forint devaluation on households owing foreign-currency denominated debt emerged as "a key concern" during the crisis and a major topic of debate (EBRD 2010: 173), in addition to the key issues of inflation and the budget deficit. The Romanian government argued that the immediate objective of its decision to request an IMF Stand-By Arrangement was "to facilitate an orderly adjustment of the external deficit, thus easing excessive pressures on the exchange rate which could otherwise cause severe balance sheet effects on the corporate and household sectors, resulting in a sharper recession and strains in the banking sector" (Government of Romania 2009: 1). Overall, the significant foreign-currency exposure of households and corporates in both countries strongly exacerbated the financial sector consequences of exchange-rate changes, thus limiting the appetite for external adjustment (Bakker and Christiansen 2011).[28]

In light of the high vulnerability of Hungarian and Romanian voters to both external and internal adjustment coupled with the initial delay in implementing serious adjustment measures, which subsequently increased the pain caused by the adjustment measures, the argument predicts that incumbent governments in these countries should have faced significant political problems and electoral challenges. This prediction is borne out both in Hungary and Romania.[29]

When the crisis hit Hungary in the fall of 2008, the country was governed by a single-party minority government headed by Prime Minister Ferenc Gyurcsány from the Hungarian Socialist Party (MSZP). Amid worsening economic conditions and the fall of the currency, the prime minister resigned in March 2009 in a surprise move and was replaced in a constructive vote of no confidence by a more technocratic government headed by the former minister of the economy and national development, Gordon Bajnai.[30] Interestingly, the main opposition party, the conservative Fidesz, did not push harder for a government of their own, despite their very high level of popularity. It has been argued that Fidesz did not want to take responsibility during a severe economic crisis, especially in light of the widespread problems with foreign-currency loans among Hungarian voters (Ilonszki and Kurtán 2009). In fact, despite its fervent criticism of the unpopular Socialist government for its economic and structural policies, Fidesz had not yet presented a reform program of their own at the time of the collapse of the government in March 2009 (EIU 2009c). The new prime minister announced (and subsequently implemented) deeper spending cuts and more far-reaching structural reforms than his predecessor and promised to ease pressure on the forint, which he said put 700,000

---

[28] In both countries, the governments also introduced measures to discourage foreign-currency borrowing, and the Hungarian government created several policy instruments designed to support debt-laden households holding foreign-currency denominated debt.

[29] In both countries governments faced political difficulties not only because of the economic crisis but also because corruption charges created a lot of disenchantment with policymakers.

[30] Gyurcsány had been in a politically difficult situation ever since his admittance had been leaked to the public shortly after the 2006 election that he had lied to the electorate about the state of the economy to stay in power.

homeowners and 1 million car owners in peril because of their foreign-currency denominated debt.[31] While the austere stabilization policies implemented by the new government succeeded in stabilizing the currency, both unemployment and inflation increased further as a result of internal adjustment. Given these continued economic problems in addition to persistent accusations of corruption against the incumbent Socialist Party, Fidesz won a landslide victory in the next regular elections in April 2010, whereas the Socialists lost about two-thirds of their seats in parliament.[32]

In Romania, a minority coalition government with a center-right orientation had been presiding over the long boom period and the accumulation of severe external imbalances, despite warnings from both the IMF and the EU that this development was unsustainable (EIU 2008c). When the Lehman Brothers collapse in September 2008 led to a sudden stop in capital inflows, resulting in a sharp depreciation of the currency and big losses on the Bucharest stock exchange, the country was just in the process of preparing for the next regular elections to be held in November 2008. As a government that had delayed adjustment despite growing imbalances and that was caught by the emergence of a balance-of-payments crisis, the incumbent parties were resoundingly defeated in the elections by the two main opposition parties, the Social Democratic Party and the center-right Democratic Liberal Party (DLP). After some difficult negotiations, these two parties formed a coalition government headed by Emil Boc from the DLP. Although the new government immediately withdrew the fiscal stimulus package proposed by the previous government, conflicts about how to address the economic crisis arose quickly between the two coalition partners, with the DLP favoring a much more austere path than the Social Democrats. The conclusion of an IMF program in March 2009, one of whose goals was to prevent (or slow down) a further depreciation of the leu, committed the governing parties to internal adjustment measures. Although these were only implemented in a half-hearted manner (Stan and Zaharia 2010), the currency stabilized. Nonetheless, the divergent policy stances of both parties led to increasing tensions within the government, which culminated in its breakdown in October 2009, a good month before the next presidential elections and amid major protests against the government's austerity measures. On October 5, a general strike was held in which 800,000 people participated, protesting especially against the wage cuts in the public sector and the increasing unemployment rate. The fall

---

[31] *The Economist*, 1 April 2009, New Leader, Same Old Constraints?
[32] In addition, the election saw the emergence of an extreme right party (Jobbik).

of the government created a political vacuum, during which Romania was governed by an interim government with limited political powers, so that adjustment stalled during this period.[33] This political crisis only ended after the reelection of the center-right President Basescu. Boc formed a new center-right government, which quickly implemented more austere adjustment measures (Aslund 2010). However, it continued to face political difficulties: In June 2010 it narrowly escaped a vote of no confidence concerning its proposal to cut public sector wages and pensions, parts of which the Constitutional Court ruled as unconstitutional a few days later.

As in the case studies of Thailand and South Korea in the previous chapter, the experiences of Hungary and Romania thus highlight the political difficulties of implementing macroeconomic adjustment in countries where voters exhibit high vulnerabilities to external and internal adjustment.

7.3.3 Uncontroversial External Adjustment: The Czech Republic and Poland

How did the politics of macroeconomic adjustment play out in the Czech Republic and Poland, the two countries that implemented predominantly external adjustment strategies? As is to be expected in light of the vulnerability profiles in both countries, this choice of adjustment path was relatively uncontroversial. Initially, the depreciation of the currencies was seen as a welcome reversal of the exchange-rate appreciation these economies had seen in the pre-crisis months. This appreciation had been controversial especially in the Czech Republic, where the export industry had complained about the strong currency and where measures had been taken since April 2008 to slow down further appreciation of the koruna.[34] As a result, the depreciation of the currency that followed the collapse of Lehman Brothers in September 2008 was not perceived as a particularly worrisome development. On the contrary, both central banks continued to cut interest rates in the fall of 2008 despite the depreciating exchange rates, and governments pursued neutral or accommodative fiscal policies during the height of the crisis. The depreciating exchange rate also does not seem to have received a lot of media attention. Given the low vulnerability of Czech and Polish voters to external adjustment, this is not surprising. Overall, a World Bank study concludes that this low level of vulnerability, especially the relatively low

---

[33] Among others, the second review of the IMF's Stand-By-Arrangement could not be completed because the outgoing administration was legally prohibited from submitting the 2010 budget (IMF 2010d).

[34] *Czech Republic Today*, 22 July 2008.

foreign-currency denomination of loans and deposits permitted especially the Czech economy "to reap the benefits of currency depreciation without experiencing major balance sheet effects" (Mitra et al. 2010: 66).

The predominant reliance on exchange-rate adjustment and the fact that the governments in both countries did not implement painful internal adjustment during the peak of the global and financial crisis in late 2008 and early 2009 suggests that given their electorates' vulnerability profiles, both governments should face little political problems. However, although this prediction is borne out in the Polish case, it applies to a much lesser extent to the Czech case.

In Poland, a centrist coalition government under Prime Minister Donald Tusk led the country throughout the crisis. Its support in the public remained comfortably high throughout the crisis (Tworzecki 2012), and the coalition partners did well both in the European Elections in June 2009 and local elections in November 2010. The government's position was further strengthened when centrist Bronislav Komorowski, the candidate from the ruling Civic Platform, won the presidential elections in July 2010, which ended a period of cohabitation between the centrist government and the conservative president. [35] One year later, in the campaign for the next parliamentary elections, the ruling government emphasized that it had steered the economy through the economic crisis relatively unharmed (Tworzecki 2012: 3).[36] In an October 2011 survey, respondents evaluated both the government's overall performance as well as its economic policy positively (CBOS Public Opinion 2011). As a result, the governing coalition gained seats in the next parliamentary elections in October 2011, making it the first to be reelected in Poland's post-communist history.

Czech crisis politics were much more muddled. When the crisis hit Eastern Europe, the Czech Republic was governed by a center-right minority government consisting of three parties. Given significant ideological differences between the governing parties, internal divisions within the largest coalition partner, the Civic Democratic Party (ODS), and volatile parliamentary support, this coalition was inherently unstable even before the crisis hit the Czech Republic (EIU 2008a). Because Czech voters had a very low vulnerability to external adjustment, the depreciation of the koruna played no role in the political debate, which was dominated by other issues,

---

[35] These elections had to be held early after the former President Lech Kaczynski had been killed in a plane crash in April 2010.

[36] Although overall, the campaign was less focused on economic issues and waged more in terms of a "culture war."

most notably the ratification of the Lisbon Treaty (Linek and Lacina 2010). Nonetheless, domestic economic policy was politically contentious, which is not surprising if one considers the high vulnerability of Czech voters to internal adjustment. Although the Czech government had implemented reforms that were far less painful than those of the other Eastern European countries and additionally implemented some stimulus measures to soften the impact of the global financial crisis, it fell in a vote of no confidence in March 2009. It was replaced by a technocratic caretaker government supported by the two main parties, the ODS and the Social Democrats, which ruled until the next regular elections in May 2010 and received high popular approval ratings (Stegmaier and Vlachová 2011).[37] In the meantime, the political scene remained turbulent. A party split of the Christian Democrats KDU-CSL, one of the previous coalition partners, led to the foundation of a new party, the rightist TOP 09. In addition, another conservative liberal party with an anti-corruption stance, Public Affairs, became an active player on the national scene. After a campaign dominated by the economic crisis, these two new parties did surprisingly well in the next elections and formed a center-right government with the ODS in the summer of 2010.

This shows that although both Poland and the Czech Republic pursued external adjustment strategies, which did not impose too much pain in their economies, the political fate of their governments differed. Whereas the Polish government was rewarded with reelection for its economic policy strategy, the Czech government broke down. This breakdown, however, was not caused by the government's crisis management, but rather resulted from a generally turbulent political environment. The Czech experience thus illustrates that adjustment can remain a second-rate issue if it does not impose significant pain on voters, leaving room for other issues to become salient in domestic politics.

7.4 Conclusion

Overall, the Eastern European experience during the first phase of the most recent global financial crisis shows that in line with this book's argument, differences in electorates' vulnerability profiles led to different policy responses in the eight new EU member states that had not yet adopted the common currency by the time the crisis hit. In the Baltic countries and Bulgaria, voters exhibited a moderate vulnerability to internal adjustment but a very high vulnerability to external adjustment. In particular, voters and

---

[37] Nonetheless, the interim Prime Minister Fischer did not stand for reelection.

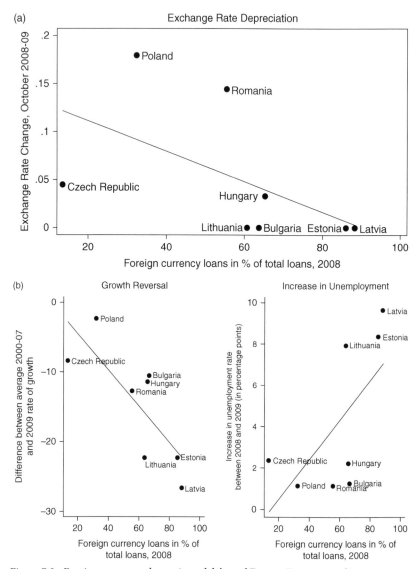

Figure 7.3. Foreign-currency denominated debt and Eastern European policy responses: a. External adjustment, b. Internal adjustment.

firms in these countries held unusually large amounts of foreign-currency denominated debt, which significantly raised the potential cost of a devaluation of the currency. As a result, governments in these countries were able to push through massive contractionary fiscal and nominal wage policies. These vulnerability profiles differed from voters' vulnerability profiles in the other four Eastern European countries (the Czech Republic, Hungary, Poland, and Romania), whose vulnerability to external adjustment was significantly lower and vulnerability to internal adjustment higher than in the Baltic countries and Bulgaria. As a result, governments in these countries chose more externally oriented adjustment strategies.

In contrast to the Asian crisis cases discussed in the previous chapter, what is striking about the Eastern European experience is the high level of voters' direct balance sheet vulnerabilities to external adjustment. Foreign-currency lending to households played a much more important role in the recent crisis than in any previous crisis. Together with foreign-currency lending to corporations, it constituted one of the key issues in Eastern European crisis management. The relationship between foreign-currency denominated debt exposure and different adjustment strategies is striking. Figures 7.3a and 7.3b show the relationship between the prevalence of private foreign-currency lending and different policy outcomes associated either with external adjustment (exchange-rate depreciation) or internal adjustment (measured as growth reversal and unemployment increases). The figures show that countries with high levels of foreign-currency denominated debt endured much sharper downturns in their domestic economies than those economies with a low exposure to foreign-currency debt. The latter in turn saw a stronger depreciation in their exchange rates.

Overall, the findings in this chapter demonstrate that differences in voters' vulnerability profiles can lead to very different policy responses to speculative pressure in countries affected by balance-of-payments crises. As a result of financial globalization, exchange-rate policy decisions have become much more politicized and are no longer an "easy solution" to balance-of-payments problems. In contrast, the policy path of internal adjustment, which hitherto has been regarded as unfeasible for democratic policymakers, has become a viable policy option when voters' vulnerabilities to external adjustment are very high.

EIGHT

Conclusions

When are policymakers willing to adjust their macroeconomic policies to address balance-of-payments problems? Which types of adjustment strategies do they choose? Under what circumstances do they delay reform, and when are such delays likely to result in currency or other financial crises?

This book has answered these questions from a political economy perspective. It has argued that the distributional consequences of macroeconomic adjustment on individual voters shape policymakers' incentives to address balance-of-payments problems, with respect both to the choice between different types of adjustment strategies and to the timing of when such strategies are seriously implemented. Building on the insight that in financially open countries, exchange-rate, monetary, and fiscal policy are intricately linked, it has shown that voters can be both directly and indirectly exposed to changes in these policies. Voters are directly vulnerable to macroeconomic adjustment when they have immediate effects on their personal finances, but also can be indirectly exposed when the policy adjustments adversely affect their employers or the economy in general. The overall impact of a certain adjustment strategy on voters therefore depends on the net effect of the direct personal and indirect employment-specific and general economic effects of macroeconomic adjustment.

The electorate's vulnerability profile, that is the distribution of voters' overall vulnerabilities to both external and internal types of adjustment, strongly influences policymakers' incentives for reform. When balance-of-payments problems emerge, policymakers facing an electorate more vulnerable to exchange-rate (or external) adjustment have incentives to favor structural reforms and adjustment of monetary, fiscal, and structural policies (or internal adjustment), and vice versa. When voters are vulnerable to both internal and external adjustment, however, policymakers face strong pressure both to stabilize the exchange rate and to leave domestic economic structures and policies untouched. Although this is impossible in the long run, policymakers can achieve this goal in the short to medium run by financing the deficit in the current account, for example, by engaging in sterilized sales of foreign-currency reserves. This creates incentives for policymakers to delay reform, especially when they expect short-term electoral advantages from such delay. However, by allowing the misalignment to accumulate, the eventual costs of adjustment rise further if the problems are caused by fundamental economic problems. Major financial crashes are particularly likely when voters are vulnerable to both external and internal adjustment policies and when electoral incentives discourage timely reform.

The quantitative and qualitative evidence presented in the book supports this argument. Focusing on the direct and indirect determinants of voters' vulnerabilities to external and internal adjustment, Chapters 3 and 4 analyzed survey data from individuals and firms, who were asked to evaluate their personal and nation's economic situation and particular macroeconomic policies, respectively. The findings of these two sets of microlevel analyses suggest that both voters and their employers evaluate different macroeconomic adjustment strategies in light of their specific vulnerability profiles to changes in the exchange and interest rate. To complement these findings, the case studies of the two most recent global financial crises – the Asian financial crisis of 1997–8 (Chapter 6) and the global financial and economic crisis (Chapter 7) – examine domestic vulnerability profiles and national crisis responses to these crises. Taken together, these case studies demonstrate that differences in the distribution of vulnerabilities among countries' electorates and their electoral calendars can translate into different policy responses to balance-of-payments problems and speculative pressure on countries' currencies.

Regarding the microlevel findings, three conclusions deserve particular emphasis. First, the analyses highlight the importance of *balance sheet considerations* for exchange-rate and monetary policymaking in financially open economies. Foreign-currency denominated liabilities have created new risks associated with exchange-rate adjustment, whereas debt tied to domestic interest rates raises the stakes with regard to monetary policy. Chapter 3 demonstrated that during the global economic and financial crisis of 2008–9, a depreciation of the currency significantly raised voters' concerns about both their personal economic situation and that of the national economy when they were living in countries in which borrowing in foreign currencies was widespread. Likewise, voters repaying a mortgage were particularly concerned about their personal situation when monetary policy was tightened and when economic growth was collapsing. They were less likely to be concerned when interest rates were lowered and the economy was only modestly affected by the crisis. Looking at the indirect, employment-specific sources of voters' vulnerabilities to different types of macroeconomic adjustment, Chapter 4 investigated how firm-specific vulnerability profiles shape firms' assessments of their countries' monetary and exchange-rate policies. It showed that balance sheet concerns, such as loans from foreign banks and firms' overall dependence on borrowing, influence firms' self-reported vulnerabilities to external and internal adjustment. In contrast to previous research (e.g., Frieden 1991b), which has mostly focused on the real price effects of exchange-rate changes, these results underline that in a financially liberalized world, exchange-rate and monetary policies additionally have significant effects on the financial situation of voters and firms. Voters' policy preferences in these areas can hence only be fully understood if both types of effects of macroeconomic adjustment are taken into account.

Second, the results suggest that voters are aware that adjustments in macroeconomic policies can affect them *directly and indirectly* and are able to differentiate between these effects. Previous research has assumed that voters have homogenous preferences regarding external adjustment and has argued that they oppose depreciation because it reduces their purchasing power. These popular preferences have been juxtaposed with those of the corporate sector, especially the manufacturing or tradables sector, which is argued to mainly favor depreciation because this can increase its international competitiveness (Blomberg et al. 2005). Likewise, voters' preferences toward internal adjustment have been assumed to be quite homogenous as well. Labor in particular (and hence a majority of voters) has been argued to uniformly oppose internal adjustment and the increase in unemployment associated with it (Eichengreen 1992, 1996; Simmons 1994). In contrast, this book has argued that voters are not indifferent to the fate of the corporate sector and the national economy in general, because their jobs and incomes are influenced by it as well, although naturally they are not blind for their personal situation either. Moreover, it has demonstrated that voters can differentiate between these effects. For example, during the 2008–9 global financial crisis, several European central banks significantly cut interest rates to support their struggling financial sectors. The evidence presented in Chapter 3 suggests that voters were aware that, even though these cuts were beneficial for their own personal situation, they signaled more serious problems in the national economy. These results also inform the debate about the relative importance of economic and distributional issues in determining individuals' policy preferences and voting decisions, which has been receiving increasing attention by international political economy scholars in recent years (e.g., Hainmueller and Hiscox 2006; Mansfield and Mutz 2009; Leblang et al. 2011). The findings presented in this book suggest that both the direct and the indirect material effects of adjustment are important determinants of individuals' evaluations of their overall vulnerability to different policy options.

Third, the data presented in Chapter 4 suggest that high levels of vulnerability to *both internal and external adjustment* are not an infrequent phenomenon. More than 20 percent of the firms in this worldwide sample reported that they were concerned about both the exchange rate and the interest rate. As the combination of vulnerability to both types of adjustment leads to resistance to any changes in economic policy, the relatively high incidence of actors with such a vulnerability profile means that policymakers can face strong incentives to delay macroeconomic adjustment – a finding echoed by the case studies of Thailand, South Korea, Hungary, and Romania presented in the second part of the book. Whereas most research to date has focused on explaining either exchange-rate policy preferences or monetary policy preferences on their own, this finding suggests that in financially open economies in which macroeconomic policies are tightly linked, a combined approach is necessary to accurately assess such policy preferences.

Overall, these microlevel findings suggest that voters' vulnerability profiles and the resulting distribution of vulnerabilities among countries' electorates can differ widely. The second part of the book therefore investigated how these differences affect actual policy choices at the country level. The two empirical chapters in this section examined the reasons for the different macroeconomic policy choices in four countries affected by the Asian financial crisis of 1997–8 (Chapter 6) and in eight Eastern European countries affected by the global financial and economic crisis of 2008–10 (Chapter 7). The case studies show that the variation in policymakers' willingness to adjust to emerging balance-of-payments pressures can be traced back to differences in distributional and electoral concerns. When voters were vulnerable to only one type of adjustment strategy, policymakers typically acted decisively when balance-of-payments pressures emerged and rapidly implemented the strategy to which their voters were less vulnerable. In those countries in which the electorate's overall vulnerability to external adjustment far exceeded its vulnerability to monetary and fiscal tightening (as in Hong Kong, the Baltic states, and Bulgaria), the authorities decisively implemented internal adjustment. When voters were much less vulnerable to exchange-rate depreciation than internal adjustment (as in Taiwan, the Czech Republic, and Poland), adjustment typically was achieved mainly through a depreciation of the currency. In contrast, electorates in a third group of countries exhibited high vulnerabilities to both depreciation and domestic economic tightening. Faced with demands to neither adjust internally nor externally, attempts at serious economic reform in Thailand, South Korea, Hungary, and Romania were initially quite muted, and the authorities heavily relied on foreign reserve sales instead. This behavior ultimately resulted in serious economic crises in these countries, all of which had to ask for outside help from the IMF. Eventually, all four countries resolved their balance-of-payments difficulties with a policy mix that involved both external and internal adjustment.

Once more, three main conclusions follow from these analyses. First, they show that distributional considerations indeed play an important role in influencing the choice of macroeconomic adjustment strategy implemented by a national government facing balance-of-payments difficulties. In all cases studied in Chapters 6 and 7, the distributional consequences of the different policy options available to policymakers were objects of serious consideration and shaped both the types of adjustment strategies ultimately chosen and the timing of their implementation. These findings underscore the importance of correctly specifying the distributional consequences of particular policies and policy mixes for a country's electorate and their influence on policymakers' willingness to implement certain policies and reforms. A better understanding of the relevant policy preferences complements and improves existing explanations, which mainly focus on the macroeconomic and institutional decision-making context that delineate the ability of policymakers to implement macroeconomic and structural policy changes.

Second, the case studies also demonstrate that distributional concerns can create strong incentives for policymakers to pursue macroeconomic policies that are detrimental in the long run. Although most existing research sees the source of such time-inconsistent behavior in institutions that encourage policymakers to discount the future (e.g., Nordhaus 1975; Rogoff 1990; Stein and Streb 2004), the approach proposed in this book suggests that a short-term bias can be rooted in distributional concerns as well. Such concerns can, of course, be exacerbated by institutional constraints such as the timing of elections. The case studies of the delayed devaluations and subsequent crises in Hungary, Romania, Thailand and South Korea demonstrate that such incentives can have serious consequences. This suggests that researchers not only need to look at the distributional consequences of certain policies at a particular point in time, but additionally need to consider the time dimension associated with these distributional effects. Moreover, the interplay between distributional and institutional incentives for time-inconsistent behavior should receive more attention.

Finally, the results show that under certain circumstances, elections can speed up rather than delay reform. Most previous research on the role of elections in the context of exchange-rate policy has argued that elections discourage depreciations, giving rise to business cycle dynamics in which depreciations and devaluations are delayed until after election day (e.g., Stein and Streb 2004; Blomberg et al. 2005; Walter 2009). The case of South Korea illustrates, however, that elections can under certain circumstances speed up the decision to adjust macroeconomic policies. As argued in Chapter 5, these circumstances chiefly involve a high probability that the effort to delay adjustment will break down before election day, making large adjustments in a crisis setting necessary shortly before elections are held. Under these circumstances, policymakers tend to be more willing to adjust economic policies to avoid a further deterioration of the situation. The effect of elections is thus conditioned by the severity of the macroeconomic problems and the probability that these will quickly escalate into a crisis.

8.1 Agenda for Future Research

The book has emphasized that in situations of macroeconomic duress, policymakers can face significant political constraints in their domestic political arena, which are rooted in the distribution of direct and indirect vulnerabilities of a country's electorate to different types of macroeconomic reform. Concentrating on the domestic politics of macroeconomic adjustment has allowed me to explore in detail the sources and effects of distributional considerations and their interaction with electoral incentives on policy decisions regarding macroeconomic adjustment designed to address balance-of-payments problems. At the same time, the selective focus on these issues entails that a number of questions are left unanswered. The book thus opens up a number of important avenues for future research.

For one, this book has investigated the variation in voters' vulnerability profiles to different types of macroeconomic adjustment, but has not focused on the sources of such variation. In particular, it has shown that financial globalization has turned the composition of balance sheets into critical determinants of voters' vulnerabilities to internal and external adjustment. Although this analysis provides us with a better understanding of the systemic risks associated with mismatched balance sheets and other sources of vulnerability to adjustment, it leaves open the question when and why crisis-prone vulnerability profiles emerge in the first place. The answers to these questions are likely to be associated with countries' institutional settings, such as the degree of capital account openness or the exchange-rate regime. By encouraging or discouraging the accumulation of vulnerabilities to both external and internal adjustment, such institutions can exacerbate or mitigate policymakers' incentives to delay macroeconomic adjustment and to choose one type of macroeconomic adjustment over the other. For instance, in an environment of fixed exchange rates individuals and firms are more likely to operate under the expectation that the exchange rate will remain stable whereas interest rates are likely to be volatile. As a result, they have incentives to invest and borrow in such a way that their vulnerability to interest-rate changes is comparatively low and their vulnerability to exchange-rate adjustments is comparatively high. In contrast, more intermediate exchange-rate regimes, such as soft pegs, frequently adjusted parities, or crawling bands, often result in relatively high levels of both exchange-rate and interest-rate stability in the short run, which encourages economic actors to accumulate vulnerabilities to both exchange-rate and interest-rate adjustments in these regimes. Intermediate exchange-rate regimes should consequently be associated with a higher incidence of joint vulnerabilities to both types of macroeconomic adjustment and should hence exacerbate policymakers' incentives to delay macroeconomic adjustment. Incidentally, this offers a possible explanation for the "unstable middle" hypothesis, which holds that intermediate exchange-rate regimes are more crisis prone than either fixed or flexible exchange-rate regimes. Future research should therefore examine how different vulnerability profiles emerge and which factors influence the strength and the direction of the distributional constraints the government is likely to face.

Moreover, in addition to distributional considerations and the timing of elections, policymakers' incentives about how and when to adjust their macroeconomic policies in response to balance-of-payments problems are influenced by other characteristics of the domestic political setting as well. Such characteristics include partisan politics, the electoral system, the number of veto players, and the degree of central bank independence. All of these factors have been shown to influence exchange-rate, monetary, and fiscal policymaking (for reviews of this literature, see, for example, Broz and Frieden 2001; Steinberg and Walter forthcoming). What remains less clear is how they interact with the distributional and electoral incentives discussed in this book. For example, different electoral systems and partisan politics might give certain groups in the electorate greater weight. Rather than the overall distribution of vulnerabilities in the electorate, the distribution of vulnerabilities among these subsets of voters would then be the decisive elements shaping policymakers' reactions to macroeconomic imbalances. The type of electoral competition is hence likely to affect the politics of adjustment. Likewise, although this book has argued that voters care about the effects of different policy options on their employers and the national economy, special interests additionally lobby for policies that do not take into account the overall vulnerability of the electorate as a whole. This raises the question how policymakers strike the balance between the demands of special interests and the needs of their electorates. Future research should therefore investigate how different assumptions about the behavior of voters and interest groups influence the distributional politics associated with the resolution of balance-of-payments problems. Moreover, whereas this book has focused on macroeconomic adjustment in largely democratic countries, balance-of-payments imbalances emerge in autocratic countries as well, and autocratic policymakers equally encounter different vulnerability profiles among their supporters. How do the resulting distributional concerns affect the politics of adjustment in autocratic political systems? Finally, even though this book has treated the choice between internal and external adjustment largely as a discrete choice between two policy options to maximize analytical clarity, this interplay between distributional and institutional factors is likely to affect the policy mix between external and internal adjustment measures as well.

In a similar vein, future research should explore in more detail how exchange-rate, monetary, and fiscal policy adjustments interact with decisions in other policy areas. The experiences of the deficit countries most affected by the euro crisis, such as Greece, Ireland, Spain, or Portugal, demonstrate the importance of such an undertaking. Faced with significant balance-of-payments problems, these countries are in the uncomfortable position that both exchange-rate and interest-rate adjustment is barred to them. This is because external adjustment would require opting out of the common currency altogether and reintroducing a national currency, whereas monetary policy is set centrally by the European Central Bank for all EMU member states. These countries are therefore forced to rebalance their economies through fiscal tightening and structural reforms in other policy fields. Examples for policy fields that are likely to be affected by governments' attempts at rebalancing the economy are labor market policy because wage restraint helps to restore domestic prices to internationally competitive levels, social policy in which measures such as benefit reductions or increases in retirement age can be implemented, or trade policy, which is most directly related to the current account. Whereas the interaction of trade policy decisions with monetary and exchange-rate decisions has been examined by past research (Simmons 1994), future research should investigate the interaction between decisions in these different policy fields and the determinants of specific mixes of adjustment policies in more detail.

Given the inherently international nature of balance-of-payments problems, future research should also investigate more closely the interplay of the domestic politics of macroeconomic adjustment with international politics. For example, the case studies presented in Chapters 6 and 7 showed that the IMF exercised a lot of influence on the adjustment strategies ultimately implemented in Thailand and South Korea, and to a lesser extent in Hungary, Romania, and Latvia, the five countries that relied on IMF financing support. In Thailand and South Korea, the IMF essentially forced the authorities to implement far-reaching internal adjustment measures despite fierce opposition from national policymakers, which was based on the grounds that their electorates were highly vulnerable to such a course of action. On the other hand, in Latvia the IMF backed an adjustment strategy, which it clearly judged second best, because the EU was strictly opposed to the IMF's proposal of having Latvia quickly adopt the euro at a depreciated rate. This suggests that to fully understand the variation in adjustment strategies, the influence of powerful international organizations such as the IMF or the EU needs to be accounted for. This is particularly important as IMF policies and conditions themselves often reflect highly politicized decisions as well (Pop-Eleches 2009; Copelovitch 2010a) and are sometimes strategically sought by domestic policymakers unable to pursue unpopular reforms by themselves (Vreeland 2003). At the same time, the possibility to receive additional funds from the IMF or other influential international actors, such as the United States or the European Union, may incentivize policymakers to delay adjustment, because this possibility increases the capacity to finance the current account deficit. Such a strategy is likely to appear particularly attractive to governments faced with an electorate vulnerable to both internal and external adjustment.

Finally, the book's focus on domestic politics also entails that the role of international financial markets and speculators has received only limited attention. Much research in economics has shown that speculation against countries' currencies is most likely to arise when financial market participants doubt the authorities' willingness and ability to address balance-of-payments problems through decisive policy adjustments (e.g., Krugman 1979; Obstfeld 1994, 1996), but can also arise because of herding behavior (e.g., Morris and Shin 1998). Policymakers consequently have to balance the demands from their electorate against those of international market participants. Once more, research into the interplay between these factors promises to yield valuable insights into the dynamics of the politics of macroeconomic adjustment and crises.

This wealth of questions opened by the book's findings shows that although the book furthers our understanding of the domestic politics of macroeconomic adjustment and crises, it also opens up many promising avenues for future study. In particular, more research is needed on the interaction between the distributional considerations emphasized in this book and other domestic as well as international factors, which affect policymakers' incentives to adjust economic policies.

8.2 Policy Implications

The findings presented in this book also have a number of policy implications, which may be of use to policymakers and policy advisors.

Most importantly, the argument and evidence presented in this book suggest that distributional concerns can provide powerful incentives to deviate from economically efficient outcomes. Rather than adjusting economic policies quickly to address balance-of-payments imbalances and the macroeconomic problems associated with such imbalances, the fear of hurting voters directly or indirectly can induce governments to delay such adjustment by financing the deficit as long as possible. This strategy is going to be particularly attractive to governments who can procure financing from external actors (such as the IMF, the EU, or other countries) without very strict conditions requiring an immediate adjustment of their policies. Greece in the ongoing euro crisis is a case in point: Faced with an electorate exhibiting excessive vulnerabilities to both external adjustment (a euro exit) and internal adjustment (fiscal tightening and serious structural reforms), the government has repeatedly tried to buy time from the international community. However, because such a strategy of delay usually leads to a worsening of the economic problems, it often results in a financial crisis, with potentially destructive effects not only for the affected country but also for the entire global financial system.

Second, the incentives for policymakers to delay necessary macroeconomic adjustment originate in their desire to survive politically. This turns these incentives into a powerful influence on policymakers' decision calculi. Policy advice, which ignores these incentives, is therefore likely to be equally ignored by policymakers. This makes the implementation of policies that make good economic sense but are associated with high political costs difficult at best and impossible at worst. The findings presented here suggest that a stronger consideration of the political constraints under which domestic policymakers operate would improve the ease with which the recommended policies can be implemented politically. Even if this results in the recommendation of economically second best, but politically feasible policy options, such policy advice is more likely to bring about policy change than economically superior but politically infeasible policy advice. This suggests that one-size-fits-all policy advice in response to crises is not the best route to pursue. Rather, policy recommendations should be based not only on a careful assessment of a country's economic situation, but on the political constraints as well.

Even though it is important to recognize these political constraints once the need for adjustment has arisen, it is equally important to understand that such constraints can be avoided or alleviated if addressed in good time. The book has shown that the combination of high levels of vulnerability to adjustments in both externally oriented policies such as exchange-rate policy and domestically oriented policies such as monetary, fiscal, and structural policies leads to the vulnerability profile, which is most likely to be associated with delayed adjustment and subsequent crisis. Such vulnerability profiles emerge, for example, when consumers, firms, or the public sector accumulate large unhedged foreign currency liabilities while at the same time incurring high levels of debt indexed to the domestic interest rate. To avoid the emergence of such precarious vulnerability profiles, policymakers should therefore introduce measures that prevent the accumulation of such liabilities in the first place. This could be achieved by implementing more carefully designed and well-sequenced capital account liberalization measures or by designing regulatory systems that encourage hedging and discourage the accumulation of large currency or maturity mismatches. In short, prudent financial regulation is key. While this is hardly a novel insight, the findings presented in this book imply that improved regulation would not only improve the economic constraints faced by policymakers during times of macroeconomic distress but alleviate political pressure as well.

References

Achen, Christopher, and Larry Bartels. 2004. Blind Retrospection. Electoral Responses to Drought, Flu, and Shark Attacks. Estudio/Working Paper 2004/199.

Agénor, Pierre-Richard. 2004. Macroeconomic Adjustment and the Poor: Analytical Issues and Cross-Country Evidence. *Journal of Economic Surveys* 18 (3): 351–408.

Aghion, Philippe, Philippe Bacchetta, and Abhijit Banerjee. 2004. A Corporate Balance-Sheet Approach to Currency Crises. *Journal of Economic Theory* 119: 6–30.

Aguiar, Mark. 2005. Investment, Devaluation, and Foreign Currency Exposure: The Case of Mexico. *Journal of Development Economics* 78: 95–113.

Alesina, Alberto, and Allan Drazen. 1991. Why Are Stabilizations Delayed? *American Economic Review* 81: 1170–88.

Alesina, Alberto, Nouriel Roubini, and Gerald D. Cohen. 1997. *Political Cycles and the Macroeconomy*. Cambridge MA: The MIT Press.

Anderson, Christopher. 2000. Economic Voting and Political Context: A Comparative Perspective. *Electoral Studies* 19: 151–70.

Asia Pulse. 1997. "Korean Industrialists Call for Money Mart Liberalization." September 23.

Aslund, Anders. 2010. *The Last Shall be the First: The Eastern European Financial Crisis, 2008–10*. Washington DC: The Peterson Institute.

Athukorala, Prema-chandra, and Peter G. Warr. 2002. Vulnerability to a Currency Crisis: Lessons from the Asian Experience. *The World Economy* 25 (1): 33–57.

Austrian National Bank. 2007. Die neue Fremdwährungskreditstatistik. Vorstellung und Analyse. *Statistiken* Q4/07: 26–30.

Aziz, Jahangir, Francesco Caramazza, and Ranil Salgado. 2000. Currency Crises: In Search of Common Elements. IMF Working Paper WP/00/67.

Baker, Andy. 2005. Who Wants to Globalize? Consumer Tastes and Labor Markets in a Theory of Trade Policy Beliefs. *American Journal of Political Science* 49 (4): 924–38.

Bakker, Bas, and Anne-Marie Gulde. 2010. The Credit Boom in the EU New Member States: Bad Luck or Bad Policies? IMF Working Paper WP/10/130.

Bakker, Bas, and Lone Christiansen. 2011. Crisis and Consolidation – Fiscal Challenges in Emerging Europe. *Proceedings of OeNB Workshops* 17 (February 28): 25–40.

Banducci, Susan A., Jeffry A. Karp, and Peter H. Loedel. 2003. The Euro, Economic Interest and Multi-Level Governance: Examining Support for the Common Currency. *European Journal of Political Research* 42 (5): 685–703.

Bank of Korea. 1999. *Annual Report 1998*. Seoul: The Bank of Korea.

Batra, Geeta, Daniel Kaufmann, and Andrew Stone. 2004. "The Firms Speak: What the World Business Environment Survey Tells Us about Constraints on Private Sector Development." In *Pathways Out of Poverty. Private Firms and Economic Mobility in Developing Countries*, eds. Gary Fields and Guy Pierre Pfeffermann. Norwell: Kluwer Academic Publishers. 193–214.

Bearce, David. 2003. Societal Preferences, Partisan Agents, and Monetary Policy Outcomes. *International Organization* 57: 373–410.

2007. *Monetary Divergence: Domestic Policy Autonomy in the Post-Bretton Woods Era*. Ann Arbour MI: University of Michigan Press.

Bearce, David, and Mark Hallerberg. 2011. Democracy and De Facto Exchange Rate Regimes. *Economics & Politics* 23 (2): 172–94.

Beck, Peter. 1998. Revitalizing Korea's Chaebol. *Asian Survey* 38 (11): 1018–35.

Beck, Thorsten, Katie Kibuuka, and Erwin Tiongson. 2010. Mortgage Finance in Central and Eastern Europe: Opportunity or Burden? IZA Discussion Papers No. 4758.

Beckmann, Ruth, Philipp Trein, and Stefanie Walter. 2010. Wählen in der Krise. Wirtschaftskrise und Wahlverhalten bei der deutschen Bundestagswahl 2009. Universität Heidelberg.

Berg, Andrew. 1999. *The Asia Crisis: Causes, Policy Responses, and Outcomes*. Washington DC: IMF Working Paper No. 99/138.

Berg, Andrew, Eduardo Borensztein, and Catherine Pattillo. 2005. Assessing Early Warning Systems: How Have They Worked in Practice? *IMF Staff Papers* 52 (3): 462–502.

Bernhard, William, J. Lawerence Broz, and William Roberts Clark, eds. 2003. *The Political Economy of Monetary Institutions*. Cambridge MA: MIT Press.

Bernhard, William, and David Leblang. 1999. Democratic Institutions and Exchange-Rate Commitments. *International Organization* 53 (1): 71–97.

2006. *Democratic Processes and Financial Markets: Pricing Politics*. Cambridge: Cambridge University Press.

Bird, Graham, and Thomas D. Willett. 2008. Why do Governments Delay Devaluation? The Political Economy of Exchange-Rate Inertia. *World Economics* 9 (4): 55–74.

Blaszkiewicz, Monika, and Wojciech Paczynski. 2003. "The Economic and Social Consequences of Currency Crises." In *Currency Crises in Emerging Markets*, ed. Marek Dabrowski. Norwell MA: Kluwer Academic Publishers. 145–68.

Bleakley, Hoyt, and Kevin Cowan. 2008. Corporate Dollar Debt and Depreciations: Much Ado About Nothing? *The Review of Economics and Statistics* 90 (4): 612–26.

Blomberg, Brock, Jeffry Frieden, and Ernesto Stein. 2005. Sustaining Fixed Rates: The Political Economy of Currency Pegs in Latin America. *Journal of Applied Economics* VIII (2): 203–25.

Bloom, Stephen. 2011. The 2010 Latvian Parliamentary Elections. *Electoral Studies* 30: 366–83.

Blustein, Paul. 2001. *The Chastening: Inside the Crisis That Rocked the Global Financial System and Humbled the IMF*. New York: Public Affairs.

Brambor, Thomas, William Roberts Clark, and Matt Golder. 2006. Understanding Interaction Models: Improving Empirical Analyses. *Political Analysis* 14: 63–82.

Brown, Martin, Steven Ongena, and Pinar Yesin. 2009. Foreign Currency Borrowing by Small Firms. *Swiss National Bank Working Papers* 2009–2.

Brown, Martin, Marcel Peter, and Simon Wehrmüller. 2009. *Swiss Franc Lending in Europe*. Zürich: Swiss National Bank.

Broz, Lawrence. 2002. Political System Transparency and Monetary Commitment Regimes. *International Organization* 56 (4): 861–87.

—— 2010. "Exchange Rates and Protectionism." Presented at *International Political Economy Society Conference 2010*. Harvard University, Cambridge MA.

Broz, Lawrence, and Jeffry Frieden. 2001. The Political Economy of International Monetary Relations. *Annual Review of Political Science* 4: 317–43.

Broz, Lawerence, Jeffry Frieden, and Stephen Weymouth. 2008. Exchange-Rate Policy Attitudes: Direct Evidence from Survey Data. *IMF Staff Papers* 55 (3): 417–44.

Burnside, Craig, Martin Eichenbaum, and Sergio Rebelo. 2000. Understanding the Korean and Thai Currency Crises. *Economic Perspectives (Federal Reserves Bank of Chicago)* QIII: 45–60.

Cardarelli, Roberto, Selim Elekdag, and Ayhan Kose. 2009. Capital Inflows: Macroeconomic Implications and Policy Responses. *IMF Working Paper* WP/09/40.

Carlson, John, and Naven Valev. 2008. Fixed Exchange Rate Credibility with Heterogenous Expectations. *Journal of Macroeconomics* 30 (4): 1712–22.

Carse, David. 1998. *The Impact of the Asian Crisis on the Hong Kong Banking Sector*. Speech held on 28 May at the Sixth Conference on Pacific Basin Business, Economics and Finance, Hong Kong.

Caves, Richard, Jeffrey Frankel, and Ronald Jones. 2002. *World Trade and Payments: An Introduction*. Boston: Addison Wesley Longman.

CBOS Public Opinion. 2011. Final Evaluation of the Government of Donald Tusk. *Polish Public Opinion*.

Chang, Roberto, and Andrés Velasco. 2001. A Model of Financial Crises in Emerging Markets. *The Quarterly Journal of Economics*: **116** (2) 489–517.

Chen, Chyong L. 2000. Why Has Taiwan Been Immune to the Asian Financial Crisis? *Asia-Pacific Financial Markets* 7: 45–68.

Chou, Ji. 2001. "Taiwan's Macroeconomic Performance Since 1980." In *Taiwan's Economic Success Since 1980*, eds. Chao-Cheng Mai and Chien-Sheng Shih. Cheltenham: Edward Elgar. 47–86.

Chu, Yun-han. 1999. "Surviving the East Asian Financial Storm: The Political Foundation of Taiwan's Economic Resilience." In *The Politics of the Asian Economic Crisis*, ed. T. J. Pempel. Ithaca NY: Cornell University Press. 184–202.

Chue, Timothy, and David Cook. 2008. Sudden Stops and Liability Dollarization: Evidence from Asia's Financial Intermediaries. *Pacific-Basin Finance Journal* 16: 436–52.

Chung, Un-Chan. 2004. "The Korean Economy Before and After the Crisis." In *The Korean Economy Beyond the Crisis*, eds. Duck-Koo Chung and Barry Eichengreen. Cheltenham: Edward Elgar.

Chwieroth, Jeffrey, and Andrew Walter. 2010. "Financial Crises and Political Turnover: A Long Run Panoramic View." In *International Political Economy Society Conference 2010*. Cambridge MA: Harvard University.

Claessens, Stijn, Simeon Djankov, and Lixin Colin Xu. 2000. East Asian Corporations, Before and During the Recent Financial Crisis. *The World Bank Research Observer* 15 (1): 23–46.

Clark, William Roberts. 2003. *Capitalism, not Globalism. Capital Mobility, Central Bank Independence, and the Political Control of the Economy. University of Michigan Studies in International Political Economy.* Ann Arbour: The University of Michigan Press.

Cleeland Knight, Sarah. 2010. Divested Interests: Globalization and the New Politics of Exchange Rates. *Business and Politics* 12 (2): Article 3.

Cohen, Benjamin J. 1995. "The Triad and the Unholy Trinity: Problems of International Monetary Cooperation." In *International Political Economy. Perspectives on Global Power and Wealth*, eds. Jeffry Frieden and David Lake. New York: St. Martin's Press. 255–66.

———— 2003. "Monetary Union: The Political Dimension." In *The Dollarization Debate*, eds. Dominick Salvatore, James W. Dean, and Thomas D. Willett. Oxford: Oxford University Press. 154–71.

Connolly, Richard. 2012. The Determinants of the Economic Crisis in Post-Socialist Europe. *Europe-Asia Studies* 64 (1): 35–67.

Cook, David. 2004. Monetary Policy in Emerging Markets: Can Liability Dollarization Explain Contractionary Devaluations? *Journal of Monetary Economics* 51: 1155–81.

Cooper, Richard. 1971. Currency Devaluation in Developing Countries. *Essays in International Finance* **86**: 276–304.

Copelovitch, Mark. 2010a. *The International Monetary Fund in the Global Economy.* Cambridge: Cambridge University Press.

———— 2010b. Master or Servant? Common Agency and the Political Economy of IMF Lending. *International Studies Quarterly* 54 (1): 49–77.

Copelovitch, Mark, and Jon Pevehouse. Forthcoming. Ties That Bind? Preferential Trade Agreements and Exchange Rate Policy Choice. *International Studies Quarterly.*

Corsetti, Giancarlo, Paolo Pesenti, and Nouriel Roubini. 1999. What Caused the Asian Currency and Financial Crisis? *Japan and the World Economy* 11 (3): 305–73.

Council for Economic Planning and Development. 2002. *Taiwan Statistical Data Book 2002.* Taipeh: Council for Economic Planning and Development,.

Cunat, Alejandro, and Marc Melitz. 2007. Volatility, Labor Market Flexibility, and the Pattern of Comparative Advantage. NBER Working Paper W13062.

Darvas, Zsolt. 2010. The Impact of the Crisis on Budget Policy in Central and Eastern Europe. *OECD Journal on Budgeting* 10 (1): 1–30.

Desai, Padma. 2003. *Financial Crisis, Contagion, and Containment: From Asia to Argentina.* Princeton NJ: Princeton University Press.

Dollar, David, and Mary Hallward-Driemeier. 2000. Crisis, Adjustment, and Reforms in Thailand's Industrial Firms. *The World Bank Research Observer* 15 (1): 1–22.

Dorrussen, Han, and Michaell Taylor. 2002. "Group Economic Voting: A Comparison of the Netherlands and Germany." In *Economic Voting*, eds. Han Dorrussen and Michaell Taylor. New York: Routledge. 92–120.

Downs, Anthony. 1957. *An Economic Theory of Democracy.* New York: Harper and Row.

Dreher, Axel. 2004. A Public Choice Perspective of IMF and World Bank Lending and Conditionality. *Public Choice* 119: (3–4): 445–64.

Dreher, Axel, and Stefanie Walter. 2010. Does the IMF Help or Hurt? The Effect of IMF Programs on the Likelihood and Outcome of Currency Crises. *World Development.* 1–18.

Duch, Raymond. 2007. "Comparative Studies of the Economy and the Vote." In *Encyclopedia of Comparative Politics*, eds. Charles Boix and Susan Stokes. Oxford: Oxford University Press. 805–44

Duch, Raymond, and Randolph Stevenson. 2008. *The Economic Vote. How Political and Economic Institutions Condition Election Results*. Cambridge MA: Cambridge University Press.

Duckenfield, Mark, and Mark Aspinwall. 2010. Private Interests and Exchange Rate Politics: The Case of British Business. *European Union Politics* 11 (3): 381–404.

Dunn, Malcom, and Eric Soong. 1998. "Structures, Policy Issues and Prospects of Taiwan's Financial Markets." In *Asian Financial Markets – Structures, Policy Issues and Prospects*, eds. Lukas Menkhoff and Beate Reszat. Baden-Baden: Nomos. 151–70.

EBRD. 2009. *Transition Report 2008*. London: EBRD.

    2010. *Transition Report 2009*. London: EBRD.

    2012. *Transition Report 2011. Crisis and Transition – the People's Perspective*. London: EBRD.

Echeverry, Juan Carlos, Leopoldo Fergusson, Roberto Steiner, and Camila Aguilar. 2003. 'Dollar' Debt in Colombian Firms: Are Sinners Punished During Devaluations? *Emerging Markets Review* 4: 417–49.

Economist Intelligence Unit. See EIU.

Eichengreen, Barry. 1992. *Golden Fetters: The Gold Standard and the Great Depression*. New York: Oxford University Press.

    1996. *Globalizing Capital. A History of the International Monetary System*. Princeton NJ: Princeton University Press.

Eichengreen, Barry, ed. 2003. *Capital Flows and Crises*. Cambridge MA: MIT Press.

Eichengreen, Barry, and Ricardo Hausmann. 2005. *Other People's Money. Debt Denomination and Financial Instability in Emerging Market Economies*. Chicago: The University of Chicago Press.

Eichengreen, Barry, Andrew Rose, and Charles Wyplosz. 1996. Contagious Currency Crises: First Tests. *Scandinavian Journal of Economics* 98 (4): 463–84.

    2003. "Exchange Market Mayhem: The Antecedents and Aftermath of Speculative Attacks." In *Capital Flows and Crises*, ed. Barry Eichengreen. Cambridge MA: Massachusetts Institute of Technology. 99–154. Original edition, Economic Policy 21 (October 1995).

EIU. 2009a. Estonia. *Economist Intelligence Unit Country Report*. March.

    2009b. Latvia. *Economist Intelligence Unit Country Report*. August.

    2009c. Lithuania. *Economist Intelligence Unit Country Report*. May.

    2008a. Czech Republic. *Economist Intelligence Unit Country Report*. October.

    2008b. Lithuania. *Economist Intelligence Unit Country Report*. November.

    2008c. Romania. *Economist Intelligence Unit Country Report*. October.

    2009a. Bulgaria. *Economist Intelligence Unit Country Report*. August.

    2009b. Bulgaria. *Economist Intelligence Unit Country Report*. April.

    2009c. Hungary. *Economist Intelligence Unit Country Report*. April.

    2009d. Latvia. *Economist Intelligence Unit Country Report*. January.

    2010. Bulgaria. *Economist Intelligence Unit Country Report*. March.

Euromonitor. 1998. *The World Economic Factbook 1988/9*. London: Euromonitor.

European Bank for Reconstruction and Development. See EBRD.

European Commission. 2009a. Cross-Country Study: Economic Policy Challenges in the Baltics. *European Economy. Occasional Papers* **58**.

2009b. *Special Eurobarometer: The Europeans in 2009*. Brussels: European Commission, Directorate for Communication.

Eurostat. 2012. *Statistics Database*. Brussels: European Commission – Eurostat.

Férnandez-Albertos, José. 2009. "Trade and Currency Policies as Substitutes: The Institutional Sources of the Preference Over Policy Instruments." In *IPES Conference 2009*. College Station TX.

Fernandez, Raquel, and Dani Rodrik. 1991. Resistance to Reform: Status Quo Bias in the Presence of Individual-Specific Uncertainty. *American Economic Review* 81 (5): 1146–55.

Fidrmuc, Jan. 2000. Economics of Voting in Post-Communist Countries. *Electoral Studies* 19: 199–217.

Fiorina, Morris. 1981. *Retrospective Voting in American National Elections*. New Haven CT: Yale University Press.

Fleming, Marcus J. 1962. *Domestic Financial Policies under Fixed and under Floating Exchange Rates*. International Monetary Fund.

Forbes, Kristin J. 2002a. Cheap Labor Meets Costly Capital: The Impact of Devaluations on Commodity Firms. *Journal of Development Economics* 69: 335–65.

2002b. How Do Large Depreciations Affect Firm Performance? *IMF Staff Papers* 49 (Special Issue): 214–37.

Fosler, Gail, and Eliza Winger. 2004. *Do Exchange Rates Matter? A Global Survey of CEOs and CFOs on Exchange Rates. of Research Report R-1349-04-RR*. New York: The Conference Board.

Frankel, Jeffrey. 1999. No Single Currency Regime is Right for All Countries or at all Times. *Essays in International Finance No. 215*. Princeton NJ: Princeton University.

2005. *Contractionary Currency Crashes in Developing Countries*. NBER Working Paper 11508. Cambridge MA: NBER.

Frankel, Jeffrey, and Shang-Jin Wei. 2004. *Managing Macroeconomic Crises: Policy Lessons*. NBER Working Paper 10907.

Freund, Caroline. 2005. Current Account Adjustment in Industrial Countries. *Journal of International Money and Finance* 24: 1278–98.

Freund, Caroline, and Frank Warnock. 2007. "Current Account Deficits in Industrial Countries. The Bigger They are, the Harder They Fall?" In *G7 Current Account Imbalances: Sustainability and Adjustment*, ed. Richard Clarida. Chicago: University of Chicago Press.

Frieden, Jeffry. 1991a. *Debt, Development, and Democracy*. Princeton NJ: Princeton University Press.

1991b. Invested Interests: The Politics of National Economic Policies in a World of Global Finance. *International Organization* 45 (4): 425–51.

1996. The Impact of Goods and Capital Market Integration on European Monetary Politics. *Comparative Political Studies* 29 (2): 193–222.

2002. Real Sources of European Currency Policy: Sectoral Interests and European Monetary Integration. *International Organization* 56 (4): 831–60.

Frieden, Jeffry, and Ernesto Stein. 2001a. *The Currency Game. Exchange Rate Politics in Latin America*. Washington DC: Johns Hopkins University Press.

2001b. "The Political Economy of Exchange Rate Policy in Latin America: An Analytical Overview." In *The Currency Game. Exchange Rate Politics in Latin*

America, eds. Jeffry Frieden and Ernesto Stein. Washington DC: Inter-American Development Bank. 1–19.

Frieden, Jeffry, Piero Ghezzi, and Ernesto Stein. 2001. "Politics and Exchange Rates: A Cross-Country Approach." In *The Currency Game: Exchange Rate Politics in Latin America*, eds. Jeffry Frieden and Ernesto Stein. Washington DC: Inter-American Development Bank. 21–63.

Frieden, Jeffry, David Leblang, and Neven Valev. 2010. The Political Economy of Exchange Rate Regimes in Transition Economies. *Review of International Organizations* 5 (1): 1–25.

Furman, Jason, and Joseph Stiglitz. 1998. Economic Crises: Evidence and Insights from East Asia. *Brookings Papers on Economic Activity* (2): 1–135.

Gabel, Matthew, and Simon Hix. 2005. Understanding Public Support for British Membership of the Single Currency. *Political Studies* 53 (1): 65–81.

Galindo, Arturo, Ugo Panizza, and Fabio Schiantarelli. 2003. Debt Composition and Balance Sheet Effects of Currency Depreciation: A Summary of the Micro Evidence. *Emerging Markets Review* 4: 330–9.

Garrett, Geoffrey. 1998. *Partisan Politics in the Global Economy*. New York: Cambridge University Press.

Gerlach, Stefan, and Frank Smets. 1995. Contagious Speculative Attacks. *European Journal of Political Economy* 11: 45–63.

Ghosh, Atish, Anne-Marie Gulde, and Holger Wolf. 2003. *Exchange Rate Regimes. Choices and Consequences*. Cambridge MA: MIT Press.

Goh, Chor-ching, Sung Jin Kang, and Yasuki Sawada. 2005. How did Korean Households Cope with Negative Shocks from the Financial Crisis? *Journal of Asian Economics* 16: 239–54.

Goldberg, Pinelopi Koujianou, and Michael Knetter. 1997. Goods Prices and Exchange Rates: What Have We Learned? *Journal of Economic Literature* 35 (3): 1243–72.

Goldfajn, Ilan, and Taimur Baig. 1998. Monetary Policy in the Aftermath of Currency Crises: The Case of Asia. *IMF Working Paper* WP/98/170.

Gourevitch, Peter. 1986. *Politics in Hard Times: Comparative Responses to International Economic Crises*. Ithaca NY: Cornell University Press.

Government of Romania. 2009. *Letter of Intent and Technical Memorandum of Understanding*.

Government of the Hong Kong SAR. 1998. *Hong Kong SAR. The First 12 Months*. Hong Kong: Hong Kong Information Services Department.

Grossman, Gene, and Elhanan Helpman. 2001. *Special Interest Politics*. Cambridge MA: MIT Press.

Guisinger, Alexandra, and David Singer. 2010. Exchange Rate Proclamations and Inflation-Fighting Credibility. *International Organization* 64 (2): 313–37.

Gwartney, James, Joshua Hall, and Robert Lawson. 2011. 2011 Economic Freedom Dataset. http://www.freetheworld.com/2011/2011/Dataset.xls.

Haggard, Stephan. 2000. *The Political Economy of the Asian Financial Crisis*. Washington DC: Institute for International Economics.

Haggard, Stephan, and Andrew MacIntyre. 2000. "Incumbent Governments and the Politics of Crisis Management." In *The Political Economy of the Asian Financial Crisis*, ed. Stephan Haggard. Washington DC: Institute for International Economics. 47–85.

Haggard, Stephan, and Jongryn Mo. 2000. The Political Economy of the Korean Financial Crisis. *Review of International Political Economy* 7 (2): 197–218.

Hainmueller, Jens, and Michael Hiscox. 2006. Learning to Love Globalization: Education and Individual Attitudes Toward International Trade. *International Organization* 60 (2): 469–98.

Hall, Michael. 2005. *Exchange Rate Crises in Developing Countries. The Political Role of the Banking Sector.* Burlington: Ashgate.

    2008. Democracy and Floating Exchange Rates. *International Political Science Review* 29 (1): 73–98.

Hardarson, Ólafur, and Gunnar Helgi Kristinsson. 2010. The Parliamentary Election in Iceland, April 2009. *Electoral Studies* 29 (3): 523–6.

Häusermann, Silja. 2010. *The Politics of Welfare State Reform in Continental Europe. Modernization in Hard Times.* Cambridge: Cambridge University Press.

Hayo, Bernd. 2005. Mass Attitudes Toward Financial Crisis and Economic Reform in Korea. *Socio-Economic Review* 3: 491–515.

Healy, Andrew, and Neil Malhotra. 2009. Myopic Voters and Natural Disaster Policy. *American Political Science Review* 103 (3): 387–406.

Hefeker, Carsten. 1997. *Interest Groups and Monetary Integration. The Political Economy of Exchange Regime Choice.* Boulder CO: Westview Press.

Helleiner, Eric. 2005. A Fixation with Floating: The Politics of Canada's Exchange Rate Regime. *Canadian Journal of Political Science* 38 (1): 23–44.

Hellwig, Timothy. 2008. Globalization, Policy Constraints, and Vote Choice. *The Journal of Politics* 70 (4): 1128–41.

Hellwig, Timothy, and David Samuels. 2007. Voting in Open Economies. *Comparative Political Studies* 40 (3): 283–306.

Henning, Randall. 1994. *Currencies and Politics in the United States, Germany, and Japan.* Washington DC: Institute for International Economics.

Hiscox, Michael J. 2002. *International Trade and Political Conflict: Commerce, Coalitions, and Mobility.* Princeton NJ: Princeton University Press.

Ho, Lok-sang. 1998. "The Rise and Fall of the Economy." In *The Other Hong Kong Report 1998*, eds. Larry Chuen- Ho Chow and Yiu-Kwan Fun. Hong Kong. 139–53.

Hobolt, Sara, and Patrick Leblond. 2009. Is my Crown Better than Your Euro? Exchange Rates and Public Opinion on the Single European Currency. *European Union Politics* 10 (2): 202–25.

Holbrook, Thomas. 2009. Economic Considerations and the 2008 Presidential Election. *PS: Political Science & Politics* 42 (3): 473–8.

Hong, Gong-Soog, Jaminie Sung, and Soon-Mi Kim. 2002. Saving Behavior Among Korean Households. *Family and Consumer Sciences Research Journal* 30 (4): 437–62.

Hong Kong Industry Department. 1999. *Hong Kong Industries.* Hong Kong: Government of the Hong Kong SAR.

Hong Kong Monetary Authority. 1998. *Hong Kong Monetary Authority Annual Report 1997.* Hong Kong: Hong Kong Monetary Authority.

Hsu, Chen Min. 2001. *How Could Taiwan Have been Insulated from the 1997 Financial Crisis?* Taipeh: NPF Research Report.

Ilonszki, Gabriella, and Sándor Kurtán. 2009. Hungary. *European Journal of Political Research* 48: 973–9.

IMF. 1994. *Thailand 1994. Article IV Consultation – Staff Report.* Washington DC: IMF.

——— 1997. *People's Republic of China – Staff Report for the Article IV Consultation Discussions Held in 1997 in Respect of the Hong Kong Special Administrative Region.* Vol. SM/97/295. Washington DC: IMF.

——— 1998a. *People's Republic of China – Hong Kong Special Administrative Region – Recent Economic Developments.* Vol. SM/98/12. Washington DC: IMF.

——— 1998b. *Republic of Korea – Selected Issues.* Vol. SM/98/99. Washington DC: IMF.

——— 1998c. *Republic of Korea – Statistical Appendix.* Vol. SM/98/98. Washington DC: IMF.

——— 1998d. *Thailand – Statistical Appendix.* Vol. SM/98/116. Washington DC: IMF.

——— 1998e. *Thailand – Statistical Appendix.* Vol. SM/98/116 (Revision 1). Washington DC: IMF.

——— 2000a. *People's Republic of China-Hong Kong SAR: Staff Report for the 1999 Article IV Consultation.* Washington DC: IMF. 00/28.

——— 2000b. Thailand: Selected Issues. *IMF Staff Country Report* 00/21.

——— 2003. *Republic of Korea: 2002 Article IV Consultation – Staff Report; Staff Supplement; Public Information Notice on the Executive.* Washington DC: IMF.

——— *International Financial Statistics.* Washington DC: IMF.

——— 2009a. *Republic of Estonia: 2008 Article IV Consultation – Staff Report; Staff Statement; Public Information Notice on the Executive Board Discussion; and Statement by the Executive Director for the Republic of Estonia.* Washington DC: IMF. 09/86.

——— 2009b. *Republic of Latvia: Request for Stand-By Arrangement – Staff Report; Staff Supplement; Press Release on the Executive Board Discussion; and Statement by the Executive Director for the Republic of Latvia.* Washington DC: IMF. 09/3.

——— 2009c. *Republic of Lithuania: Staff Report for the 2009 Article IV Consultation.* Washington DC: IMF. 09/322.

——— 2010a. *Bulgaria: 2010 Article IV Consultation – Staff Report; Staff Supplement; Public Information Notice on the Executive Board Discussion; and Statement by the Executive Director for Bulgaria.* Washington DC: IMF. 10/160.

——— 2010b. *Bulgaria: Selected Issues.* Washington DC: IMF. 10/159.

——— 2010c. Romania: Financial Sector Stability Assessment. *IMF Country Report* 10/47.

——— 2010d. *Romania: Second and Third Reviews under the Stand-By Arrangement, Request Rephasing and Waiver of Nonobservance of Performance Criterion; Statement by the IMF Staff Representative; and Press Release on the Executive Board Discussion.* Washington DC: IMF. 10/49.

——— 2011. *Bulgaria: 2011 Article IV Consultation – Staff Report, Public Information Notice on the Executive Board Discussion, and Statement by the Executive Director for Bulgaria.* Washington DC: IMF. 11/179.

——— 2012a. Latvia's Successful Recovery Not Easy to Replicate. *IMF Survey online.* 11 June.

——— 2012b. *Republic of Latvia: Fifth Review under the Stand-By Arrangement and Financing Assurances Review, Request for Waiver of Nonobservance of a Performance Criterion, and Proposal for Post-program Monitoring.* Washington DC: IMF. 12/31.

International Currency Review. 1998. South Korean Won. *International Currency Review* 24 (4): 137–44.

International Monetary Fund. See IMF.

Jacobs, Alan. 2011. *Governing for the Long Term: Democracy and the Politics of Investment.* Cambridge: Cambridge University Press.

Jao, Y. C. 1997. *Hong Kong as an International Financial Center. Evolution, Prospects and Policies.* Hong Kong: City University of Hong Kong Press.

    1998. "Money and Banking." In *The Other Hong Kong 1998*, eds. Larry Chuen- Ho Chow and Yiu-Kwan Fun. Hong Kong.

Jeanne, Olivier. 2003. Why do Emerging Market Economies Borrow in Foreign Currency? IMF Working Paper WP/03/177.

Jorda, Oscar, Moritz Schularick, and Alan Taylor. 2010. Financial Crises, Credit Booms, and External Imbalances: 140 Years of Lessons. *NBER Working Paper Series* 16567.

Kalra, Sanjay, Dubravko Mihaljek, and Christoph Duenwald. 2000. Property Prices and Speculative Bubbles: Evidence from Hong Kong SAR. *IMF Working Paper* 00/2.

Kaminsky, Graciela L., and Carmen M. Reinhart. 1999. The Twin Crises: The Causes of Banking and Balance-of-Payments Problems. *The American Economic Review* 89 (3): 473–500.

Kaminsky, Graciela, Saul Lizondo, and Carmen M. Reinhart. 1998. Leading Indicators of Currency Crises. *IMF Staff Papers* 45 (1).

Kawai, Masahiro, and Ken-ichi Takayasu. 1999. "The Economic Crisis and Banking Sector Restructuring in Thailand." In *Rising to the Challenge in Asia: A Study of Financial Markets. Volume 1 -Thailand*, ed. Asian Development Bank. 37–49.

Key, V. O. 1966. *The Responsible Electorate.* New York: Vintage Books.

Kinder, Donald, and Roderick Kiewit. 1979. Economic Discontent and Political Behavior: The Role of Personal Grievances and Collective Economic Judgements in Congressional Voting. *American Journal of Political Science* 23 (3): 495–527.

Kinderman, Daniel. 2008. The Political Economy of Sectoral Exchange Rate Preferences and Lobbying: Germany from 1960–2008, and Beyond. *Review of International Political Economy* 15 (5): 851–80.

Kirk, Donald. 1999. *Korean Crisis. Unraveling of the Miracle in the IMF Era.* New York: St. Martin's Press.

Klein, Michael W., and Nancy P. Marion. 1997. Explaining the Duration of Exchange-Rate Pegs. *Journal of Development Economics* 54: 387–404.

Kraay, Aart. 2003. Do High Interest Rates Defend Currencies During Speculative Attacks? *Journal of International Economics* 59: 297–321.

Krugman, Paul. 1979. A Model of Balance of Payments Crises. *Journal of Money, Credit and Banking* 11 (3): 311–25.

Krupavicus, Algis. 2010. Lithuania. *European Journal of Political Research* 49: 1058–75.

    2011. Lithuania. *European Journal of Political Research* 50: 1045–57.

Kuklinski, James, Pauk Quirk, Jennifer Jerit, David Schwieder, and Robert Rich. 2000. Misinformation and the Currency of Democratic Citizenship. *Journal of Politics* 62 (3): 790–816.

Kuokstis, Vyautas, and Ramunas Vilpisauskas. 2010. Economic Adjustment to the Crisis in the Baltic States in Comparative Perspective. Presented at the 7th Pan-European International Relations Conference, Stockholm.

Kwon, S. 2001. Economic Crisis and Social Policy Reform in Korea. *International Journal of Social Welfare* 10 (1): 1–10.

Labán, Raúl, and Federico Sturzenegger. 1994. Distributional Conflict, Financial Adaptation and Delayed Stabilizations. *Economics & Politics* 63 (3): 257–76.

Leblang, David. 1999. Domestic Political Institutions and Exchange Rate Commitments in the Developing World. *International Studies Quarterly* 43 (4): 599–620.

2003. To Devalue or to Defend? The Political Economy of Exchange Rate Policy. *International Studies Quarterly* 47 (4): 533–59.

2005. "Pegs and Politics." In *American Political Science Association Annual Meeting.* Washington DC.

Leblang, David, Joseph Jupille, and Amber Curtis. 2011. The Mass Political Economy of International Public Debt Settlement. Presented at the Political Economy of International Finance (PEIF) meeting 2011, Berlin.

Lee, Jisoon. 1998. Causes for Business Failures: Understanding the 1997 Korean Crisis. *Journal of Asian Economics* 9 (4): 637–51.

Levasseur, Sandrine. 2012. Labour Market Adjustments in Estonia During the 2008/20122 Crisis. *Eastern Journal of European Studies* 3 (1): 123–43.

Lewis-Beck, Michael, and Richard Nadeau. forthcoming. Pigs or Not? Economic Voting in Southern Europe. *Electoral Studies.*

Lewis-Beck, Michael S., and Martin Paldam. 2000. Economic Voting: An Introduction. *Electoral Studies* 19: 113–21.

Lewis-Beck, Michael, and Mary Stegmaier. 2000. Economic Determinants of Electoral Outcomes. *Annual Review of Political Science* 3: 183–219.

2007. "Economic Models of Voting." In *The Oxford Handbook of Political Behavior,* eds. Russell Dalton and Hans-Dieter Klingemann. Oxford: Oxford University Press.

LG Economic Research Institute. 1997. *Korean Economic Briefing September 1997: Market Interest Rates.* Seoul: LG Economic Research Institute.

Lim, Linda Y. C. 1999. "Free Market Fancies: Hong Kong, Singapore, and the Asian Financial Crisis." In *The Politics of the Asian Economic Crisis,* ed. T. J. Pempel. Ithaca: Cornell University Press. 101–15.

Linek, Lukás, and Tomás Lacina. 2010. Czech Republic. *European Journal of Political Research* 49: 939–46.

MacKuen, Michael, Robert Erikson, and James Stimson. 1992. Peasants or Bankers? The American Electorate and the U.S. Economy. *American Political Science Review* 86 (3): 597–611.

Mansfield, Edward, and Diana Mutz. 2009. Support for Free Trade: Self-Interest, Sociotropic Politics, and Out-Group Anxiety. *International Organization* 63 (2): 425–57.

Marer, P. 2010. The Global Economic Crises: Impacts on Eastern Europe. *Acta Oeconomica* 60 (1): 3–33.

Masso, Jaan, and Kerly Krillo. 2011. "Labour Markets in the Baltic States During the Crisis 2008–2009: The Effect on Different Labour Market Groups." The University of Tartu.

Masson, Paul, and Mark Taylor. 1993. *Policy Issues in the Operation of Currency Unions.* Cambridge: Cambridge University Press.

McKinnon, Ronald. 1963. Optimum Currency Areas. *The American Economic Review* 53 (4): 717–25.

McNamara, Kathleen. 1998. *The Currency of Ideas: Monetary Politics in the European Union*. Ithaca: Cornell University Press.

Mendoza, Enrique G., and Marco E. Terrones. 2008. An Anatomy of Credit Booms: Evidence from Macro Aggregates and Micro Data. *NBER Working Paper* 14049.

Menkulasi, Jeta, Jacques Miniane, and Tigran Poghosyan. 2011. Republic of Lithuania – Selected Issues Paper. *IMF Country Report* No. 11/327.

Mishkin, Frederic. 1996. "Understanding Financial Crises: A Developing Country Perspective." In *Annual World Bank Conference on Development Economics*, eds. Michael Bruno and Boris Pleskovic. Washington DC: World Bank. 29–62.

Mitra, Pradeep, Marcelo Selowsky, and Juan Zalduendo. 2010. *Turmoil at Twenty: Recession, Recovery, and Reform in Central and Eastern Europe and the Former Soviet Union*. Washington DC: The World Bank.

Morris, Stephen, and Huyun Song Shin. 1998. Unique Equilibrium in a Model of Self-fulfilling Currency Attacks. *The American Economic Review* 88 (3): 587–97.

Muller, Aline, and Willem Verschoor. 2006. Foreign Exchange Risk Exposure: Survey and Suggestions. *Journal of Multinational Financial Management* 16 (4): 385–410.

Mundell, Robert. 1961. A Theory of Optimum Currency Areas. *American Economic Review* 51 (4): 657–64.

Myant, Martin, and Jan Drahokupil. 2012. International Integration, Varieties of Capitalism and Resilience to Crisis in Transition Economies. *Europe-Asia Studies* 64 (1): 1–33.

Nannestad, Peter, and Martin Paldam. 1999. What do Voters Know about the Economy? A Study of Danish Data, 1990–1993. *Electoral Studies* 19 (2).

Nguyen, Pascal. 2007. Macroeconomic Factors and Japan's Industry Risk. *Journal of Multinational Financial Management* 17: 173–85.

Noble, Gregory, and John Ravenhill. 2000. *The Asian Financial Crisis and the Architecture of Global Finance*. Cambridge: Cambridge University Press.

Nordhaus, W. 1975. The Political Business Cycle. *Review of Economic Studies* 42: 169–90.

Nukul Commission. 1998. *Analysis and Evaluation on Facts Behind Thailand's Economic Crisis (Nukul Commission Report)*. English Language Edition. Bangkok: Nation Multimedia Group.

Oatley, Thomas. 1999. How Constraining is Capital Mobility? The Partisan Hypothesis in an Open Economy. *American Journal of Political Science* 42 (4): 1003–27.

Obstfeld, Maurice. 1994. *The Logic of Currency Crises*. NBER Working Paper 4640. Cambridge: National Bureau of Economic Research.

1996. Models of Currency Crises with Self-Fulfilling Features. *European Economic Review* 40: 1037–47.

1998. The Global Capital Market: Beneface or Menace? *Journal of Economic Perspectives* 12 (4): 9–30.

Organization of Economic Co-operation and Development. 2010. *OECD Economic Surveys. Hungary*. Paris: OECD.

Overholt, William H. 1999. Thailand's Financial and Political Systems: Crisis and Rejuvenation. *Asian Survey* 39 (6): 1009–35.

Park, Won-Am, and Gongpil Choi. 2004. "What Caused the Crisis? A Post Mortem." In *The Korean Economy Beyond the Crisis*, eds. Duck-Koo Chung and Barry Eichengreen. Cheltenham: Edward Elgar.

Pattie, Charles, Daniel Dorling, and Ron Johnston. 1997. The Electoral Geography of Recession: Local Economic Conditions, Public Perceptions and the Economic Vote in the 1992 British General Election. *Transactions of the Institute of British Geographers* 22 (2): 147–61.

Pepinsky, Thomas. 2009. *Economic Crises and the Breakdown of Authoritarian Regimes: Indonesia and Malaysia in Comparative Perspective*. 1st ed. Cambridge: Cambridge University Press.

2012. The Global Economic Crisis and the Politics of Non-Transitions. *Government and Opposition* 47 (2): 135–61.

Perng, Fai-nan. 1999. *Responding to the Challenges: Financial Development and Structural Change in the ROC Economy*. Planned speech at the Chinatrust Dinner on the Eve of the International Monetary Fund/World Bank Annual Meetings (Dinner was canceled), Twin Oaks Garden, Washington DC.

Pierson, Paul. 1994. *Dismantling the Welfare State? Reagan, Thatcher, and the Politics of Retrenchment*. New York: Cambridge University Press.

Pop-Eleches, Grigore. 2009. *From Economic Crisis to Reform: IMF Programs in Latin America and Eastern Europe*. Princeton NJ: Princeton University Press.

Powell, Bingham, and Guy Whitten. 1993. A Cross-National Analysis of Economic Voting: Taking Account of the Political Context. *American Journal of Political Science* 37 (2): 391–414.

Pratap, Sangeeta, Ignacio Lobato, and Alejandro Somuano. 2003. Debt Composition and Balance Sheet Effects of Exchange Rate Volatility in Mexico: A Firm Level Analysis. *Emerging Markets Review* 4: 450–71.

Przeworski, Adam. 1991. *Democracy and the Market. Political and Economic Reforms in Eastern Europe and Latin America*. Cambridge: Cambridge University Press.

Purfield, Catriona, and Christoph Rosenberg. 2010. Adjustment under a Currency Peg: Estonia, Latvia and Lithuania during the Global Financial Crisis 2008–09. *IMF Working Paper* WP/10/213.

Radelet, Steven, and Jeffrey Sachs. 1998. The East Asian Financial Crisis: Diagnosis, Remedies, Prospects. *Brookings Papers on Economic Activity* 1998 (1): 1–90.

Reinhart, Carmen, and Vincent Reinhart. 2008. Capital Flow Bonanzas: An Encompassing View of the Past and Present. *NBER Working Paper* 14321.

Reinhart, Carmen, and Kenneth Rogoff. 2004. The Modern History of Exchange Rate Arrangements: A Reinterpretation. *The Quarterly Journal of Economics* 119 (1): 1–48.

2010. *This Time is Different: Eight Centuries of Financial Folly*. Princeton NJ: Princeton University Press.

Roberts, Andrew. 2008. Hyperaccountability: Economic Voting in Central and Eastern Europe. *Electoral Studies* 27: 533–46.

Rodrik, Dani. 1996. Understanding Economic Policy Reform. *Journal of Economic Literature* XXXIV (1): 9–41.

1999. Where did all the Growth go? External Shocks, Social Conflict, and Growth Collapses. *Journal of Economic Growth* 4 (4): 385–412.

Rogoff, Kenneth. 1990. Equilibrium Political Budget Cycles. *American Economic Review* 80 (1): 21–36.

Rogoff, Kenneth, and Anne Sibert. 1988. *Elections and Macroeconomic Policy Cycles*. NBER Working Paper 1838. Cambridge MA: National Bureau of Economic Research.

Rogowski, Ronald. 1989. *Commerce and Coalitions: How Trade Affects Domestic Political Alignments*. Princeton NJ: Princeton University Press.

Sachs, Jeffrey, Aarón Tornell, and Andrés Velasco. 1996. The Mexican Peso Crisis: Sudden Death or Death Foretold? *Journal of International Economics* 41 (3–4): 265–83.

Sattler, Thomas, and Stefanie Walter. 2009. Globalization and Government Short-term Room to Maneuver in Economic Policy. An Empirical Analysis of Reactions to Currency Crises. *World Political Science Review* 5 (1): article 16.

Satyanath, Shankar. 2006. *Globalization, Politics, and Financial Turmoil: Asia's Banking Crisis*. Cambridge: Cambridge University Press.

Schamis, Hector E., and Christopher R. Way. 2003. The Politics of Exchange Rate-Based Stabilization. *World Politics* 56: 43–78.

Scheve, Kenneth. 2004. Public Inflation Aversion and the Political Economy of Macroeconomic Policymaking. *International Organization* 58 (1): 1–34.

Scotto, Thomas, Harold Clarke, Allan Kornberg, Jason Reifler, Marianne Stewart, and Paul Whiteley. 2010. The Dynamic Political Economy of Support for Barack Obama During the 2008 Presidential Election Campaign. *Electoral Studies* 29 (4): 545–56.

Shambaugh, George E. 2004. The Power of Money: Global Capital and Policy Choices in Developing Countries. *American Journal of Political Science* 48 (2): 281–95.

Sikk, Ivar. 2011. *Fiscal Consolidation in Estonia*. OECD: Ministry of Finance of the Republic of Estonia.

Simmons, Beth. 1994. *Who Adjusts? Domestic Sources of Foreign Economic Policy During the Interwar Years*. Princeton NJ: Princeton University Press.

Sims, Christopher. 2003. Implications of Rational Inattention. *Journal of Monetary Economics* 50 (3): 665–90.

Singer, David. 2010a. Migrant Remittances and Exchange Rate Regimes in the Developing World. *American Political Science Review* 104 (2): 307–23.

Singer, Matthew. 2010b. Who Says "It's the Economy"? Cross-National and Cross-Individual Variation in the Salience of Economic Performance. *Comparative Political Studies* 44 (3): 284–312.

Singer, Matthew, and Francois Gélineau. 2012. "Heterogenous Economic Voting: Evidence from Latin America 1995–2005." In *MPSA Annual Conference 2012*. Chicago.

Smith, Alastair, and James Raymond Vreeland. 2003. "The Survival of Political Leaders and IMF Programs: Testing the Scapegoat Hypothesis." In *Globalization and the Nation State. The Impact of the IMF and the World Bank*, eds. Gustav Ranis, James Raymond Vreeland, and Stephen Kosack. New York: Routledge. 263–89.

Soroka, Stuart. 2006. Good News and Bad News: Asymmetric Responses to Economic Information. *Journal of Politics* 68 (2): 372–85.

Stan, Lavinia, and Razvan Zaharia. 2010. Romania. *European Journal of Political Research* 49: 1139–53.

Steenbergen, Marco, and Bardford Jones. 2002. Modeling Multilevel Data Structures. *American Journal of Political Science* 46 (1): 218–37.

Stegmaier, Mary, and Klára Vlachová. 2011. The Parliamentary Election in the Czech Republic, May 2010. *Electoral Studies* 30: 223–44.

Stein, Ernesto, and Jorge Streb. 2004. Elections and the Timing of Devaluations. *Journal of International Economics* 63 (1): 119–45.

Steinberg, David. 2008. "Currencies, Compensations, and Coalitions: The Politics of Exchange Rate Valuation in Argentina, 1963–2007." In *IPES Conference*. Philadelphia.

2009. "Interest Group Influence in Authoritarian States: The Political Determinants of China's Undervalued Exchange Rate." In *APSA Annual Meeting 2009*. Toronto, Canada.

Steinberg, David, and Stefanie Walter. 2013. "The Political Economy of Exchange Rates." In *Handbook of Safeguarding Global Financial Stability: Political, Social, Cultural, and Economic Theories and Models*, ed. Gerard Caprio. Oxford: Elsevier. 27–36.

Stierli, Markus. 2006. "Institutions, Credibility, and Economic Policy." University of Zurich.

Stiglitz, Joseph. 2002. *Globalization and Its Discontents*. London: Penguin Books.

Stone, Randall. 2008. The Scope of IMF Conditionality. *International Organization* 62: 589–620.

The Economist. 2009. "Foreign-currency mortgages. The Bills are Alive." October 8.

Tiongson, Erwin, Naotaka Sugawara, Victor Sulla, Ashley Taylor, Anna Guerguieva, Victoria Levin, and Kalanidhi Subbarao. 2010. *The Crisis Hits Home. Stress-testing Households in Europe and Central Asia*. Washington DC: The World Bank.

Tsurimi, Hiroki. 2000. Asian Financial Crisis. Prologue and the Case of Thailand. *Asia-Pacific Financial Markets* 7: 1–9.

Tworzecki, Hubert. 2012. The Polish Parliamentary Elections of October 2011. *Electoral Studies* **31** (3): 617–21.

Vreeland, James Raymond. 2003. *The IMF and Economic Development*. Cambridge: Cambridge University Press.

Walter, Stefanie. 2008. A New Approach for Determining Exchange-Rate Level Preferences. *International Organization* 62 (3): 405–38.

2009. The Limits and Rewards of Political Opportunism. How Electoral Timing Affects the Outcome of Currency Crises. *European Journal of Political Research* 48 (3): 367–96.

2012. Distributional Politics in Times of Crisis. Eastern European Policy Responses to the Global Financial and Economic Crisis 2008–10. Presented at the EPSA Annual Convention, Berlin.

Walter, Stefanie, and Thomas Willett. 2012. Delaying the Inevitable. A Political Economy Model of Currency Defenses and Capitulation. *Review of International Political Economy* 19 (1): 114–39.

Weaver, Kent. 1986. The Politics of Blame Avoidance. *Journal of Public Policy* 6 (4): 371–98.

Weisbrot, Mark, and Rebecca Ray. 2010. *Latvia's Recession: The Cost of Adjustment with an "Internal Devaluation."* Washington DC: Center for Economic and Policy Research.

Willett, Thomas. 1988. *Political Business Cycles: The Political Economy of Money, Inflation, and Unemployment*. Durham NC: Duke University Press.

1998. The Credibility and Discipline Effects of Exchange Rates as Nominal Anchors. The Need to Distinguish Temporary from Permanent Pegs. *The World Economy* 21 (6): 803–26.

2003. "The OCA Approach to Exchange Rate Regimes. A Perspective on Recent Developments." In *The Dollarization Debate*, eds. Dominick Salvatore, James Dean, and Thomas Willett. Oxford: Oxford University Press. 154–71.

2006. Optimum Currency Area and Political Economy Approaches to Exchange Rate Regimes: Towards a Framework for Integration. *Current Politics and Economics of Europe* 17 (1): 25–52.

2007. Why the Middle is Unstable: The Political Economy of Exchange Rate Regimes and Currency Crises. *The World Economy* 30 (5): 709–32.

Willett, Thomas, Ekniti Nitithanprapas, Isriya Nitithanprapas, and Sunil Rongala. 2005. The Asian Crises Reexamined. *Asian Economic Papers* 3 (3): 32–87.

Williams, John. 1990. The Political Manipulation of Macroeconomic Policy. *American Political Science Review* 84 (3): 757–74.

Woodruff, David. 2005. Boom, Gloom, Doom: Balance Sheets, Monetary Fragmentation, and the Politics of Financial Crisis in Argentina and Russia. *Politics & Society* 33 (1): 3–45.

World Bank. 2011. *The Jobs Crisis. Household and Government Responses to the Great Recession in Eastern Europe and Central Asia*. Washington DC: The World Bank.

Yam, Joseph. 1998a. The Hong Kong Dollar Link. Speech Held on 3 March at the Hong Kong Development Council, Financial Roadshow in Tokyo.

1998b. "Why We Intervened." In *The Asian Wall Street Journal*.

Yang, Ya-Hwei, and Jia-Dong Shea. 1999. "Evolution of Taiwan's Financial System." In *East Asia's Financial Systems: Evolution and Crisis*, eds. Seiichi Masuyama, Donna Vandenbrink, and Chia Siow Yue. Tokyo: Nomura Research Institute. 260–90.

Yao, Y. C. 1998. Money and Finance in Hong Kong: Retrospect and Prospect. *EAI Occasional Paper* No. 2.

Yu, Min-Teh. 1999. "Banking Environment and Reform Measures of Taipei, China during the Asian Financial Crisis." In *Rising to the Challenge in Asia. A Study of Financial Markets. Vol 3: Sound Practices*, ed. Asian Development Bank. Manila: Asian Development Bank. 142–65.

Index

Made in the USA
Middletown, DE
02 May 2017